PROPERTY AND KINSHIP

PROPERTY AND KINSHIP

Inheritance in Early Connecticut
1750-1820

Toby L. Ditz

PRINCETON UNIVERSITY PRESS

PRINCETON, NEW JERSEY

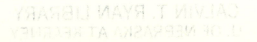

CONTENTS

LIST OF TABLES

ACKNOWLEDGMENTS

Doing my first empirical study was both exhilarating and daunting. I could not have done it without help. The research was partially supported by the National Science Foundation under grant no. NSF SES-79-11068. Columbia University and the Danforth Foundation also provided much-needed fellowships. I am grateful to all of them.

A special thanks to Gloria L. Main and Jackson Turner Main, who may not realize that their expert and perfectly timed advice on probate records and research sites was the catalyst that got me to the archives. The Connecticut State Library in Hartford houses most of the documents used in this study. I thank Bob Claus, State Archivist at the time of my research, and Eunice DiBella, Assistant Archivist, for their patience and good advice; Ann Barry and Julia Schwartz, who know the probate records inside-out; and Marvin Thompson, then Associate Editor of the Jonathan Trumball Papers, who, when I mused over a gap in my work, would reappear within a few hours with a reference or document that solved the problem. I also thank Christopher Bickford, Director of The Connecticut Historical Society, who provided vital documents and texts almost before I knew I needed them, and Mary Kay Schnare, who did much to make Hartford seem a second home.

The book is a much revised version of my dissertation. I am indebted to several people who were at Columbia University when I was a graduate student: Jonathan Cole, who has known me since my first day of classes; Andrew Beveridge, whose knack for formulating unanticipated counterarguments much improved the early drafts; Stuart Bruchey and Rosalind Rosenberg, both of whom offered very insightful comments on the final draft of the dissertation; and George Sweeting, who was an exceptionally lucid guide through the labyrinth of computer data management and analysis. But I am especially grateful to Allan Silver, my former advisor. He encouraged the project when I could only articulate a sentence or two about it, later introduced me to the world of academic presses, and provided the usual help at all the stages in between. He has, more generally, the gifted advisor's talent for giving form and direction to one's own intellectual inclinations.

I also want to thank other colleagues and friends who read all or parts of the manuscript: Lois Carr, Helena Flamm, John Higham, Michael Merrill, John Pocock, Marylynn Salmon, Carol Shammas, and

Robert Zussman. Bruce Daniels and James Henretta, who read the manuscript for Princeton University Press, deserve special mention for their thorough and very helpful comments. The manuscript is better as a result of everyone's comments, although perhaps not in precisely the ways each might have anticipated.

I salute my family for their admirable forbearance. They never gave the least indication that they doubted I would finish what I had started. Hardly ever, at any rate. Mark Martin, who has lived with the daily ups-and-downs of research, writing, and publication, finds much of it interesting and rarely complains about the rest. I thank him specifically for his astute criticism and editing of the manuscript.

PREFACE

The American North is Janus-faced. At least it appears to be so. Dichotomous images of family and community life in the preindustrial countryside predominate. "American exceptionalism" and the tone it has given to subsequent discussion are partly responsible. As the tradition of Turner and Hartz has it, conditions special to the American North from the era of first settlement, especially the abundance of land and a nonseigneurial social structure, produced distinctively modern values and institutions. Specifically, these conditions encouraged isolated, nuclear families, early independence of children, and individual social and geographic mobility. But there is a counterimage: the values and behavior of rural dwellers did not differ fundamentally from those of peasants and farmers in western Europe. In particular, American families were patriarchal and "lineal" in orientation, kin ties were extensive and strong, and mobility was family-sponsored.

The American exceptionalism motif long antedates the emergence of family studies as a specialized subdiscipline. We shall return to it in more detail in due course. Certain trends within American family studies are worth mentioning first, though, because they have reinforced the polar reasoning that even this brief reference to the American exceptionalism thesis suggests. For the last decade at least, family historians and sociologists have been engaged in a great dismantling operation. They have undermined one of the commonplaces of Parsonian functional theory: that fundamental transformations in family life were the result of adaptation to the "requirements" of an urban and industrial economy. Since Peter Laslett's early studies, empirical research on both western Europe and America has shown that many characteristics associated with family life in the industrial West—non-Malthusian demographic rhythms, nuclear households, child-centered patterns of socialization, companionate ideals concerning the conjugal bond—predate factory production and rapid urbanization.[1]

Indeed, the model of historical development that produced the erro-

---

[1] Peter Laslett, *The World We Have Lost*, 2nd ed. (New York: Scribner's, 1973); Peter Laslett, ed., *Household and Family in Past Time* (Cambridge, Eng.: Cambridge University Press, 1972). A comprehensive review useful from the perspective of inheritance studies is Michael Anderson, *Approaches to the History of the Western Family, 1500-1914* (London: Macmillan, 1980).

neous commonplace now stands charged with a variety of intellectual sins. Parsonian systems theory posits a linear and necessary path of social evolution. Hence it dismisses as insignificant the persistent, patterned differences in family organization within preindustrial Europe. It denies that families or classes are historical agents, failing to focus on social groups that, through the interplay of their interests and actions, might foster or resist change. Instead it uses the reified language of "institutional differentiation" and "societal prerequisites" to explain historical change. In short, systems theory neglects central aspects of historical variation, and its ambitious attempt to achieve universal explanatory power engenders only empty formalism.[2]

Family historians, like other social historians, are also skeptical about Parsonian methodology. Parsons and his followers usually make total societies their object of study. Family historians for the most part argue that analysis of total societies cannot adequately identify the opportunities and constraints to which most individuals respond. They declare that local settings are a more promising context for understanding historical change. New methodologies and research techniques suited to the neighborhood, the village, and the town have emerged, focusing on family reconstitution, the generational cohort, the family's developmental cycle, and the individual's life course.

But a dismantling operation has its own dangers. Historians using the new techniques have produced detailed mappings of well-defined aspects of family life in particular regions and eras, but they often leave the local settings analytically "unmoored." There is no sustained view of the larger institutional context. As a result, these studies have yet to replace discarded generalizations with a more adequate analysis of connections between family life and economic development.[3] In addition, hazily defined local settings produce seeming contradictions when there may be none. One researcher finds that patriarchal fathers are well-served by dutiful sons; another that children neglect elderly parents. Do these contrasting reports simply reflect the differing interpretive perspectives of researchers? Or are we discovering meaningful variation in family behavior—variation rooted in significant differ-

[2] Michael Anderson, "Sociological History and the Working Class Family: Smelser Revisited," *Social History*, no. 3 (October 1976): 317-34; Colin Creighton, "Family, Property, and Relations of Production in Western Europe," *Economy and Society* 9 (May 1980): 129-67; Hans Medick, "The Proto-Industrial Family Economy: The Structural Function of Household and Family during the Transition from Peasant Society to Industrial Capitalism," *Social History*, no. 3 (October 1976): 293-94.

[3] For a good formulation of this point, see Glen Elder, "Approaches to Social Change and the Family," in *Turning Points: Historical and Sociological Essays on the Family*, ed. John Demos and Surane Spence Boocock. Supplement, *American Journal of Sociology*, vol. 84 (Chicago: University of Chicago Press, 1978), pp. S12-S19.

ences within the rural economy of the American North? Unless settings are described in clear, analytic terms that link them to the larger context, we cannot know. As it stands, conflicting findings reinforce the either-or portraits associated with the American exceptionalism thesis.

There is another danger. In order to give theoretical significance to their findings, many American family historians invoke the concept of "modernization."[4] In so doing, they flirt with Parsonian systems theory, often unwittingly, even as they reject the specific idea that industrialization constituted a major turning point in the history of family life. The dismantling operation is less thorough than it seems. When used as an explanatory device, the concept of modernization often only summarizes basic aspects of northern American development in the late colonial and early national eras: increasing articulation of mercantile trade networks, growth of indigenous manufactures, democratization of political life. Used in this way, modernization is a spongy organizing concept. It points to market development in an era of spreading commercial capitalism and to the consolidation of a constitutional republic, but does not identify the direct relation between these developments and changes in family life.

As in the case of hazily defined settings, the overly broad concept of "modernization" also encourages either-or reasoning. Indeed, in the American context modernization theory is the exceptionalism thesis updated. In a widely cited essay attempting to persuade other American historians of the usefulness of modernization theory, Richard Brown wrote the following about eighteenth-century Americans: "The striving, competitive, calculating American continued to move around, speculate, and transmit his restless ambitions to his offspring."[5] His portrait of the American personality uses Parsonian theory to update Hartz's Lockean liberal and Turner's democratic frontiersman. The implicit logic, of course, is that conditions unique to the American colonies encouraged especially early and gradual cultural modernization.

Those skeptical of this portrait of the American psyche seem to be trapped by the terms of its underlying argument. They counter the "cal-

[4] See, for example, Carl Degler, *At Odds: Women and the Family in America from the Revolution to the Present* (Oxford: Oxford University Press, 1981), pp. 8-9; Michael Gordon, "Introduction," in *The American Family in Social-Historical Perspective*, 2nd ed., ed. Michael Gordon (New York: St. Martin's, 1978), pp. 1-16; also see Lawrence Stone, "Family History in the 1980s: Past Achievements and Future Trends," *Journal of Interdisciplinary History* 7 (Summer 1981): 71-77, who uses the concept of modernization to organize his review of competing explanations for shifts in family values and affective life.

[5] Richard D. Brown, "Modernization and the Modern Personality in Early America, 1600-1865: A Sketch of a Synthesis," *Journal of Interdisciplinary History* 2 (Winter 1972): 213.

culating" American with a traditional, custom-bound peasant prone to magical thinking.[6] This is anti-exceptionalism of a sort. But it tacitly endorses the linear, bipolar logic of modernization theory. Americans and Europeans made the same historical journey. Traditional society was the point of departure, modernity the destination. The only real issue is whether Americans traveled an appreciably more direct route.

Family history, in short, is just emerging from a debunking phase. This phase has produced a characteristic tension. Lack of conceptual clarity has hindered efforts to situate new findings about family life in a larger context, and exasperation with the resulting muddle threatens to give renewed credibility to Parsonian assumptions. As a result, American family history has both fallen back on and perpetuated the dichotomous images surrounding the American exceptionalism thesis.

Anyone studying family and economy in the American North runs the risk of merely adding to these conflicting images. To minimize this risk, this study adopts a comparative method. The comparative strategy is meant to avoid both the "unmoored" study and overly abstract depictions of the larger society. In brief, the study rests on an intraregional comparison of inheritance patterns. It analyzes family property relations in two types of rural Connecticut communities in the 1750s, 1770s, and 1820s. They shared features typical of rural society in the American North, such as widespread family-farm ownership. They were, however, distinguished by their relationship to developing regional and export markets and by accompanying differences in internal social organization. The upland towns were comparatively self-sufficient, "subsistence-plus" agricultural communities. Their economies did not heavily depend on production for nonlocal markets. In contrast, the agriculture and occupational structure of the river-valley town was becoming highly commercialized. The community became increasingly dependent on regional and export markets.

Thus, although the research sites are New England towns, the true units of comparison are economic subregions: subsistence-plus and commercial agriculture areas. The economic region and systematic variation within it provides an organizing framework at the appropriate analytic level.[7] It is specific enough to identify those aspects of the

[6] See, for example, Kenneth Lockridge, "Social Change and the Meaning of the American Revolution," in *Colonial America: Essays in Politics and Social Development*, 2nd ed., ed. Stanley Katz (Boston: Little, Brown, 1976), pp. 403-39.

[7] Research using regions or subregions as units of comparison is common in European social history, but it is rare in American family studies. A recent example that also relies on the strategic selection of local sites, rather than on regional-level data, is Margaret Spufford, *Contrasting Communities: English Villagers in the Sixteenth and Seventeenth Centuries* (Cambridge, Eng.: Cambridge University Press, 1974). John W. Cole and Eric

economic and social environment to which families directly respond. But it is broad enough to allow for meaningful links between family behavior and economic life.

The central comparative question is whether variation in inheritance patterns accompanied the differences in the economic organization of rural communities. Viewed in the light of inheritance practices found among owner-producers in western Europe, the answer should address the matter of American exceptionalism. If conditions special to the American North created distinctive family property arrangements, inheritance patterns ought to be similar in both types of towns precisely because they shared the features typical of the northern countryside. By the same token, they ought to differ markedly from the practices of Europeans in family-farm areas. Should inheritance practices in both areas resemble those of rural European producers, however, one could reject the exceptionalist position on family organization.

The comparison of inheritance patterns in subsistence-plus and commercial agriculture communities also permits one to consider one positive alternative to the exceptionalist position. This is that commercialization of agricultural life, rather than conditions distinctive to the American North, eroded the connection between inheritance and life-chances. Should this be correct, individualized approaches to the management of property and its intergenerational transfer ought to emerge only in areas of commercialized agriculture. Conversely, families in subsistence-plus communities should pursue inheritance strategies involving complex ties of dependency and inequality among heirs, and transfers of family property should be closely tied to critical life events such as marriage and retirement. In sum, because the early growth of regional markets promoted uneven development in the countryside, different strategies for managing family property ought to emerge in commercial and subsistence-plus agriculture areas.

In Chapter One I discuss the American exceptionalism motif, regional economic development, and the specific sites chosen. I have said little about inheritance yet, other than to indicate a faith that what may seem at first an esoteric subject serves as a particularly good vantage point for studying family and economy. In Chapter Two I introduce the trans-Atlantic perspective on inheritance and market development, and define basic types of inheritance strategies. I argue that concepts widely used to typify family organization, including family property relations, misconstrue kin ties in precommercial family-farm regions. I offer al-

R. Wolf do the same in *The Hidden Frontier: Ecology and Ethnicity in an Alpine Valley* (New York: Academic Press, 1974). Also see David Levine, *Family Formation in an Age of Nascent Capitalism* (New York: Academic Press, 1977).

ternatives that provide a firmer foundation for analyzing the inheritance practices of small and middling landholders.

By then, inheritance should no longer seem esoteric. Chapter Three
begins the second, empirical part of the study. These chapters take up
equality and inequality in the distribution of property among kin, with
special attention to gender-based inequalities; the kin ties created in
virtue of the obligations and services accompanying inherited property;
the twinning of property transfers with marriage and retirement; and
the activities surrounding the probate process. Always, the major empirical aim is to establish whether degree of town integration into the
developing regional and export market system is associated with variation in basic inheritance strategies. The final chapter briefly summarizes
the results and relates them to American republican ideology.

PROPERTY AND KINSHIP

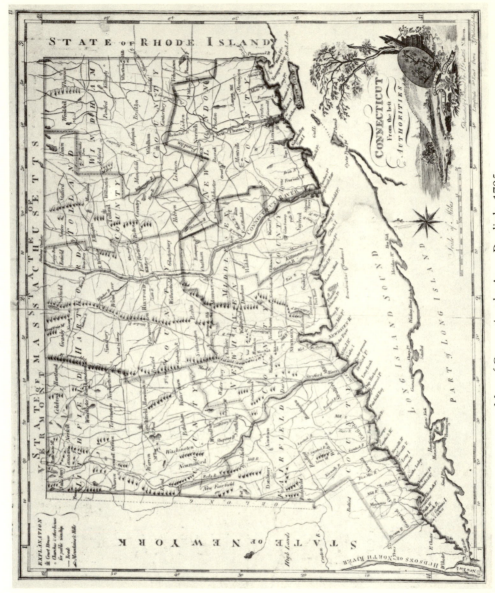

Map of Connecticut by Amos Doolittle, 1795

CHAPTER ONE

AMERICAN EXCEPTIONALISM AND THE NORTHERN COUNTRYSIDE

When historians group together the New England and mid-Atlantic colonies, they are, explicitly or implicitly, using the criterion of agricultural enterprise type to demarcate a region dominated by family-farming from southern plantation areas, from manorial and tenancy systems, and from large-scale capitalist agriculture systems that would later appear in parts of the West. The distinction between family-farm systems and others rests on the distribution of property rights and allied economic decision-making powers between producers and others—rentiers, lords, masters, employers. The key feature of family-farm economies is the unification of legal powers to make economic decisions in the hands of those who actually work the land.[1] Owner-producers dominated the agriculture of the American North. The legal rights of heads of households to make production decisions were largely constrained only by village ordinances, and their rights to returns from such production were limited only by local and colonial taxes.

The distinction according to agricultural enterprise type is schematic, but it does capture two important points. First, it emphasizes that the household is the basic economic unit in family-farm regions. In manorial or tenancy systems the basic decision-making unit is actually a vertical relation between the family of the lord or rentier and the family of the peasant dependent. In slave economies and those depending on hired labor, of course, producers have few, if any, significant rights in productive property. Second, by emphasizing property rights, the distinction according to enterprise type underscores the importance of inheritance. In regions dominated by owner-producers, inheritance transfers are a primary mechanism for allocating economic decision-making powers.

RURAL ECONOMIC DEVELOPMENT AND FAMILY FARMS

Northern farm productivity increased only slightly in the last half of the eighteenth century, with the absolute increase in farm output barely

[1] Arthur Stinchcombe, "Agricultural Enterprise and Rural Class Relations," in *Class,*

keeping pace with a rapidly growing and geographically expanding population. As a consequence, per capita wealth increased only modestly. But the sluggish rate of economic growth did not substantially impede ongoing and notable change in the structure of northern markets. Differentiated zones of agricultural production appeared and consolidated as maturing trade networks between the colonies and both Europe and the West Indies, and between the North and the South, reinforced demand for northern agricultural goods. The more fertile mid-Atlantic colonies became the leading producers of exported grains, while in New England dairy and livestock became chief exports. Further, by the first quarter of the nineteenth century, zones of intensive market gardening appeared near cities.[2]

The proportion of total agricultural output destined for extra-local markets probably increased only slightly. Even in those areas identified as most commercialized in the late eighteenth and early nineteenth centuries, the surplus available for interregional and export markets constituted at best forty percent of annual farm production; the rest was consumed locally. And twenty percent was the more typical figure.[3] The increase in available surplus that did occur was sustained in part by the adoption of more intensive agricultural techniques, especially in the perishable foodstuffs zones and, by the early nineteenth century, in the more "commercialized" grain-producing areas. But northern farm families continued to practice diversified farming everywhere, and most observers attribute the low proportional increase in the surpluses for extra-local markets largely to this failure to specialize.[4]

Status, and Power, 2nd ed., ed. Reinhard Bendix and Seymour Martin Lipset (New York: Free Press, 1966), pp. 183, 186-88.

[2] Stuart Bruchey, *The Roots of American Economic Growth, 1607-1860: An Essay in Social Causation* (New York: Harper Torchbooks, 1968); Clarence Danhof, *Change in Agriculture in the Northern United States, 1820-1870* (Cambridge, Mass.: Harvard University Press, 1969), p. 13; James Henretta, "Wealth and Social Structure," in *Colonial British America,* ed. Jack P. Greene and J. R. Pole (Baltimore: Johns Hopkins University Press, 1984), pp. 269-82. For estimates of farm productivity, see Terry L. Anderson, "Economic Growth in Colonial New England: 'Statistical Renaissance'," *Journal of Economic History* 39 (March 1979): 243-58; Duane E. Ball and Gary M. Walton, "Agricultural Productivity Change in Eighteenth-Century Pennsylvania," *Journal of Economic History* 36 (March 1976): 102-17.

[3] Bruchey, *Economic Growth,* pp. 20-22; Danhof, *Change in Agriculture,* pp. 9-12; Bruce C. Daniels, "Economic Development in Colonial and Revolutionary Connecticut: An Overview," *William and Mary Quarterly,* 3rd ser., 37 (July 1980): 434-35; James T. Lemon, *The Best Poor Man's Country: A Geographical Study of Early Southeastern Pennsylvania* (Baltimore: Johns Hopkins University Press, 1972), p. 27.

[4] Bruchey, *Economic Growth,* pp. 26-31; Danhof, *Change in Agriculture,* pp. 17-23, 144-47, 253-56, 268-69; Daniels, "Development in Connecticut," pp. 433-34; Lemon, *Poor Man's Country,* pp. 150-83.

The first quarter of the nineteenth century was also the formative period for the development of rural industry in New England. Putting-out systems, centralized textile mills, and small manufacturing companies that produced for interregional and export markets had become important features of New England's economy by the 1820s. Typically employing laborers who retained a foothold on land, these new forms of enterprise spread rapidly enough in some sectors to overshadow the domestic and artisanal production that had served local markets.[5]

Although there is general agreement about the formation of these broad zones, historians dispute whether or not they indicate thorough commercialization of agriculture because they disagree about the economic orientations and behavior of farmers themselves. These disagreements about the economic outlook of rural dwellers are, in turn, closely related to the issue of American exceptionalism. I first raised this issue with specific reference to family life, but American exceptionalism also impedes efforts to conceptualize northern agrarian social order as a whole.

Perhaps the most sustained statement of the American exceptionalism thesis is that of Seymour Martin Lipset. Even the title of his book, *The First New Nation*, makes a strong case. He writes,

> Two themes, equality and achievement, emerged from the interplay between the Puritan tradition and the Revolutionary ethos in the early formation of America's institutions. . . . the thesis is advanced that the dynamic interaction of these two predominant values has been a constant element in determining American institutions and behavior.[6]

Not only did these values, and the tension between them, define a distinctive "American character," they persist as "constant" core elements of our culture or "national identity." Indeed, in his account, these values, forged in the family-farm regions of the American North, endure as underlying causes of contemporary European-American differences in political institutions and "status systems," despite trans-Atlantic similarities in occupational structure, degree of urbanization, and level of technological development.[7]

Lipset refers to many features of the early American context that

---

[5] Christopher Clark, "Household Economy, Market Exchange and the Rise of Capitalism in the Connecticut Valley, 1800-1860," *Journal of Social History* 13 (Winter 1979): 170-71; Danhoff, *Change in Agriculture*, p. 20; Curtis Nettels, *The Emergence of a National Economy, 1775-1815* (White Plains, N.Y.: M. E. Sharpe, 1962), pp. 275-77.

[6] Seymour Martin Lipset, *The First New Nation: The United States in Historical and Comparative Perspective* (Garden City, N.Y.: Doubleday Anchor, 1967), p. 115.

[7] Lipset, *First New Nation*, pp. 139-40.

contributed to the crystallization of this distinctive value pattern, but he does not clearly indicate which of these were the most important. He does, however, use the summary phase "the absence of a feudal past" associated with the Hartz thesis.[8] For Louis Hartz, the initial conditions of settlement and the seventeenth-century natural rights doctrines brought by the first settlers produced a social formation that had no history. There had been no legally distinct upper class; there was, therefore, no gulf between elite and nonelite styles of life or intellectual culture, and there was no legacy of conflict between aristocratic interests and the growth of a centralized political administration. Material abundance, distance from England's cosmopolitan culture, and the subsequent war of independence only reinforced the result: ideology and values were, and continue to be, formed within the tradition of "Lockean liberalism."[9]

Historians who echo the American exceptionalism thesis usually stress the relative abundance and widespread ownership of land, a social structure relatively open in its opportunities for vertical mobility, and a decentralized and sometimes lax imperial administration as factors crucial to the formation of the mentality of American farmers. All of them share with Lipset and Hartz the view that these factors gave rise to patterns of behavior and orientations that were individualistic and profit-seeking, as well as egalitarian.

In his widely quoted statement about the rural population of eighteenth-century southeastern Pennsylvania, James Lemon takes an extreme position:

> A basic stress in these essays is on the "liberal" middle-class orientation of many of the settlers. . . . "Liberal" I use in the classic sense, meaning placing individual freedom and material gain over that of public interest . . . , the people planned for themselves much more than they did for their communities. . . . Undoubtedly their view was fostered by a sense that the environment was "open."[10]

Lemon has recently adopted a more moderate tone, warning others, for example, not to overemphasize the weakness of community organization in the mid-Atlantic colonies. But his larger point still remains that freeholding communities in both New England and the mid-Atlantic colonies sheltered accumulative, acquisitive behavior. Other social historians draw similar conclusions. Charles Grant identifies a "drive for

[8] Ibid., p. 148.

[9] Louis Hartz, *The Liberal Tradition in America* (New York: Harvest-Harcourt Brace, 1955).

[10] Lemon, *Poor Man's Country*, p. xv.

profits" in his study of eighteenth-century Kent, while Richard Bushman's interpretation of the Great Awakening in Connecticut is predicated on the emergence of patterns of economic behavior that were individualist and oriented to accumulation.[11]

In this view, the development of an integrated market system provides the framework of opportunities for realizing such preexisting orientations. Richard Hofstadter once argued that if farmers practiced subsistence agriculture, they did so only reluctantly and because of transitory conditions (the hardships attendant upon initial settlement) or conditions beyond their control (the immaturity of markets or exceptionally poor factor endowments). Using such logic, others have since interpreted, for example, the proliferation of artisanal activity during the colonial period as evidence of an entrepreneurial and profit-seeking mentality frustrated by lack of outlets for farm produce.[12] As such outlets did develop, eager farmers made the most of them. Indeed, the demarcation of "zones" of specialized production for export indicates that commercially oriented northern farmers were experimenting with the allocation of their productive resources along lines of competitive advantage.

But others deny that freehold tenure, abundant unsettled land, or a nonseigneurial social structure gave rise to market-oriented economic calculations or liberal and individualist values. Widespread ownership of viable farms sustained instead a social formation resistant to market rationality. The heart of the rural economy was household production founded on a secure landed base and a highly integrated local system of exchange. A small flow of outside goods supplemented the village economy, but local production met most basic living needs. The agricultural surplus that constituted the bulk of the goods handled by export merchants was simply that left over after most local needs had been satisfied.[13] It may be that farmers were sharp in their dealings with one an-

[11] Richard L. Bushman, "The Great Awakening in Connecticut," in *Colonial America: Essays in Politics and Social Development*, 2nd ed., ed. Stanley Katz (Boston: Little, Brown, 1976), pp. 334-44; Charles S. Grant, *Democracy in the Connecticut Frontier Town of Kent* (New York: Columbia University Press, 1961), pp. 31-54; James Lemon, "Spatial Order: Households in Local Communities and Regions," in *British Colonial America*, ed. Jack P. Greene and J. R. Pole (Baltimore: Johns Hopkins University Press, 1984), pp. 102, 110-14. Also see Stephanie Grauman Wolf, *Urban Village: Population, Community, and Family Structure in Germantown, Pennsylvania* (Princeton, N.J.: Princeton University Press, 1976).

[12] Richard Bushman, *From Puritan to Yankee: Character and the Social Order in Connecticut, 1690-1765* (New York: Norton, 1970), pp. 108-109; Grant, *Kent*, pp. 40-44; Richard Hofstadter, "The Myth of the Happy Yeoman," *American Heritage*, April 1956, pp. 43-53.

[13] James Henretta, "Family and Farms: 'Mentalité' in Pre-Industrial America," *Wil-*

other and sensitive to the selling price of the surplus they brought to
storekeepers who acted as intermediaries in the flow of goods between
merchants and farmers (or the price it brought when they themselves
did travel to market). But they did not seek or calculate profit, if by this
is meant a search for the largest returns in relation to input and a willingness to change inputs in order to maximize net profit.[14]

In this view the tenacity of diversified farming is unsurprising. Increased market opportunities failed to induce greater specialization,
not because farmers were technologically ignorant or blindly attached
to customary practices, but because diversified production helped to
sustain a valued way of life based on largely self-sufficient villages. Similarly, the growth of artisanal activity, gristmills, and sawmills signifies
the consolidation of a local rural economy in which needs were met
within the confines of a town-centered system of production and exchange. Finally, investment in extra-local land was less a "speculative"
drive than a form of saving for the future inheritances of children.[15]

For these historians, the absence of a landed elite has very different
implications than it has for those within the tradition of Turner and
Hartz. As Robert Mutch argues, although rural villages had comparatively egalitarian class structures, family-farm regions as a whole had a
special class structure. Merchants engaged in intercolonial and export
trade played a prominent, even dominant role in provincial politics and
economic life. Such merchants were certainly an elite. But, unlike
landed elites, merchants did not possess direct authority over rural producers. They were not a "ruling class." Located mainly in primary and
secondary port centers, they did not dominate the countryside. They
did not live there or have a significant hold on land there, and they handled rural surplus through intermediaries—the ubiquitous peddlers
and storekeepers. The absence of an elite that could mediate between
town and country encouraged a heterogeneous American character; it
reinforced the segmentation of provincial and local culture and institutions.[16]

---

liam and Mary Quarterly, 3rd ser., 35 (January 1978): 3-31; Michael Merrill, "Cash is
Good to Eat: Self-Sufficiency and Exchange in the Rural Economy of the United States,"
Radical Historian's Review (Winter 1977): 42-66; Robert E. Mutch, "Yeoman and Mer-
chant in Pre-Industrial America: Eighteenth Century Massachusetts As a Case Study,"
Societas 7 (Autumn 1977): 279-302.

[14] Danhof, Change in Agriculture, pp. 23-24, 130; Mutch, "Yeoman and Merchant,"
pp. 284-86. For analogous reasoning in the western European context, see Hans Medick,
"The Proto-Industrial Family Economy: The Structural Function of Household and Family during the Transition from Peasant Society to Industrial Capitalism" Social History,
no. 3 (October 1976): 298-99.

[15] Henretta, "Families and Farms," pp. 11-24.

[16] Mutch, "Yeoman and Merchant"; Robert Mutch, "The Cutting Edge: Colonial

This view of provincial and rural social relations complements the work of those who stress the cohesion or highly articulated institutional structure of colonial New England towns, and present a picture of a finely graded system of internal stratification in which families were ranked not only by wealth but by moral standing and the extensiveness of their local kin network. Local leaders were selected from "good families" and were older men with a history of prior service in lesser offices.[17] The hierarchy of local standing was finely graded, but social relations were also cooperative and democratic, in part because of the underlying parity among families established by their ownership of viable farms. Some historians even argue that these were essentially one-class or classless settings despite their complex status systems. They locate the main axis of domination and subordination within households—male control over the labor of wives and children and possibly over young servants or apprentices—rather than between households.[18]

James Henretta's position is a representative summary. According to him the rural communities of the American North were

> . . . distinguished by age and wealth stratification and [usually] by ethnic or religious homogeneity, while on the family level there was . . . a household mode of production, limited economic possibilities and aspirations. . . .
> The lineal family—not the conjugal unit and certainly not the unattached individual—thus stood at the center of economic and social existence in northern agricultural society.[19]

Local social relations and orientations, the argument continues, inhibited the impact of market forces on farm communities. The existence of the frontier merely stabilized the structure and culture of these communities by preventing them from being engulfed by population pres-

America and the Debate about the Transition to Capitalism," *Theory and Society* 9 (November 1980): 847-63.

[17] Edward M. Cook, Jr., *The Fathers of the Towns: Leadership and Community Structure in Eighteenth Century New England* (Baltimore: Johns Hopkins University Press, 1976), pp. 81-94; Bruce C. Daniels, *The Connecticut Town: Growth and Development, 1635-1790* (Middletown, Conn.: Wesleyan University Press, 1979), pp. 119-39. (They would not make the same overall interpretive argument discussed here.) Also see John Waters, "Patrimony, Succession, and Social Stability: Guilford, Connecticut, in the Eighteenth Century," *Perspectives in American History* 10 (1976): 159-60. Michael Zuckerman, *Peaceable Kingdoms: New England Towns in the Eighteenth Century* (New York: Knopf, 1970), pp. 187-219.

[18] Merrill, "Cash is Good to Eat," pp. 64-65; Mutch, "Cutting Edge," pp. 848-53.

[19] Henretta, "Families and Farms," pp. 20-31.

sure on locally scarce resources.[20] According to this viewpoint, although a minority may always have been entrepreneurs, the spread of an entrepreneurial and individualist orientation toward management of farm production becomes problematic—a phenomenon in need of explanation, as is the process by which the majority of rural Americans became integrated into an increasingly complex market system.

In short, polar images of agrarian life in the American North prevail.[21] A good deal of the difficulty may lie in our tendency to mistake the part for the whole and to overstate the homogeneity of rural life. For exceptionalists this is inherent in the initial thesis. Material abundance and an egalitarian social structure promoted a culture in which market development could take place evenly and gradually, suffusing and percolating throughout the countryside. Everyone was a would-be entrepreneur or petty capitalist. But many who reject this view also homogenize the rural landscape. For some, the flattening effect appears to result from a tacit acceptance of Gemeinschaft/Gesellschaft logic: if we were not all entrepreneurs, we must have been peasants. For others, the starting point seems to be that, except in the anomalous case, market penetration of initially self-sufficient family-farm areas cannot occur without resistance. The subsistence-plus way of life did not come under severe pressure, and resistance did not emerge, until the Federal, even the Jacksonian, era.

One suggested resolution is that the anti-exceptionalist interpretation holds good for New England and New England alone. On this argument, a distinctive culture, structure of political administration, and natural environment combined to make New England a backward enclave in an otherwise swiftly commercializing Anglo-American world. Compared with the mid-Atlantic colonies, the township system was more elaborate and more easily became the focus of its inhabitants' loyalties. Townships retained effective jurisdiction over their farmers, who did not scatter quite so widely as their mid-Atlantic counterparts. County government, which tended to be the effective unit of political administration elsewhere, was weak in New England, and, throughout most of the colonial era, congregation and town dovetailed more closely than in the mid-Atlantic colonies. This distinctive township system together with lingering Puritan communal ideals and greater ethnic

[20] Ibid., p. 7; Kenneth Lockridge, "Land, Population, and the Evolution of New England Society, 1630-1790," *Past and Present*, no. 39 (April 1968): 62-80.

[21] For further discussion of these conflicting imageries, see Richard L. Bushman, "Family Security in the Transition from Farm to City, 1750-1850," *Journal of Family History* 6 (Fall 1981): 238-56; Lemon, "Spatial Order," pp. 101, 110-12. Carole Shammas, "How Self-Sufficient Was Early America?" *Journal of Interdisciplinary History* 8 (Autumn 1982): 247-73.

homogeneity is said to have discouraged market development in a region that was ill-equipped by nature to produce agricultural exports. New Englanders may have become Yankees in the end, but commercial orientations and activities spread more slowly and against greater odds than elsewhere.[22]

This position rightly stresses the unevenness of economic development in the colonial and early national periods. But the interpretive debates about market orientations and behavior cannot be resolved so neatly. Although the political and cultural differences between the colonies were substantial, they can easily be exaggerated. New England towns were not closed, corporate communities in 1750, and it may well be, as Lemon has recently pointed out, that we have overemphasized the looseness of community structure in the mid-Atlantic colonies. Moreover, uneven development was a feature of both New England and the mid-Atlantic colonies. Early market growth reinforced subregional differences in the organization of rural communities. The variation went beyond the neat formula of intensive development in the older areas, extensive growth on the frontiers: the extent of commercialization varied within the older, longer-settled areas themselves.[23]

A proper distinction between subsistence-plus and commercial agriculture can be of value because it recognizes that economic development was uneven in the early American North. Commercial agriculture communities coexisted with subsistence agriculture areas within the countryside. Certainly, the spread of commercial agriculture and crafts did not occur uniformly in rural New England.

Let us now take a closer look at the distinction between subsistence-plus and commercial agriculture.

FIVE CONNECTICUT TOWNS: THE SITES

Commercialization of agriculture has sometimes been equated with the decline of *household* self-sufficiency in foodstuffs and other necessities. Defined this broadly, commercialization refers to any notable thickening in the pace of exchange among rural producers. As used here, however, commercialization is a commitment of a substantial proportion of resources—land, labor, and capital—to production of commodities for exchange outside of the community. It does not refer to local exchanges

[22] Gary Nash, "Social Development," in *British Colonial America*, ed. Jack P. Greene and J. R. Pole (Baltimore: Johns Hopkins University Press, 1984), pp. 235-37, makes a recent case for New England "exceptionalism." But see Bettye Hobbs Pruitt, "Self-Sufficiency and the Agricultural Economy of Eighteenth Century Massachusetts," *William and Mary Quarterly*, 3rd ser., 41 (July 1984): 333-64.

[23] Lemon, "Spatial Order," pp. 91-92, 102.

of cash, goods, or services when these are destined for use within the local community. It follows that subsistence-plus agriculture refers not to household, but to village self-sufficiency or near self-sufficiency.

The universality of the peddler and the storekeeper does indicate that the completely self-sufficient town was an oddity in the northern countryside. Indeed, the term subsistence-*plus* is in part meant to underline this fact. Only when a substantial proportion of the community's resources are devoted to production for extra-local exchange rather than local use can we expect something more than minor changes in the institutional context of economic life, including inheritance patterns.[24]

Subsistence-plus and commercial agriculture remain controversial terms, even among those who share this understanding of their meaning. Several historians have developed typologies of colonial towns based on systematic, quantitative evidence. Apart from urban and newly settled "frontier" towns of the American North, Jackson Turner Main distinguishes subsistence-plus from commercial agriculture towns according to wealth and concentration of wealth, degree of occupational diversification, and what might be called material life factors: topography, soil type, and location in relation to the main arteries of transport. Main and others have found that towns located in areas of poor soil and poor access to markets were marked by low proportions of both landless and large landholders as well as little interfamilial economic specialization. Towns with fertile soil and good market access, on the other hand, had greater concentrations of wealth and were marked by greater occupational differentiation.[25]

But there are difficulties with the use of the terms "commercial" and "subsistence-plus" agriculture to describe towns grouped by these characteristics. Although the presence or absence of agricultural specialization is said to underlie the association between material factors

[24] I thank Professor Stuart Bruchey for clarifying my use of the term "commercialization." One could also quantify this definition of commercialization (that is, x proportion of productive resources devoted to production of commodities for exchange outside of the community by y proportion of a community's families). Economic historians have just begun to turn their attention to the complex task of developing the appropriate indices. The literature does not contain precise or commonly agreed-on measures of "specialized" or "commercialized" farm production. Economic historians are developing indices of *productivity* using probate records, but productivity is not the same as specialization or commercialization.

[25] Jackson Turner Main, *The Social Structure of Revolutionary America* (Princeton, N.J.: Princeton University Press, 1965), pp. 17-34, 177-86, 277-82. Daniels, *Connecticut Town*, pp. 162-63; Lemon, *Poor Man's Country*, pp. 8-11; Gloria L. Main, "Inequality in Early America: The Evidence from Probate Records of Massachusetts and Maryland," *Journal of Interdisciplinary History* 7 (Spring 1977): 561-62. For a summary, see Henretta, "Wealth and Social Structure," pp. 275-79.

and degree of concentration of wealth, this link is not demonstrated. Rather, there appears to be an assumption that relatively advantageous factor endowments coupled with market opportunities translated easily into shifts in agricultural production. Or, it is simply assumed that concentration of wealth and occupational diversification are indications of such shifts. However, concentration of wealth and occupational differentiation within rural communities are not reliable indications of dependency on extra-local markets. These criteria may simply draw distinctions among towns practicing subsistence-plus agriculture, distinguishing between the relatively prosperous and stable towns and the poorer and less developed ones. Moreover, commercialization did not always produce higher concentrations of wealth. The precise relation between market dependency and the local distribution of wealth depended on the type of commercialization and on a host of secondary factors, such as age of settlement, the structure of credit, and the strength and volatility of relevant market demand.[26]

Given these difficulties, I decided the best strategy for this study was to select a rural town that meets more stringent criteria for commercial agriculture or market integration. I will compare the inheritance practices of its population with those of towns typical of a subsistence-plus agriculture area. Not only are the sites I have chosen distinguished by the material life factors and levels of wealth ordinarily used to differentiate commercial and subsistence-plus agriculture, but there is direct evidence that the town representing commercial agriculture was developing intensive farming oriented toward extra-local markets.

In addition, I use another criterion of market integration. There were always some rural towns whose relation to extra-local trade was more direct than was typical of family-farm regions as a whole. Although they remained primarily agricultural, they were home to a group of landed families directly engaged in interregional and export trade. These were "tertiary" port towns; their ships' tonnage and volume of goods traded were small compared with larger ports such as New London and New Haven in Connecticut, and, of course, minute when compared with the primary ports of Boston, New York, and Philadelphia.[27]

Commercial activity had a double meaning in these towns. They contained a group of families directly engaged in "commercial" or extra-local trade, and this stratum constituted an indigenous pull toward commercialized or market-dependent, cash-crop agricultural production. These men retained local and landed interests (unlike most of their

[26] Henretta, "Wealth and Social Structure," pp. 278-79; Merrill, "Cash is Good to Eat," pp. 43-44.

[27] Daniels, *Connecticut Town*, pp. 141-42, 150-52; Nettels, *National Economy*, pp. 302-304.

counterparts in primary and secondary port centers), and were farmers themselves. But they also had direct interests in larger and cheaper agricultural cargoes. Thus they coped with the pull of two worlds—that of the autonomous village based on diversified farming and that of cash-crop production and the resulting market dependency. In these towns merchant and farmer had a direct relationship with one another both in the person of the merchant himself and in the effect of his presence on his neighbors.

Upland and Valley

In this study I compare inheritance practices in towns located in the upland and interior of eastern Connecticut with those in Wethersfield, a "tertiary" port town located on the Connecticut River. The central empirical question of the study—how are differences in the economic life of agrarian freeholding communities related to inheritance practices?—dictated my choice of sites within a colony. Using economic areas within a single colony holds constant basic tenure patterns, the law of succession, and the structure of judicial administration. Furthermore, Connecticut developed within its borders the well-marked economic zones characteristic of the northern countryside as a whole. The Connecticut River bisects the state north to south. Its lowland, alluvial valley is from six to thirty-five miles wide, and, above the coastal plain that forms Connecticut's southern border, it is flanked on both sides by rugged uplands. Almost all discussions of economic differentiation distinguish the fertile area of the Connecticut River Valley and the coastal lowlands from the infertile, upland interior.

The dimensions of this contrast are many: the upland was the area of poor and easily exhausted soils, low surplus, and extensive agriculture. Although New England as a whole has been described as turning to dairying and livestock in the late colonial period, the uplands devoted a much greater proportion of its farmland to pasture than did the Valley.[28] Of the extensive agriculture in most of New England, the reformer, Jared Eliot, commented scathingly,

A Man that spends more than his Income altho' that be very great, yet he will grow poor; so in Land, if the Exhaustion be more than

[28] See figures in Percy Wells Bidwell and John I. Falconer, *History of Agriculture in the Northern United States, 1620-1860*, reprint ed. (New York: Peter Smith, 1941), pp. 119-20; Eric L. Jones, "Agricultural Origins of Industry," *Past and Present*, no. 40 (July 1968): 67-71; Albert Lavern Olsen, *Agricultural Economy and the Population in Eighteenth Century Connecticut*, Tercentenary Series, no. 40 (New Haven: Yale University Press, 1935), pp. 10-13; George Schumacher, *The Northern Farmer and His Markets during the Late Colonial Period* (New York: Arno, 1975), pp. 21-25.

the Assistance it receives by Dung or Tillage, the Land will not gain but grow poor: That which is called hoeing scarce deserves the Name of Tillage, for really it is but scraping.[29]

But towns in the valley and coastal area practiced more intensive techniques; by the nineteenth century many of these towns had turned to market gardening.[30]

The population statistics reflected these contrasts. In the late eighteenth century the population of the upland stabilized at lower densities than in the area of higher surplus, primarily through disproportionate westward and northward emigration. For example, Bruce Daniels's data show a growth rate of between 13.5 and 18.7 percent for the five Connecticut counties containing fertile coastal or river valley land, while eastern and interior Windham County had a growth rate of only 2.2 percent in the eight years following the Revolution. This slower rate occurred despite the fact that Windham also supported a population density in 1790 that was lower than that of the other five counties (40.43 per square mile versus 45.35 to 55.06 per square mile).[31]

The towns included in this study reflect these contrasts between upland and valley. Wethersfield, the town selected to represent commercial agriculture, was settled in the seventeenth century. It is bordered on the east by the Connecticut River, a main artery of transport in the colonial and early national period, and on the north by Hartford, the provincial and state capital. The River Valley has a soil and topography well suited for food crops, and, by Bruce Daniels's estimate, "Wethersfield had the best farming land in the colony."[32] This very large rural town, with a population of 3,489 in 1774, had the highest population density of any nonurban Connecticut town throughout the late colonial period. Its density rose from over 85 to 106 persons per square mile by 1820, although its population growth rate dropped dramatically after the Revolution (see Table 1.1).

Since they are small, it was necessary to choose at least four towns to

[29] *Essays Upon Field Husbandry in New England as it is or May Be Ordered*, quoted in Wayne D. Rassmussen, ed., *Agriculture in the United States: A Documentary History*, vol. 1 (New York: Random House, 1975), p. 201.

[30] Compare John Adams's praise of Connecticut Valley agriculture with the comments of Eliot: "Here is the finest ride in America, I believe; nothing can exceed the beauty and fertility of the country. The lands upon the river, the flat lowlands, are loaded with rich, noble crops of grass and grain and corn." *Life and Works of John Adams*, quoted in Sherman W. Adams and Henry R. Stiles, *The History of Ancient Wethersfield*, 2 vols., reprint ed. (Somersworth: New Hampshire Publishing Co., 1974), 1: 721.

[31] Daniels, *Connecticut Town*, pp. 52-54; Olsen, *Agricultural Economy*, pp. 10-35; Robert V. Wells, *The Population of the British Colonies in America before 1776: A Survey of the Census Data* (Princeton, N.J.: Princeton University Press, 1975), pp. 88-93.

[32] Daniels, *Connecticut Town*, p. 56.

TABLE 1.1

SITES: POPULATION AND DENSITY

Town	1756 Pop.[a]	1774 Pop.[b]	1774 Density[c]	1820 Pop.[d]	1820 Density[c]
Wethersfield	2,483	3,489	85.87	3,825	106.43
Bolton	766	1,001	30.5	1,697[e]	51.14[e]
Coventry	1,635	2,056	45.37	2,058	45.42
Union	500	514	17.31	757	25.49
Willington	650	1,001	30.52	1,246	37.99

[a] Figures from the colonial census of 1756, as found in Evarts B. Green and Virginia D. Harrington, *American Population before the Federal Census of 1790* (New York: Columbia University Press, 1932), pp. 58-60.
[b] Figures from the colonial census of 1774, ibid.
[c] Density per square mile. Figures derived from Edward M. Cook, *The Fathers of the Towns* (Baltimore: The Johns Hopkins University Press, 1976), Appendix II.
[d] Figures from the U.S. Bureau of the Census, 4th Census, *Population for the Year 1820 in the State of Connecticut*, vol. 1 (Hartford County), vol. 8 (Tolland County).
[e] Population for the town of Vernon included.

represent "subsistence-plus" agriculture in order to generate enough probated estates to compare with those of Wethersfield. Given this, my tactic was to choose towns within the same locale that represented a range of material conditions characteristic of subsistence-plus agriculture in the eastern uplands.

The four upland towns, incorporated between 1712 and 1734 in the first wave of settlement of the northeastern interior, are all located in what is now Tolland County, east of the Connecticut River Valley and separated from it by a ridge of mountains.[33] Material conditions in the selected towns ranged from the truly mountainous, heavily forested, and stony, infertile soil of tiny Union (population 514 in 1774) to the relatively large country town of Coventry (population 2,056 in 1774). The upland, hilly terrain of the latter supported pockets of decent ara-

[33] The northern half of one of the towns, Bolton, became Vernon in 1808; Vernon is included in the portion of the study covering 1820-21. In addition, a small portion of Wethersfield became part of Berlin, a town incorporated in 1785. In the 1820-21 portion of the study, two estates from this corner of Berlin were included. It would have been desirable to control for time of settlement. As was typical of all the colonies, however, the best farm lands and those near river transport were settled first. In fact, part of the reason I chose towns in the eastern rather than the western interior of Connecticut is that the former was settled earlier.

ble land in otherwise stony soil. Daniels, in his typology of Connecticut towns, developed a productivity index relating soil type and terrain to adaptability to various types of crops, including pasturage, given the agricultural techniques known then. Wethersfield rates a highest ranking of "8" on his overall index, while Coventry gets a "3," Bolton "2," and Willington and Union each a "1."[34]

In 1756 Union was among the least densely populated of the nonurban towns in Connecticut, and Coventry was among the more crowded. The towns still retained their relative ranking in 1790.[35] Although all the upland towns except Coventry had population growth rates higher than Wethersfield's between 1774 and 1820, none had reached even half the density of Wethersfield by the latter date (see Table 1.1).

Economic Life

I emphasize that this study seeks to establish an association between inheritance and one *particular* form of commercialization. The definition of commercialization with which I began is sufficiently abstract to embrace a variety of distinctive economic formations, including those based on large-scale monoculture using hired or coerced labor. Wethersfield, the river-valley town studied here, was a family-farm community, and it was never a purely agricultural village. Not only did its agricultural production become increasingly oriented to sales on extra-local markets, but the town supported an array of occupations ancillary to its merchants' regional and export trade.

Distinguishing "secondary centers" from "country towns" in part on the basis of levels of commercial activity, Daniels calls Wethersfield the largest secondary center on the Connecticut River.[36] Throughout the period of this study, some Wethersfield families played a significant role in export trade. The town had wharves and shipyards from which goods were carried not only to the primary port towns but directly to the West Indies and occasionally to other foreign ports. At least sixty Wethersfield men were owners or part owners of ships engaged in

[34] Daniels, *Connecticut Town*, pp. 186-90. Bolton, Union, and Willington had between 85 and 95 percent of their acreage in stony, hilly land or very stony and mountainous land. Coventry had 60 percent of its acreage in such land.

[35] Ibid., pp. 58, 60, 62.

[36] Ibid., pp. 151-52. Agricultural towns that had some port activity or towns that were major inland market centers are "secondary centers" in Daniels's classification. According to J. Main, Wethersfield is a prototypical "commercial" agriculture town. It had the comparatively high average wealth, concentration of wealth, and degree of occupational specialization that distinguish "commercial" from "subsistence-plus" agriculture towns in his classification; see J. Main, *Social Structure*, p. 34n.

coastal or export trade between 1750 and 1820, and at least seventy-five ships constructed by Wethersfield builders participated in export trade between 1740 and 1830. Families such as the Boardmans, the Bulkleys, the Kelloggs, the Robbinses, and the Williamses also developed interests in shipping and trade centered in the primary ports: their cargoes linked them to the harbors of these ports, and they had credit relations with merchants there.[37] Although the level of shipping activities could not compare with that of Connecticut's major ports, the men of Wethersfield constituted a pull—indigenous to the countryside—toward extra-local market production.

This direct participation in trade networks linking the colonies to each other and to foreign ports had its correlates in Wethersfield's greater integration into the political life of the province. For example, although province and county-level officeholders were recruited largely from men living in Connecticut's largest port towns and in the capital, Wethersfield contributed three members to the upper house of the legislature in the period 1750-1819 (compared to New London's five or Hartford's seven),[38] and its men served twenty-five years as county justices, the highest county-level judicial position, between 1725 and 1774.[39] From the upland towns, in contrast, only Jesse Root of Coventry filled one of these offices. In this regard, Union was politically very isolated. Before the Revolution, the town had never paid taxes to the colonial government and was therefore never represented in the colonial assembly.[40]

This pattern of greater integration for Wethersfield and isolation for the upland towns confirms what Daniels found to be true for the colony as a whole in the case of Assistants. (The governor, deputy governor, and twelve assistants, all elected at-large, composed the upper house of the legislature.) Between 1701 and 1784 Connecticut's five urban towns contributed 40 percent of the members of the upper house, and the seventeen secondary towns contributed 50 percent, while the other seventy-nine towns contributed only the remaining 10 percent.[41]

It already has been noted that, compared with the valley, the upland

[37] Stiles and Adams, *Ancient Wethersfield*, 1: 541, 545-46, 555-95. Because of gaps in Customs House records, the figure for seagoing ships built in Wethersfield (not all necessarily on behalf of Wethersfield owners) understates the actual number.

[38] Connecticut General Assembly, *Register and Manual of the State of Connecticut, 1889* (Hartford, 1889), pp. 69-74, 98-101.

[39] Cook, *Fathers*, pp. 154-56, 162, 200.

[40] Charles Hammond, *The History of Union, Connecticut* (New Haven, 1893), p. 128. Union was not alone in foregoing the privilege of electing deputies to the General Assembly in exchange for tax abatements. Some historians use such evidence to argue for the localist and insular nature of rural town life.

[41] Daniels, *Connecticut Town*, pp. 163-64.

was a relatively low surplus area. For his typology of New England towns, Cook developed an index of prosperity or productivity based on each town's share of its colony's taxes (in Connecticut's case, for the year 1774) divided by the town's total acreage. In this index Wethersfield gets the highest ranking in the colony, 1.301, while the upland towns range from Coventry's .724 to Union's zero.[42] Judged by its population density and value of its assessed property, Coventry was indeed a relatively prosperous country town; it did not, however, perform the function of an inland market center. In fact, according to Daniels, all of the upland towns in this study were "country towns"; that is, they neither engaged directly in the export of goods nor served as market centers for other towns.[43]

At the other end of the subsistence-plus spectrum, Union petitioners claimed, in their pleas for relief from taxes imposed by the revolutionary General Assembly, that they had no surpluses whatsoever. The affidavits and petitions of 1776 and 1778 pleaded,

> The truth is it is a miserable poor township of land. . . . It is unhappy and disagreeable to be in such a state of poverty, yet it is a fact they are obliged to own. This situation is not for want of industry or frugality . . . but is the result of their circumstances.[44]

Given their purpose the petitioners were likely to have overstated their case, but Union's poor "circumstances" were generally recognized.

By 1820 Wethersfield was an outstanding example, in the minds of contemporaries, of specialized crop production. It was famous for its extraordinary production of onions, but it was also a leader in general market gardening in the state, and would remain so according to the federal census of 1840. Its onion crop, estimated around 1820 at about one million bunches or ropes annually (about 61,000 bushels),[45] inspired the undoubtedly hyperbolic remark that it alone supplied the South with three-quarters of its supply.[46]

---

[42] Cook, *Fathers*, pp. 79-80, 200-201. He argues that this is actually an index of "commercialization," but if land is worked intensively and thus supports a higher population than land elsewhere, this is a measure not of commercialization but of productivity. See the recalculation of Cook's data in Daniel Scott Smith, "A Malthusian-Frontier Interpretation of United States Demographic History before 1815," in *Urbanization in the Americas*, ed. Woodrow Borah, Jorge Hardoy, and Gilbert Stelter (Ottawa: University of Ottawa Press, 1980); and discussion in Lemon, "Spatial Order," p. 110, and Henretta, "Wealth and Social Structure," p. 272.

[43] Daniels, *Connecticut Town*, p. 145.

[44] Hammond, *Union*, pp. 128-29.

[45] John C. Pease and John M. Niles, *Gazetteer of the States of Connecticut and Rhode Island* (Hartford, 1819), p. 89.

[46] Unattributed. Cited in Howard S. Russell, *A Long, Deep Furrow: Three Centuries*

On his 1823 tour of the eastern states, President Dwight of Yale College made the following comments about Wethersfield's intensive, "specialized" agriculture:

> They are lands . . . ordinarily fashioned with a degree of neatness and elegance, which is unrivaled. . . . The regular production of a considerable staple production is, I suspect, attended with several disadvantages to those by whom it is produced. It becomes an object of particular attention to the merchant, and will be more exposed to systematized schemes of over-reaching, than a mass of mixed and various produce.[47]

Dwight's comments on "neatness and elegance" echoed European visitors' favorable comparisons of valley agriculture with English techniques and contrasted with disparaging comments about the extensive agriculture practiced by most American farmers. He also expressed a widely held aversion to specialized agriculture: market involvement could mean dangerous dependence on merchants. The volatile nature of the still-forming national market was personified in the "scheming" merchant. And, more generally, any dependence was dangerous: full adult or independent stature was equated not only with owning productive land, but with retaining actual control over it.

In fact, market gardening was not incompatible with diversified farming. As in Wethersfield, small plots could be farmed intensively to produce cash crops in perishable foodstuffs, while outlying fields could be used to meet local needs for other agricultural goods. That market penetration of farm production should have taken this form rather than large-scale specialization fits the preexisting situation of widespread land ownership characteristic of northern rural life.

In addition, Wethersfield may have been undergoing a process of occupational "dediversification" by 1820. Wethersfield supported a wide array of artisanal services in the colonial era, but by 1819 almost all its nonfarm enterprises, such as its five distilleries, four tanneries, and two sawmills, were devoted to processing agricultural goods or to some aspect of shipbuilding. Its three fulling mills and the two carding machines were the only exceptions; in all likelihood they served only local residents. Further, Wethersfield had, in relation to its population, fewer gristmills and fulling mills, crucial services for families practicing diversified farming and producing cloth for home consumption, than did

---

of Farming in New England (Hanover, N.H.: University Press of New England, 1976), p. 374.

[47] Dwight's Travels in New England and New York, quoted in Stiles and Adams, Ancient Wethersfield, 1: 724.

the upland towns.[48] One author has concluded that Wethersfield's farm families were giving up home production of cloth and were even purchasing flour.[49]

Less is known about agricultural activities in the upland towns. None of them produced any crop sufficiently noteworthy to catch the attention of either the agricultural historians or those who wrote the sketchy town histories I consulted.[50] As noted earlier, some concentration on dairying and livestock was typical of the upland areas as a whole. The lands of Bolton, Willington, Coventry, and Union were well adapted to grazing, and a contemporary gazetteer reports that dairying constituted the "leading agricultural interest" in Coventry and Bolton. Union and Willington also engaged in lumbering.[51]

Population growth and recalcitrant land encouraged the growth of nonagricultural enterprises in the upland. By 1820 all the upland towns had small manufactures and mills that produced goods for regional and export trade. The Bolton-Vernon area, which subsequently became a leading textile center, already supported two cotton mills and one woolen mill. Two paper mills, a glass company, a shop that built carding machines, and a spinning mill had all recently opened in Coventry. Willington was also the site of a glass company and a woolen mill.[52]

These were small-scale, unstable businesses. Several changed hands more than once or closed temporarily in the economically volatile decade following the War of 1812. But they were symptomatic of the fu-

[48] Daniels, *Connecticut Town*, pp. 194-95; Pease and Niles, *Gazetteer*, pp. 89-90, 291-92, 300-301, 303.

[49] Grace P. Fuller, "An Introduction to the History of Connecticut As a Manufacturing State," *Smith College Studies in History* 1 (1915): 10.

[50] The following were used: On Bolton, George S. Brookes, *Cascades and Courage: The History of the Town of Vernon and the City of Rockville, Connecticut* (Rockville, Conn.: T. F. Rady, 1955); Henry C. Smith, comp., *Centennial of Vernon-Rockville* (Rockville, Conn.: T. F. Rady, 1908). On Coventry, Mrs. William Minor, *Coventry in Retrospect, 1712-1963* (n.p., n.d.); Maude G. Peterson, "Historical Sketch of Coventry, Connecticut," Program, Bicentennial Celebration (Coventry, 1912); Marvin Root, "History of Coventry through the Revolutionary Period," typescript, The Connecticut State Library, Hartford, 1958. On Union, George Curtiss, *History of the Congregational Church of Union, Connecticut* (n.p., 1914); Hammond, *Union*. On Willington, John Merrick, *Recollections of John Merrick, a Native of Willington, 1833-1865*, ed. Isabel Weigold (Storrs, Conn.: Parousia Press, 1978); Willington Historical Society, Comp., *Chronology of Willington, Connecticut, 1727-1927* (Storrs, Conn.: Parousia Press, 1977). The town sketches in J. R. Cole's *History of Tolland County, Connecticut* (New York, 1888) were also helpful. These and Fuller, "Manufacturing State," were used to supplement the Pease and Niles account of agricultural enterprise circa 1820, and to verify that the nonagricultural enterprises they listed as engaged in "extensive" production were producing for extra-local markets.

[51] Pease and Niles, *Gazetteer*, pp. 291-92, 300-303.

[52] Ibid., pp. 89-90, 291-92, 300-301, 303.

ture economic trajectories of the upland communities. Nonagricultural production, especially textiles, rivaled or supplanted agriculture by 1845, when textiles alone accounted for 31 to 71 percent of the total value of all goods produced in the upland towns. In contrast, market gardening was still a mainstay in Wethersfield, with agriculture contributing over three quarters of the value of Wethersfield's output, and textiles adding a scant 7 percent.[53]

Farm families in low surplus areas, when faced with population pressure on land, soil exhaustion, and a squeeze on margins over subsistence, often turned to rural industry as a source of supplementary income. Whatever its long-term effects, rural industry is at first compatible with a landed economy that is organized around a long period of dependency for its young people and domestic work by women. It allowed smaller and less productive holdings to maintain families, evened out the seasonal rhythms inherent in agriculture, and supported and shortened the "waiting period" before marriage.[54]

Much work needs to be done on mapping precisely which rural areas of New England developed nonagricultural production for extra-local markets. Wethersfield's underdeveloped nonagricultural production relative to the upland towns suggests that commercial agriculture zones are relatively immune to rural industry, while subsistence agriculture areas become increasingly susceptible to this form of extra-local market dependency.[55]

The Towns: A Summary

Wethersfield and the four upland towns meet the criteria that distinguish "commercial" and "subsistence-plus" agriculture towns and display the contrasts characteristic of Valley and upland. Wethersfield was blessed with especially rich soil: the upland towns struggled with thin soil and rocky ground. Wethersfield had immediate access to river transport; the upland towns did not. Wethersfield turned to intensive

[53] Connecticut, Office of the Secretary of State, *Statistics of the Condition and Products of Certain Branches of Industry in Connecticut for the Year Ending October 1, 1845* (Hartford, 1846). Also Clive Day, *The Rise of Manufacturing in Connecticut, 1820-1850*, Tercentenary Series, no. 44 (New Haven: Yale University Press, 1935).

[54] Clark, "Household Economy," pp. 178-82; Medick, "Family Economy"; Franklin F. Mendels, "Agriculture and Peasant Industry in Eighteenth Century Flanders," in *European Peasants and Their Markets*, ed. William Parker and Eric L. Jones (Princeton, N.J.: Princeton University Press, 1975), p. 90.

[55] Clark, "Household Economy"; Jones, "Origins of Industry"; Jones, "Afterword," in *European Peasants and Their Markets*, pp. 327-60. Franklin F. Mendels, "Proto-Industrialization: The First Phase of the Industrialization Process," *Journal of Economic History* 32 (March 1972): 241-61.

agricultural practices and sustained a dense population. The upland towns relied on dairying and livestock, sustaining less substantial populations.

In addition, Wethersfield was distinguished by the presence of a mercantile stratum that engaged directly in interregional and export trade. It was thus directly integrated into the economic and political activities that defined colonial Connecticut's developing relations with other colonies, foreign ports, and Britain. The upland towns were only indirectly connected to the economic and political life that dominated in the provincial capital and ports.

By the early nineteenth century, Wethersfield and the upland towns had started on the divergent courses that marked their alternative routes to integration into the developing national economy. Wethersfield was already a commercial farm community; its families increasingly relied on intensive agriculture and market gardening, and would continue to do so throughout the first half of the nineteenth century. The upland towns were still subsistence-plus farm communities, though they varied in the level of their prosperity; but they were beginning to develop the rural industries on which their populations would increasingly rely in the first half of the nineteenth century and beyond.

CHAPTER TWO

INHERITANCE AND LIFE-CHANCES
IN COMPARATIVE PERSPECTIVE

When most families own productive property, inheritance is a particularly promising way to study family and economy. Certainly every society has methods for regulating intergenerational succession to the use
and control of various resources. Jack Goody has said,

> The inheritance system of any society . . . is the way by which
> property is transmitted between the living and the dead, and es-
> pecially between the generations. It is part of the wider process
> whereby property relations are reproduced over time (and some-
> times changed in so doing), a process I speak of as devolution.[1]

Of course, there are ways other than inheritance to manage the "devolution" of property. In advanced capitalist societies, for example, inheritance is becoming less important because corporate ownership provides a principle of continuity for economic enterprise that is
independent of the fates of particular families.[2] And, although many
forms of productive and fiscal property can be inherited, most families
do not possess them. For those who own only consumption goods and
for those who are virtually propertyless—that is, for the great majority
of families—direct inheritance of tangible goods is of little or no importance. In the early American North, inheritance was a basic method
for regulating the "devolution" of productive property in two senses:
most of the occupied land was held in the form of securely heritable
tenures, and most families had such property.

Americans also had wide latitude in varying their inheritance practices. Once the principle of inheritance is firmly entrenched, inheritance
law and custom may regulate the choice of successors more or less
closely. Permissive inheritance systems[3] grant to individual holders the

[1] Jack Goody, "Introduction," in *Family and Inheritance: Rural Society in Western
Europe, 1200-1800*, ed. Jack Goody, Joan Thirsk, and E. P. Thompson (Cambridge,
Eng.: Cambridge University Press, 1976), p. 1.

[2] Daniel Bell, *The End of Ideology*, rev. ed. (New York: Free Press), pp. 39-42; Marvin
B. Sussman, Judith N. Gates, and David T. Smith, *The Family and Inheritance* (New
York: Russell Sage, 1970), pp. 1-5.

[3] In this text "inheritance system" refers to (1) the legal rules (national statutory or case
law and local or customary law) governing inheritance—those defining heirship, spouses'

ability to alienate property permanently during their lifetimes and to deviate from the legal or customary rules governing succession to estates held at death. Permissive systems enlarge the private powers of the individual holder, but the holder's freedom, a freedom that is a core aspect of the concept of ownership, is at the expense of the legally backed claims of other family members to use, control, and succeed to property.

The Anglo-American inheritance system was highly permissive with respect to most forms of landholding. Unless they were married women, landholders generally had broad leeway to divide property as they saw fit during their lifetimes and to select their successors at death.[4] The overall powers of seventeenth- and eighteenth-century English and colonial landholders were not the equivalent of contemporary powers, but they were greater than those of most Continental landholders. These developments had their most complete expression in the northern American colonies, where most heads of families who tilled the soil held their land under "free and common socage," a form of tenure granting the fullest rights in land then possible in Anglo-American society.[5]

By one standard the Anglo-American inheritance system was more permissive than those of contemporary Western and industrial socie-

---

shares, and testamentary powers; (2) the legal rules governing lifetime powers of alienation. It also includes the laws and customs governing (3) various types of land tenure, and (4) the property-holding capacities of different classes of persons (for example, marriage laws). This usage basically corresponds to that of Lutz Berkner and Franklin Mendels, "Inheritance Systems, Family Structure, and Demographic Patterns in Western Europe, 1700-1900," in *Historical Studies of Changing Fertility*, ed. Charles Tilly (Princeton, N.J.: Princeton University Press, 1978), pp. 211-12, except that they also include the imputed social norms governing actual practices.

[4] There were exceptions. See, for example, Richard T. Vann, "Wills and the Family in an English Town: Banbury, 1550-1800," *Journal of Family History* 4 (Winter 1979): 347, who describes restrictions on testamentary powers to deprive heirs of their legacies in York as late as 1800.

[5] It was in this form that the corporate colonies received their land. Their legislative assemblies, in turn, granted land in "socage" tenure to towns and individuals. The token of the Crown's superior proprietary right was nominal or merely formal (under Connecticut's charter, for example, one fifth of the profits of nonexistent gold and silver mines). After the American Revolution, it took a simple, bold declaration, not complex property reforms, to abolish tenure altogether in favor of allodial property—to transform all who held fee-simple estates into holders "independent of any Superior." Zephaniah Swift, *A System of the Laws of the State of Connecticut*, 2 vols. (Windham, Conn., 1795-96), 1: 238; Connecticut General Assembly, *The Public Statute Laws of the State of Connecticut. Revised 1821* (Hartford, 1821), p. 300; Marshall Harris, *Origins of the Land Tenure System in the United States* (Ames: Iowa State College Press, 1953), pp. 59-61, 116, 144-49; S.F.C. Milsom, *Historical Foundations of the Common Law* (London: Butterworth, 1969).

·ties. In the service of policies that view circulation of property as a public good and in the name of the autonomy of the living, modern English and American systems incorporate the results of a trend, detectable in the early modern period but accelerated thereafter, toward reducing "ancestrally" created restraints on alienation. In the eighteenth century, however, property holders had some scope to dictate to future generations. The Anglo-American system at the time of this study was thus doubly permissive: the holder of heritable rights, unless a married woman, had wide powers to vary the sequence of heirship and some power to define the order of succession for future generations.

Unity and Provision

Whenever the life-chances of children depend on family-held productive property, families must somehow balance the requirements for maintaining the viability of the working farm or other enterprise with their concern for "setting-up" their children; continuity or loss of class standing depends on how successfully families manage to do so. In western Europe this tension between "unity" and "provision" gave a characteristic shape to inheritance strategies within broad social classes. Certainly, families adjusted their inheritance practices as a host of demographic and economic factors altered the terms of the unity and provision problem. Yet so long as family-held property was the key to the well-being of the next generation, the fundamental tension left a well-defined impress on inheritance strategies.[6]

Among small and middling holders who had at least some flexibility in choosing their successors through wills or transfers of land during their lifetimes, inheritance practices tended to settle on a "favored heir plus burdens" pattern. Such practices preserved family property by limiting the number of children who inherited the working land and by rigorously subordinating the claims of wives to those of children. Excluded heirs, however, received claims on productive property in the form of shares in property that were less central to the integrity of the holding or in burdens imposed on preferred heirs.[7] A father who gave

[6] William J. Goode, "Family and Mobility" in *Class, Status, and Power*, 2nd ed., ed. Reinhard Bendix and Seymour Martin Lipset (New York: Free Press, 1966), p. 592; Jack Goody, "Introduction," pp. 4-5; H. J. Habbakuk, "Family Structure and Economic Change in Nineteenth Century Europe," *Journal of Economic History* 15 (1955): 1; E. P. Thompson, "The Grid of Inheritance: A Comment," in *Inheritance in Western Europe*, pp. 345-46.

[7] For examples of such practices in England, see Cicely Howell, "Peasant Inheritance Customs in the Midlands, 1200-1700," in *Inheritance in Western Europe*, pp. 112-55; David Levine and Keith Wrightson, *Poverty and Piety in an English Village: Terling 1525-1700* (New York: Academic Press, 1979); Margaret Spufford, "Peasant Inherit-

his two eldest sons all of his land, requiring them to care for their re-tired parents (or to honor life-estates created for their parents) and to provide marriage portions and legacies for their remaining siblings out of revenues from the land, practiced one classic form of the "favored heir plus burdens" strategy. Families who used this strategy tried to provide for each child indirectly by imposing burdens on the main tak-ers.

The striking feature of such arrangements, apart from the favored treatment of some male heirs, is that overlapping rights in property typ-ically created legally enforceable ties between parents and adult chil-dren, and among siblings. Although the main heirs may have held title to the land, obligations to others encumbered it, and rights to use the land or its revenues often did not belong exclusively to these heirs. The issue now is whether the inheritance practices of American family farmers ought to have had substantially similar characteristics.

Long before Tocqueville argued that partible inheritance promoted political and social democracy, American republicans pointed with pride to the egalitarian inheritance practices of northern yeomen, ob-serving that land abundance had promoted divisibility. Certainly, uni-geniture, the inheritance of all land by one heir, was rare in the Ameri-can colonies. Tocqueville also associated partible inheritance with a weakened sense of family solidarity. Commenting on what he supposed was the decline of great estates after the American Revolution, he wrote,

> When the law ordains equal shares, it breaks that intimate con-nection between family feeling and preservation of the land; the land no longer represents the family, for, as it is bound to be di-vided up at the end of one or two generations, it is clear that it must continually diminish and completely disappear in the end. . . .
>
> As the family is felt to be a vague, indeterminate, uncertain con-ception, each man concentrates on his immediate convenience; he

ance Customs and Land Distribution in Cambridgeshire from the Sixteenth to the Eight-eenth Centuries," in *Inheritance in Western Europe*, pp. 156-76. Berkner and Mendels, "Inheritance Systems," pp. 213-14, summarize such practices in permissive inheritance areas of eighteenth- and nineteenth-century France. On these areas of France at an earlier date, see Emmanuel Le Roy Ladurie, "Family Structures and Inheritance Customs in Six-teenth Century France," in *Inheritance in Western Europe*, pp. 42-45, 48-51. For refer-ences to France, Germany, and Austria, see Lutz Berkner, "Inheritance, Land Tenure, and Peasant Family Structure: A German Regional Comparison," in *Inheritance in West-ern Europe*, pp. 71-95; Berkner, "The Stem Family and the Developmental Cycle of the Peasant Household: An Eighteenth Century Austrian Example," *American Historical Review* 77 (April 1972): 398-418.

thinks about getting the next generation established in life but nothing further.[8]

Here Tocqueville yokes divisibility to individualism. Note that in his conception, individualism depends on a foreshortened perspective on intergenerational family ties. Among other things, individualism is a narrow preoccupation with the dictates of private and natural affections that extend no further than one's own children. It is a nuclear-family orientation.

Some go further than Tocqueville, maintaining that inheritance ceased to be a major determinant of life-chances very early in the American experience. Referring to the late eighteenth century, Jackson Turner Main writes, "perhaps most important to the average American was the fact that class did not depend on inheritance but upon property. Since anyone could acquire property, anyone could rise."[9] Land abundance and opportunities for emigration coupled with a nonseigneurial social structure meant that short-range vertical mobility was a matter of opportunities seized by individuals, who, at most, were aided by a "head start" in the form of skills or a small inheritance.[10] The tension between unity and provision never prevailed because unique Amerian conditions sundered the connection between family property and life-chances.

Others reject this view of family orientations and inheritance in the American North. For James Henretta, emigration due to failure to receive a landed portion was exile: a last resort forced by the same insufficiency of local land that consigned some "parents . . . to endure a harsh old age, sharing their small plot with the remaining heir." Henretta continues, "the basic character of the farm family" did not change in the preindustrial period:

> The agricultural family remained an extended lineal one; each generation lived in a separate household, but the character of production and inheritance linked these conjugal units through a myriad of legal, moral and customary bonds. Rights and responsibilities stretched across the generations. . . . The line was more

---

[8] Alexis de Tocqueville, *Democracy in America* (New York: Doubleday-Anchor, 1969), p. 53.

[9] Jackson Turner Main, *The Social Structure of Revolutionary America* (Princeton, N.J.: Princeton University Press, 1965), pp. 219-20.

[10] James Lemon, *The Best Poor Man's Country: A Geographical Study of Early Southeastern Pennsylvania* (Baltimore: Johns Hopkins University Press, 1972), and Stephanie Grauman Wolf, *Urban Village: Population, Community and Family Structure in Germantown, Pennsylvania, 1683-1800* (Princeton, N.J.: Princeton University Press, 1976), also write in this vein.

important than the individual; the patrimony had to be conserved for lineal purposes.[11]

The implication is that American family farmers faced fundamentally the same tension between unity and provision that European producers did. Henretta bases his view in part on local studies of inheritance, indicating that as the eighteenth century wore on—as local land was parceled out and as the population grew—extensive partitioning became less common. More men excluded some sons from any share in parental land, and many limited ownership of at least their home lots to one or two sons. Families in Andover and Ipswich, Massachusetts, in Guilford, Connecticut, and elsewhere practiced preferential partibility, and they apparently imposed obligations on favored heirs. The same studies agree that daughters were unlikely to inherit land and that, as a rule, widows were limited to life-estates in land.[12] Thus their practices appear to have been variants of the "favored heir plus burdens" pattern described by the Europeanists.

The reader will recognize that these conflicting interpretations bear the impress of the American exceptionalism thesis and its critics. On the one hand, farmers, freed by American abundance to snub even the authority of their fathers, confined their loyalties to their immediate families, maintaining only loose bonds with kin and neighbors residing beyond the roof. On the other hand, yeomen, obsessed with the need to preserve their patrimonies in a threatening environment, created complex family ties in an effort to balance the tension between unity and provision.

[11] James Henretta, "Families and Farms: 'Mentalité' in Pre-Industrial America," *William and Mary Quarterly*, 3rd ser., 35 (January 1978): 22, 24-26. Also see Henretta, "Wealth and Social Structure," in *Colonial British America*, ed. Jack P. Greene and J. R. Pole (Baltimore: Johns Hopkins University Press, 1984), p. 266.

[12] The following contain detailed discussions of inheritance in particular northern towns and regions: On New England, Linda Auwers, "Fathers, Sons, and Wealth in Colonial Windsor, Connecticut," *Journal of Family History* 3 (Summer 1978): 136-49; Philip J. Greven, Jr., *Four Generations: Population, Land, and Family in Colonial Andover, Massachusetts* (Ithaca, N.Y.: Cornell University Press, 1972); Christopher M. Jedrey, *The World of John Cleaveland: Family and Community in Eighteenth-Century New England* (New York: Norton, 1979), pp. 74-94; John Waters, "Patrimony, Succession, and Social Stability: Guilford, Connecticut in the Eighteenth Century," *Perspectives in American History* 10 (1976): 131-60. On the mid-Atlantic colonies, see Barry Levy, " 'Tender Plants': Quaker Farmers and Children in the Delaware Valley, 1681-1735," *Journal of Family History* 3 (Summer 1978): 116-55; Lemon, *Poor Man's Country*, pp. 94-95; Daniel Snydacker, "Kinship and Community in Rural Pennsylvania, 1749-1820," *Journal of Interdisciplinary History* 8 (Summer 1982): 41-61. On wives and widows, see Alexander Keyssar, "Widowhood in Eighteenth-Century Massachusetts: A Problem in the History of the Family," *Perspectives in American History* 8 (1974): 103-106, as well as occasional comments in the studies already cited.

DEFINING INHERITANCE STRATEGIES

Those who reject the idea that Americans were "born modern" have staked out their positions by interpreting the property orientations of American family farmers as patrilineal. Notice that Henretta identifies a widespread "extended lineal" family orientation. John Waters, in his local studies of Barnstable, Massachusetts, and Guilford, Connecticut, interprets the frequent practice of splitting the home lot between two male heirs as patrilineal, and he even uses the term "primogeniture" to refer to distributions of land that merely favor the eldest son.[13]

To equate partibility—even preferential partibility—with lineal family orientations is to reverse Tocquevillian logic. In classic formulations, such as Tocqueville's, partibility is antithetical to family strategies seeking to conserve estates for "lineal" purposes. Further, when Tocqueville spoke of inheritance practices that preserved patrimonies, he was referring to aristocratic devices such as entails and the English strict settlement.[14] Were the inheritance strategies of the "middling sort" patrilineal? Were they the plain people's version of the inegalitarian practices prevailing among landholding elites? I think not. To avoid the conclusion that family property relations were modern and individualist, some have reasoned as if patrilineal arrangements were the only alternative. In this section I make a distinction between patrilineal and "extended cognate" inheritance strategies that provides a firmer foundation for analyzing American inheritance practices and for making trans-Atlantic comparisons of inheritance patterns.

Patrimonial Inheritance Strategies

Among European landholding elites "patrimonial" inheritance strategies were widespread. Using this strategy, holders sought to preserve

[13] Waters, "Patrimony," pp. 139, 149-50, 159-60; also John Waters, "The Traditional World of the New England Peasant: A View from Seventeenth-Century Barnstable," *New England Historical and Genealogical Register* 30 (January 1976): 4-5. Also see Jedrey, *World of John Cleaveland*, pp. 78-79.

[14] Those who study the inheritance practices of American landed elites, including those of the South, are struck by the infrequency with which their practices involved the creation of life-estates for males, entails, and other "aristocratic devices." See Bernard Bailyn, "Politics and Social Structure in Colonial Virginia," in *Colonial America: Essays in Politics and Social Development*, 2nd ed., ed. Stanley N. Katz (Boston: Little, Brown, 1976), pp. 136-39; James Deen, Jr., "Patterns of Testation: Four Tidewater Counties in Colonial Virginia," *American Journal of Legal History* 16 (1972): 154-77; C. Roy Keim, "Primogeniture and Entail in Colonial Virginia," *William and Mary Quarterly*, 3rd ser., 25 (October 1968): 545-86; Daniel Blake Smith, *Inside the Great House: Planter Family Life in Eighteenth-Century Chesapeake Society* (Ithaca, N.Y.: Cornell University Press, 1980), pp. 231-48.

and to augment their estates by creating a complex array of rights in property among members of past, present, and future generations. These practices vest management of the main estate in a narrow band or "line" of successive male heads, but do not give them full powers to transfer property or its proceeds. Families treat the core of the estate as a trust for members of successive generations. The line of male heads manage it, but they must honor other family members' claims to use or to enjoy the revenues from this patrimony.[15]

The strict settlement, which became standard practice among English elites in the eighteenth century, is one example of such patrimonial inheritance strategies. Typically, the marriage of the eldest son was the occasion for renegotiating major issues concerning succession to great estates. The strict settlement ordinarily provided that the eldest son would become a life-tenant of his father's main estate at the expiration of his father's tenancy, while his future firstborn son was designated a "tenant entail." In principle, a life-tenant was entitled only to the income from an estate; but in fact, almost all settlements also granted the main heir some powers to mortgage, lease, or even sell peripheral land. These limited powers gave the heir managerial flexibility, but their primary purpose was to empower him to raise sums for his wife's maintenance (jointure) and for his younger children's portions. Such an estate would also in all likelihood be encumbered with obligations to the main heir's sisters and brothers. Finally, the settlement normally would provide for alternative heirs should the main line of succession be broken.[16]

There are, for our purposes, two key features of patrimonial inheritance strategies. First, relations between main heirs and their siblings are typically ones of subordination and dependency in relation to claims upon ancestral property. Not only are the claims of women as daughters and wives subordinate to those of brothers and husbands, but the claims of some brothers are subordinate to others. Patrimonial

---

[15] See H. J. Habbakuk, "Marriage Settlements in the Eighteenth Century," *Transactions of the Royal Historical Society*, 4th ser., 32 (1950): 15-30, and Eileen Spring, "The Strict Settlement of Land in Nineteenth Century England," *American Journal of Legal History* 8 (1964): 209-23, on such practices among the English gentry and aristocracy. See J. P. Cooper, "Patterns of Inheritance and Settlement by Great Landowners from the Fifteenth to the Eighteenth Centuries," in *Family and Inheritance*, pp. 192-327, on English and Continental aristocracies, and Ralph Geisey, "Rules of Inheritance and Strategies of Mobility in Prerevolutionary France," *American Historical Review* 82 (April, 1977): 271-89, on the eighteenth-century *haute bourgeoisie*.

[16] Habbakuk, "Marriage Settlements"; Spring, "Strict Settlement." Also see references to the evolution of the strict settlement in Lawrence Stone, *The Family, Sex, and Marriage in England, 1500-1800* (New York: Harper Colophon, 1979), pp. 70-73, 136-37, 166-68, 221-22.

inheritance practices are highly inegalitarian. Second, preestablished entitlements for members of future generations restrict the will of any given incumbent. Overlapping claims in real property extend at least three generations.

In this study the terms "patrimonial" and "strongly patrilineal" refer to those inheritance practices that not only favor some male heirs, but also contain this corporate or dynastic element in patterns of rights creation. Such practices are patrilineal in a double sense.[17] They give control over property to paternally related males, and they attempt to keep property within the line by curtailing the ability to alienate it and to designate its successors.

Extended Cognate Inheritance Strategies

To identify the "favored heir plus burdens" strategies found among European owner-producers as patrilineal is to create conceptual confusion. To be sure, the inheritance practices of European producers in some regions were at first glance highly inegalitarian. When pressure on land was severe and other sources of support for children were few, holders tended not to divide their land. But at least among brothers, inequalities were forced. Intergenerational accumulation was not the aim. Had the goal been accumulation, impartible practices would have continued well beyond the point required to maintain a viable farm. This seems not to have occurred.[18] The father with fifteen acres may have practiced impartibility, but he who had forty usually divided his property. Further, the father who passed his farm to his eldest son did not ordinarily restrict his son's rights in property by creating claims for future generations. The son ordinarily received property unencumbered by claims created on behalf of his own children. In short, these practices were not strongly patrilineal, and they were not analogous to the patrimonial practices of landholding elites.

In a recent study of eighteenth- and nineteenth-century English elites, Randolph Trumbach argues that social historians have not taken seriously enough the cognate organization of kinship. The English kinship system has always traced descent through both mothers and fathers,

[17] There is a sense in which almost all European inheritance systems and actual practices are "lineal." In most, direct descendants take before collaterals. For contrasts with lateral descent systems, see Jack Goody, "Strategies of Heirship," *Comparative Studies in Society and History* 15 (January 1973): 3-7. Social historians often use the term patrilineal to refer to any inheritance strategy that heavily favors males.

[18] Howell, "Inheritance in the Midlands," pp. 117, 154-55; Spufford, "Inheritance and Land in Cambridgeshire," pp. 164-69; Thompson, "Grid of Inheritance," pp. 341-49.

and it recognizes affines as kin. He finds that even among elites patrilineal orientations were largely restricted to the sphere of inheritance, as
in the strict settlement. Even there they were diluted. In other spheres
of action such as marriage and political alliances, patrilineal principles
were weak or did not operate at all. Instead, individuals called upon
shifting networks of maternal and paternal kin and in-laws, depending
on social context.[19]

When lineal kin orientations are absent, it is too often assumed that
strong ties ordinarily unite only parents and unmarried children and
that only nuclear or conjugal kin orientations remain. But cognate kinship systems can support complex kin ties. Although it may not show
clearly on kinship diagrams, there is a world of difference between family arrangements that stress primary loyalty to spouses and young children and those that reinforce significant bonds between parents and
adult children and among adult siblings. Parents who simply parcel out
their property among all their children are reinforcing the autonomy of
families of "procreation." The parental household and the families of
grown children remain separate; inheritance does not connect them.
But inheritance practices that require grown sons to care for aged parents, to provide legacies for other adult sisters and brothers, and to co-
operate with each other in the running of inherited enterprises reinforce
extended kin ties. This is especially the case when the inheriting children are already married or are about to be married. Such practices do
not reinforce intergenerational solidarities beyond that of parents and
children; they are not "lineal" in this sense. But because sisters, brothers, and siblings' spouses can be very significant figures, these practices
contribute to extended same-generation solidarities.[20] In deference to
what are cognate though not narrowly conjugal patterns of kin recognition, we shall call these practices "extended cognate" inheritance
practices.

This study reserves the term "extended cognate" for those inheritance practices that do not restrict the authority of main takers with respect to their own offspring, but do impose obligations on the heirs to
main holdings. One can summarize the differences between patrimonial and extended cognate strategies by stating that they manage the
tension between unity and provision differently. One emphasizes accumulation and continuity at the expense of equality; the other, equal-

[19] Randolph Trumbach, *The Rise of the Egalitarian Family: Aristocratic Kinship and
Domestic Relations in Eighteenth Century England* (New York: Academic Press, 1978),
p. 13.

[20] Ibid., pp. 1-11, 12-18, 288-89. Also see Conrad M. Arensberg and Solon Kimball,
Family and Community in Ireland (Cambridge, Mass.: Harvard University Press, 1940),
pp. 61-97, for discussion of cognate kin orientations among rural peasant families.

ity of standing at the expense of accumulation and at the risk of loss of continuity. The former routinely creates inequalities among families headed by siblings in efforts to bind property to successive generations of the paternal line. In the latter, families strive to establish a landed base for as many children as they can. They give each child direct shares in the main holding or claims on it that establish ties between main takers and other siblings. And, at the time of transfer, holders give new family heads autonomy with respect to the fates of third and future generations.

As we have seen, partibility by itself can be interpreted to fit the predilections of almost any analyst. Some Americanists have also been tempted to minimize the extent of partitioning in order to avoid the conclusion that inheritance practices were individualist or modern. The distinction between patrilineal and extended cognate practices takes some of the interpretive burden away from property distribution by emphasizing rights creation. Thus, for example, although the practices of most families in eighteenth-century Andover and Guilford lacked strongly lineal features, they were certainly not egalitarian and individualist share-and-share-alike practices. Rather, they were variants of the "favored heir plus burdens" pattern and would be classified here as extended cognate practices.

INHERITANCE AND MARKETS

Among European producers, when agriculture was not commercialized and labor markets were little developed, "favored heir plus burdens" strategies dominated. Still, the degree of inequality in the partitioning of land varied greatly. So long as the laws governing inheritance allowed producers some flexibility in disposing of their holdings, property holders adapted their inheritance practices to population pressure on land. Variation in the extent of partitioning apparently was a response to threats to the viability of the productive unit, whose fragmentation jeopardized everyone's entitlement to be set-up out of family property. Preferential partibility became impartibility only when land was scarce.[21]

Of course, sheer demographic pressure itself did not impose limits on partibility. Local conceptions of a subsistence living coupled with the productive capacity of the land when worked with given agricultural

---

[21] Berkner, "Inheritance, Tenure, and Family," pp. 83-84; Habbakuk, "Family and Economic Change," pp. 11-12; Howell, "Inheritance in the Midlands," pp. 117, 154-55; Ladurie, "Family and Inheritance Customs," pp. 43-46, 48-57; Spufford, "Inheritance and Land in Cambridgeshire," pp. 164-69; Thompson, "Grid of Inheritance," pp. 341-49.

techniques helped define the threshold of viability. Viability, moreover, was not simply a function of the amount of property held under given cultural and technological conditions. It also depended on other local resources not subject to individual inheritance. When possession of land, or even simply residence, entitled families to the use of common lands, to grazing rights, to woodlands, and to fishing places, families could subsist on smaller parcels of land than would have been otherwise possible.[22] In addition, when nonagricultural sources of support, such as domestic outwork for local industry, did become available, they allowed small parcels to sustain families, and therefore permitted continuation of partible practices. Even when sources of income were distant, farm families sometimes used them not as alternatives to landed status, but as supplements, as in seasonal migration from the countryside into cities.[23] All these conditions formed what E. P. Thompson calls the "grid of inheritance": those elements of the larger environment in reference to which inheritance strategies are planned and become effective solutions to the unity-provision problem.[24]

The development of labor markets and the commercialization of agricultural production discouraged "favored heir plus burdens" strategies. In the long run, markets reduced, even eliminated, the tension between unity and provision. Orientation to cash returns established new standards for efficient production that discouraged the accumulation of land for heirs at the expense of sound mixes of movable capital and land. By the same token, it penalized practices that separated land from other productive property (cows and plows to one, land to another). It also discouraged the creation of burdens that reduced the flexibility of agricultural enterprise or diminished the liquidity of assets.[25]

At the same time, when people in rural communities became highly dependent on nonlanded sources of income, these ceased to be merely part of the larger "grid of inheritance." In areas that were densely settled, the son who was apprenticed to a craftsman and the daughter who worked in a mill were often reduced to a mere hope of gaining landed status. When such alternatives were attractive, or the local population pressure on land was compelling, the possibility of permanent nonlanded employment encouraged holders to keep their land intact and

[22] Spufford, "Inheritance and Land in Cambridgeshire"; Thompson, "Grid of Inheritance."

[23] Habbakuk, "Family and Economic Change," pp. 6-9; David Levine, *Family Formation in an Age of Nascent Capitalism* (New York: Academic Press, 1977), p. 13; Thompson, "Grid of Inheritance," p. 342.

[24] Thompson, "Grid of Inheritance."

[25] Creighton, "Family and Production," pp. 154-56; Howell, "Inheritance in the Midlands," pp. 149-55.

to reduce the burdens on main heirs by giving other heirs consumption goods or small legacies.[26]

Such practices attempted to maximize the economic success of the family enterprise by eliminating claims that limited its manager's flexibility. Holders did so by giving unencumbered ownership rights in the enterprise to one or some family members considered capable of management, while confining the rights of others to residual property. These strategies did not use overlapping rights to link family members. Because the life-chances of children did not depend so heavily on family property, holders were free to put their primary emphasis on the integrity of their business concerns.

"Favored heir plus burdens" strategies can also collapse in another way. When families no longer depend on family-held productive property, "share-and-share-alike" notions of equity can become the main considerations that guide inheritance strategies. Holders simply disperse family property and make no sharp distinctions among different types of property.[27] Because children do not depend on parental property to assure their livelihoods, spouses are likely to take before children, and daughters are likely to inherit equally with sons. Just when productive property ceases to be important, women's status with respect to control over property improves. Such share-and-share-alike strategies are characteristic of contemporary families who own only consumption or fiscal property. They also may have been typical in areas dominated by putting-out industries, that is, in households that had come to rely primarily on piece-rates or wages rather than on productive property.[28]

In the case of provisioning strategies, the effective scope of kin reference for the purpose of inheritance transfers extends no further than nuclear families. For the great majority of those who have accumulated

---

[26] Howell, "Inheritance in the Midlands," pp. 152-53; Michel Verdon, "The Stem Family: Toward a General Theory," *Journal of Interdisciplinary History* 10 (Summer 1979): 93-98, 101.

[27] One variant does not disperse property. Using the modern trust, families attempt to create a provisioning fund that extends to members of future generations. In such arrangements, in contrast to patrimonial arrangements, management *and* powers to transfer property combine, typically in the hands of outsiders, while "enjoyment" of the revenues is separated from the use of property. See Lawrence Friedman, "Patterns of Testation in the Nineteenth Century: A Study of Essex County Wills," *American Journal of Legal History* 8 (1964): 34-53.

[28] Habbakuk, "Family and Economic Change," p. 10; Sussman, Gates, and Smith, *The Family and Inheritance*; Hans Medick, "The Proto-Industrial Family Economy: The Structural Function of Household and Family during the Transition from Peasant Society to Industrial Capitalism," *Social History*, no. 3 (October 1976): 310-13; Thompson, "Grid of Inheritance," pp. 242-45.

savings, arrangements concerning property influence relations only between spouses. Parents primarily influence their children's life-chances
indirectly, by "bequeathing" intangibles that procure advantageous labor-market positions or marriage to one who has such a position: sub-
culture, education, influence. They provide a head start in life.

In sum, developed markets dissolve the tension between unity and
provision. Efforts to maintain the class standing of members of successor generations shift from the terrain of property; direct inheritance of
tangible goods is no longer a central mechanism in the reproduction of
class. Even when families do own an enterprise, its success depends on
responsiveness to market forces. Property arrangements that permit
this responsiveness are possible because the next generation's fate no
longer depends on direct inheritance of productive property.

MARKETS AND INHERITANCE IN
THE AMERICAN NORTH

The comparison of subsistence-plus and commercial agriculture communities seeks to link inheritance, family organization, and market development. In light of the European experience, I expect to find that
farmers in Wethersfield and the uplands pursued different inheritance
practices. Such a finding would anchor inheritance and related aspects
of family life neither in unique American conditions nor in a tradition-
alism impervious to economic development, but in early market processes that heightened differences in rural social organization.

Given that New England was a family-farm region, patrimonial
strategies should be rare. Elites likely to adopt lineal and corporate
strategies for maintaining family standing did not, for the most part,
live in northern family-farm communities. Beyond this, inheritance
practices should have been more homogeneous and stable in the subsistence-plus or upland area. The economic autarky of the communities
in this area—their insulation from extra-local market pressures, their
unspecialized production and relatively small surpluses, their undifferentiated occupational structure, that is, the extraordinary dependence
of every community member on the local land—ought to have generated a sharp tension between unity and provision.

Estate holders should have settled as many children on the land as
was consistent with maintaining the integrity of their working farms.
They were likely to confine daughters and spouses to secondary claims
on core holdings (such as use rights) and to impose obligations on main
takers. Local pressure on land at the end of the colonial period may
have resulted in less partitioning and in correspondingly heightened

burdens on preferred heirs. In sum, subsistence-plus agriculture should have encouraged extended cognate inheritance practices.

Commercial development in Wethersfield should have led to more variation in inheritance practices. As concern for liquidity of assets, flexibility of agricultural enterprise, and creditworthiness increased, holders should have been more reluctant to limit the economic decision-making power of main heirs. Inheritance practices that separated the use and ownership of land should have declined. Portions or legacies should have come from revenues already accumulated or from sales of residual property. They were less likely to take the form of claims on main takers for future revenues.

Smaller holders in Wethersfield faced an economic environment quite different than that of their counterparts in the upland towns. Small holdings were more vulnerable in market-oriented Wethersfield. At the same time, increasingly specialized services and shipping activity provided more local sources of nonlanded, permanent employment. As a consequence, holders were under less pressure to practice extensive partitioning and to impose obligations on main heirs. In sum, extended cognate strategies ought to have declined in Wethersfield as commercialization dissolved the tension between unity and provision.

If, as expected, extended cognate practices declined in Wethersfield but endured in the upland, then inheritance strategies followed the dynamics suggested by the European literature. Differences in inheritance practices and in the structure of kin ties reinforced by these practices would be rooted in uneven market development. Such findings would help to delimit the scope of the claims concerning family and economic life made on both sides of the American exceptionalism debate.

What would it mean, however, if practices in Wethersfield and the upland were similar? Inheritance practices may have failed uniformly to display any tension between unity and provision. Holders in both areas may have dispersed their assets on a share-and-share-alike basis, failing to create overlapping rights in their property. Such a pattern would support the thesis that the American North was a crucible in which frontier conditions, land abundance, and a nonseigneurial social structure forged distinctive and modern forms of American family and community life. There is an alternative. Practices of the "favored heir plus burdens" type may have prevailed everywhere, indicating that tension between unity and provision persisted in commercialized Wethersfield and in upland towns alike. This would suggest that neither distinctive regional conditions nor early forms of commercialization severed the connection between inherited property and life-chances in northern—or at least New England—family-farm communities.

Probate Populations and Methodology

This study includes the inheritance practices of all individuals whose estates began probate in the years 1753-55, 1772-74, and 1820-21, and who died in the selected towns.[29] In the 1753-55 cluster this yielded thirty-nine estates for Wethersfield, and twenty-five for the subsistence-plus (or upland) towns; in 1772-74, thirty-two and twenty-three estates, respectively; and in 1820-21, thirty-six and thirty-one estates, respectively.

The procedure for collecting and analyzing data on inheritance practices adopted here is a compromise between two very different approaches. Procedures based on intergenerational reconstruction of family histories select a population and trace the history of families for a given period.[30] This study is not based on intergenerational reconstruction of family histories for several reasons. When the time period is long and families are large, one must either begin with a very small number of families or concentrate on the practices of selected members of these families (for example, sons). In addition, such studies focus on the practices of a special population: families who stay put generation after generation. Since the emphasis here is on the inheritance patterns that prevailed in given economic areas, it was inappropriate to use a procedure that would so limit the range of estate holders and their kin. Instead, the following chapters analyze the practices of all decedents (from the selected towns) whose estates were probated in a given series of years.

A second major approach to the study of inheritance practices covers much larger populations and geographic areas than is possible in studies that reconstitute family histories. It examines the probate and land records without reference to the background characteristics of the individuals involved and without coordination of lifetime and post mortem transfers.[31] When family heads transfer significant amounts of property to offspring (or others) during their lifetimes, however, examination of wills or the distribution of intestate estates alone can give a distorted picture of intergenerational succession. The same is true if one does not know the age of the estate holders or the sex, number, and marital statuses of their children. For example, the interpretation of the meaning of a testamentary transfer of equal amounts of land to two

[29] In 65 percent of the cases, year of death is known exactly. The figure does not fall below 50 percent in any time or area. In all cases where year of death is known, probate occurred in the same year. It is therefore safe to assume that the population which entered probate at the same time also died at the same time.

[30] See, for example, Greven, *Four Generations*.

[31] See, for example, Keim, "Primogeniture and Entail."

sons alters depending upon the sons' family responsibilities. Use of land records is also severely limited without this information. It is often impossible to identify family transactions when they take place between in-laws or even between parents and married daughters. Therefore, this study includes such background information on the probate population and it analyzes their recorded lifetime transfers. This "partial reconstruction" of families allows for controls fundamental to a satisfactory analysis of inheritance practices.[32]

Probated but intestate populations, whose inheritance practices can be analyzed with the approach used here, should be distinguished sharply from that population whose transfers of property go unexamined because its members are unregistered in the probate records. Throughout the period of study, Connecticut statutes required that the estates of all who died owning personal or real property be probated, stipulated stiff fines for failure to comply, and allocated the resulting monies in such a way as to provide an incentive for both town officials and parties interested in the estate to comply or to report instances of noncompliance.[33]

Despite these legal inducements to comply, scholars using New England colonial probate records estimate that anywhere from 40 to 70 percent of the adult male population died without having their estates probated.[34] Unless one is willing to assume that all adult "nonprobate"

[32] Appendix C describes sources and procedures for generating the probate population in more detail.

[33] Failure to exhibit a known will within thirty days of the testator's death entailed a penalty of 5 pounds per month against the named executor in 1750 and 17 dollars per month in 1820. It is unclear who was to be fined for failure to report the death of an intestate to the probate court (this may have been the duty of a town official or of the family member charged by law with the duty of reporting deaths to the town clerk), but once letters of administration were assigned or the executor's bond was taken, failure to produce an inventory within two months met with the same monthly fine. One half the proceeds of these fines were to go to the town in which the decedent died and one half to the person who reported the noncompliance. See Connecticut General Assembly, *Acts and Laws of His Majesty's English Colony of Connecticut in New England in America* (New London, 1750), pp. 49-50 (hereafter cited as *Acts & Laws 1750*); Connecticut General Assembly, *The Public Statute Laws of the State of Connecticut, Revised 1821* (Hartford, 1821), pp. 200-203 (hereafter cited as *Public Statutes 1821*).

[34] Daniel Scott Smith finds that in Hingham, Massachusetts, 46 percent of the men dying left neither wills nor inventories in the period 1726-86; see "Underregistration and Bias in Probate Records: Analysis of Data from Eighteenth Century Hingham, Massachusetts," *William and Mary Quarterly*, 3rd ser., 32 (January 1975): 104. Gloria L. Main reports that estimates for the period 1650 to 1720 are that 75 percent of Boston men's estates were unprobated, but 90 percent of men's estates in the rural town of Medford were probated. On the eve of the Revolution, 40 percent of all Massachusetts men's estates were probated; see "Probate Records As a Source for Early American History," *William and Mary Quarterly*, 3rd ser., 32 (January 1975); 97-99. Alice Hanson Jones

types were propertyless, an assumption no one working with probate records is willing to make, the procedure outlined here does miss the practices of one important type of property holder: those whose estates were allocated informally among kin at their deaths. This study can speak with authority only about the inheritance practices of probated holders. In key respects they differed from unprobated holders. They were legal "compliers," and one can probably assume that they transferred a smaller proportion of their property during their lifetimes. Beyond this, the characteristics of those who died unprobated are educated guesswork. They probably had fewer debts, fewer close kin, and less wealth than their probated counterparts.[35] Whether their strategies, apart from timing and legal form, differed from those of the probated population is a matter for further study.

The comparative strategy is well suited to address the relationship between inheritance and market development. But there is a methodological cost. By definition, probate populations are not representative of living populations, and, as just discussed, they may not be fully representative of all those who die in a given time and place. The compar-

---

estimates that in 1774 the estates of 67.3 percent of New England's adult property holders were unprobated, but notes that her sampling procedures may have missed some probated estates; see "Wealth Estimates for the New England Colonies about 1770," *Journal of Economic History* 32 (March 1972): 115-17. Jackson Turner Main notes that at mid-century about 67 percent of Connecticut men had their estates probated—a decline from 1700, when close to 90 percent were probated; see "The Distribution of Property in Colonial Connecticut," in *The Human Dimensions of Nation-Making: Essays on Colonial and Revolutionary America*, ed. James Kirby Martin (Madison: State Historical Society of Wisconsin, 1976), p. 56. Finally, John Waters found that of 136 men on the East Guilford tax lists between 1732 and 1740, 63 percent had their estates probated in some district in Connecticut; see "Patrimony," pp. 138, 142.

For the nineteenth century, Lawrence Friedman proposes a figure of 10 percent probated in a New Jersey county in 1850; see "Patterns of Testation." Most assume a dropping rate of probate from the late eighteenth through the nineteenth centuries. Also see William H. Newell, "The Wealth of Testators and its Distribution: Butler County, Ohio," in *Modeling the Distribution and Intergenerational Transmission of Wealth*, ed. James D. Smith (Chicago: University of Chicago Press, 1980), pp. 95-138.

[35] A. Jones, in "New England Colonies," pp. 116-18, is willing to assume that the average wealth at death of nonprobates was one quarter to one half that of probated estate holders. Bruce Daniels writes only that it is "safe" to assume that the estates of the nonprobated in Connecticut fell within the bottom two thirds of the economic spectrum; see "Money-Value Definitions of Economic Classes in Colonial Connecticut, 1770-1776," *Histoire Sociale-Social History*, no. 8 (November 1974): 347. Daniel Scott Smith found that noninventoried men held on average only one third the real property held by inventoried men; see "Underregistration," p. 106. Other factors making it less likely that an estate would be probated are low indebtedness, a thin kin network, and time of year and distance from court; see Daniels, "Money-Value," p. 347; A. Jones, "New England Colonies," p. 115; G. Main, "Probate Records," p. 98. See Appendices A and B for further discussion of bias in the probate populations of Wethersfield and the upland towns.

ative approach adds another layer of complexity. The probate populations in Wethersfield and the upland are unlikely to be biased in
precisely the same way, especially given the small samples used here.
Appendices A and B discuss in detail the sex, marital status, family responsibilities, and wealth of the probate populations in Wethersfield
and the upland. Whenever possible, the appendices distinguish between random differences in the two probate populations and those
that are the consequence of the underlying dissimilarities between subsistence-plus and commercial agriculture communities. The next sections provide a brief profile of all estate holders based on the more extensive presentation in the appendices. Although we cannot always
identify precisely the biases in this group of probates, we can at least
control for the accidental differences that can affect inheritance practices.

Sex, Marital Status, and Children

The probate population was composed largely of married men who
had children capable of inheriting.[36] Women were never more than a
quarter of the probate population, and the percentages of probated
women were always very similar in Wethersfield and the upland (see
Appendix B, Table B.2). Almost all colonial probates (over 90 percent)
had children. The exception was Wethersfield in the 1750s, though
even there only 21 percent of the probates died without children capable of inheriting. There was a striking increase in the number of property holders who had no children in the 1820s, particularly in Wethersfield (47 percent, compared to 26 percent in the uplands). Appendix B
offers some possible explanations for the change in the proportions of
childless holders.

Estate holders with children capable of inheriting are critically important since, in their case, intergenerational transmission of property
is direct. Accordingly, the following chapters will usually provide a separate analysis of this group's practices. Women were few and their percentage in the populations of the two areas are very similar at any given
time; in most cases their practices will not be treated separately in the

[36] In this study, holders are considered childless when they had no children capable of
inheriting. A child "capable of inheriting" is a child who is alive at the time of the distribution of the decedent's estate or who has direct descendants who can take in his or her
place. When lifetime transfers of property are taken into account, as in this study, other
definitions are possible. One could, for example, include all children who reach the age
of twenty-one before the decedent's death, though they may die childless before their parents. Fortunately, a definition limited to children alive at their parent's deaths or capable
of inheriting through representatives is possible because, in fact, no decedent ever gave
land during his or her lifetime to a child not also subsequently capable of sharing in his
or her parent's probated estate either directly or through children.

quantitative analysis. When women's practices did differ from those of men, qualitative analysis will note it.

Since this study focuses on inheritance and market integration, it is important to establish that differences in inheritance patterns are not reducible to the very different provisioning problems faced by families at different stages in their developmental cycles. For example, estate holders with young or unmarried children are more likely to make arrangements that resemble trusts than those whose children are married. They will not, of course, have had the opportunity to transfer property to their children during their lifetimes. The percentage of Wethersfield and upland estate holders who had minor and unmarried children to provide for when they died were very similar in each time period (see Appendix B, Tables B.3 and B.4). Over three quarters of all holders in both areas who had children had at least one unmarried child in the 1750s and the 1820s. In the 1770s fewer but still a majority were in this position (69 percent in Wethersfield; 59 percent in the upland). The large majority also died leaving at least one minor child in the 1750s (75 percent in Wethersfield, 68 percent in the upland). After that, most probated parents in Wethersfield and the upland had only adult children. About two thirds of the probates who had children had no minors to provide for in the 1770s and 1820s.

Wealth

Appendix B also provides data on the gross wealth of all holders in this study (Table B.6). Average wealth was at all times substantially higher in Wethersfield; it was also more concentrated, particularly in the 1820s (when the wealthiest quarter of all probates held 82 percent of the gross total wealth, compared to 56 percent in the uplands). There were very few landless men in either area,[37] but there were more who had neither a skilled trade nor sufficient land to constitute a working farm. Such men would have had to hire themselves out or rent land in order to live (Table B.7). In the colonial era most dependent men were young and single. Few heads of families were casual laborers or land-poor artisans and farmers (between 6 and 15 percent). But in early nineteenth century Wethersfield, 29 percent of those men who had children had too little productive property to sustain their families (compared to 10 percent in the upland).

For colonial Wethersfield, the picture is one of a relatively prosperous probate population that contained a smattering of very wealthy men. The upland estate holders were not, however, steeped in poverty.

[37] That is, very few men died landless having never passed land to potential heirs during their lifetimes.

Their average and median wealth approached colonywide norms (Appendix A). They merely lacked a particularly wealthy stratum. The range of wealth, especially among male holders, was simply narrower in the upland. Furthermore, the pattern of wealth distribution among the upland holders in the 1820s more closely resembled that of the colonial era than it did the pattern for contemporary Wethersfield. In Wethersfield in the 1820s more dependent men and the overshadowing presence of a few very wealthy holders accounted for the much more concentrated distribution of wealth. These inter-area differences in wealth are consistent with studies finding that commercial towns sustained both a wealthy few and a notable population of semidependent land poor or landless men, while the relatively self-enclosed and occupationally undifferentiated subsistence-plus communities had neither a sizable semidependent population nor strikingly wealthy men.[38]

Testacy and Intestacy

The fates of potential and actual heirs depended on estate holders who made lifetime land transfers or wills and on the probate court justices who implemented the law of intestacy and oversaw creditor claims. The proportion of willmakers (Table 2.1) was fairly constant at half or close to half of the probated decedents in any given area and time, ex-

TABLE 2.1

TESTACY AND DEED USE

| | Testate | | | Informally Testate* | | | | | |
| | All Estates | | | All Estates | | | Estates w/ Chldrn. | | |
	(N)	Yes (%)	No (%)	(N)	Yes (%)	No (%)	(N)	Yes (%)	No (%)
1750s									
Wethersfield	39	38	62	39	44	56	30	47	53
Upland	25	48	52	25	52	48	23	48	52
1770s									
Wethersfield	32	50	50	32	66	34	28	71	29
Upland	23	52	48	23	70	30	21	76	24
1820s									
Wethersfield	36	47	53	36	56	44	19	63	37
Upland	31	45	55	31	61	39	22	61	39

* Holders used deeds or wills or both.

[38] Lemon, *Poor Man's Country*, pp. 6-12, 90-98; J. Main, *Social Structure*, pp. 17-34, 177-86; but see James Henretta, "Wealth and Social Structure."

cept in Wethersfield in the 1750s (when testators accounted for only 38 percent of the probated holders). The proportion of holders who used either deeds or wills to confirm or override the law of intestate distribution was naturally higher, but the use of deeds made a substantial difference only in the 1770s and in the early nineteenth-century upland. At those times about two thirds of the probated population was informally testate. Among those holders who had children capable of inheriting, rates of "informal" testacy in Wethersfield and the upland were nearly identical in each time period. Again, this homogeneity between areas is important. Although there will be occasion to distinguish will makers from others or deed users from others, some of the quantitative analysis will not make such distinctions. Nevertheless, significant interarea differences in patterns of rights creation or in the distribution of property will not be reducible to differences in rates of testacy.

The heart of this study is an intraregional comparison of inheritance patterns. Given this aim, the study is as inclusive as possible: it examines the practices of all types of probated estate holders in the two areas, in the given years. The analysis also attempts to ensure that interarea differences found in inheritance patterns are not simply reducible to "accidental" differences in the characteristics of the probated populations.

The profile of the probated populations shows that although there were fluctuations over time, in most basic respects the probated populations resembled each other in any given time period. Wethersfield and the uplands produced similar proportions of probated men and women, and legally and "informally" testate holders. With the exception of the 1820s, similar percentages of estate holders had children. The analysis of inheritance practices will often treat estate holders who had children separately from the childless. Among holders who did have children capable of inheriting, the percentages of those in each area who had minors and those who had some unmarried children to provide for were similar.

The two populations did differ in their patterns of wealth distribution, but this has essential relation to the differences in the economies of the two types of agricultural communities studied. The direction and order of magnitude of these wealth differences are as one would expect for commercial and subsistence-plus communities within this family-farm region. They are also consistent with figures drawn from studies using larger probated populations.[39]

[39] See Appendix A for a comparison of this small sample with a much larger sample of probates.

CHAPTER THREE

UNIVERSAL FEATURES OF INHERITANCE IN CONNECTICUT

Although this study emphasizes distinctions between the upland communities of Connecticut and Wethersfield, these towns had much in common throughout the period 1750 to 1820. Family farms dominated agricultural production just as they did in the majority of rural towns in the American North. The political and social organization of these towns also developed within the broad confines established by the provincial political administration. These were not only northern towns; they were, in particular, Connecticut towns. Given these commonalities, it would be surprising if patterns of inheritance in Wethersfield and the upland shared no important features.

Invariant aspects of inheritance are the central concerns of this chapter. Data on partibility of land will establish that unigeniture was rare. Heirs were also selected from a larger universe of kin in a standard order that varied little. This standard order was rigidly observed in admission to ownership of real property. I will argue that these universal features of inheritance practices are aspects of cognate, not patrilineal, strategies. They also indicate that although practices were not patrilineal, neither were they necessarily narrowly "conjugal" or "nuclear."

PARTIBILITY AND IMPARTIBILITY: A PRELIMINARY VIEW

There was some public advocacy of unigeniture in colonial Connecticut. A minister from Stonington advised the following:

> . . . keep your Estate in one Hand; never divide it or cut off any, especially Lands. Let every one who succeeds, make what Additions he can; which add to the former, & keep all intire. And by this Means with Frugality & Industry, the Estate will increase vastly in a few descents. 'Tis not good to be upon a Level, or under the Foot of every Scoundrel.
>
> As for the other Children, if there are several, give them Trades, Merchandizg., Physic, &c. . . . This I think is better for every one,

than to have a little Scrap of Land to Starve upon, and the Estates ruined, & the Family sink into Obscurity.[1]

Here, Thomas Chesebrough has neatly captured the rationale for unigeniture. He stresses intergenerational accumulation. He also emphasizes family rank and distinction, here expressed as a warning about the ever-present possibility of ruin and "Obscurity." It is worth stressing again that unigeniture is the tool not only of the securely established landed elite, but of those who hope through patient intergenerational effort to rise in status—for example, the French *haute bourgeoisie* and the English gentry. In Chesebrough's phrase "under the Foot of every Scoundrel," one can detect the typically Anglo-American view that without the immunity provided by a sufficient estate, one becomes a dependent man, subject to the schemes of immoral, power-seeking others.

Thomas Chesebrough was free to concentrate his attention on the unity of estates and to think less about the problem of providing for children. A childless man, he died in 1754 leaving his estate to his brother. In the same year, Jacob Whaples of Wethersfield died leaving his thirty-acre farm, all its buildings, his oxen and tackling, and all his "Husbandry Business" tools to his only son, Waitstill. There was a condition attached: Waitstill, a minor, was to pay legacies to his three half-sisters and his full sister when he became twenty-one. Meanwhile, Jacob Whaples's second wife got the use of all his property, but she became owner only of a cow and all the "Goods and Chattels," she brought with her when they married.[2]

But Jacob Whaples was one of the few who passed a landed estate intact. There were 136 landed estates (for which complete distributions are known) altogether. Ownership of all real estate passed to one person in only nineteen. Moreover, holders pursued a deliberate policy of maintaining property intact in the blood line in only ten of these nineteen estates. In the remaining cases the sole heir was the only son or brother, or testators chose spouses rather than available brothers. Just 5 of the 104 landed holders who had more than one child capable of inheriting passed on their land to only one son. In two of these families, there were no other sons, and in a third the terms of the transfer suggest that the excluded son was crazy.

Neither the land rich nor the land hungry, neither artisans nor mer-

---

[1] Thomas Chesebrough, Memoir in Ezra Stiles, *Extracts from the Itineraries and Other Miscellanies of Ezra Stiles, D.D., LL.D., 1755-1794, with a Selection from His Correspondence*, ed. Franklin Bowditch Dexter (New Haven: Yale University Press, 1916), p. 1.

[2] Jacob Whaples treated the daughters of the two marriages evenhandedly, but some decedents did not; see Jacob Whaples, will, signed July 23, 1754, folio 5892, Hartford Probate District, Estate Papers.

chants were sufficiently alarmed by "scoundrels" or "obscurity" to turn to unigeniture. This was a universal aspect of inheritance patterns; the few cases of unigeniture did not cluster. Judging from this population of probates, impartibility was a marginal feature of family property relations in both the upland and Wethersfield throughout the era studied here. In short, a key feature of strongly patrilineal practices was virtually absent. Partitioning is not compatible with inheritance strategies aiming to preserve property within the blood line. Those who consider division of land among only two heirs a highly restrictive practice could not make a case for patriliny here either.[3] Among those holders who had more than two children or siblings, only about one quarter restricted partitioning to one or two blood kin.[4] Chapter Four will examine partitioning further by focusing on inequalities among children.

THE SCOPE OF KIN RECOGNITION

The Law

The pattern of heirship was the combined result of the direct actions of holders who made wills and lifetime transfers, of heirs and other kin who cooperated to make heir agreements or intervened to reclaim indebted property, and of judges who applied the law of intestate distribution. Before turning to actual patterns of heirship, a brief discussion of the rules of intestate succession is in order. In the population studied here, intestacy produced a search for heirs that extended beyond siblings in only two cases; I outline only those rules that governed the order of heirship in the situations faced by most families.[5] Keep in mind that Connecticut's inheritance system was permissive. With the exception of married women, all holders could, by using wills or deeds, alter the pattern of heirship established by the law.

[3] See, for example, John Waters, "Patrimony, Succession, and Social Stability: Guilford, Connecticut, in the Eighteenth Century," *Perspectives in American History* 10 (1976): 131-60; David P. Gagan, "The Indivisibility of Land: A Microanalysis of the System of Inheritance in Nineteenth Century Ontario," *Journal of Economic History* 36 (March 1976): 126-41.

[4] These "two-heir" strategies did not cluster, either. No more than 27 percent and no fewer than 21 percent of the upland or Wethersfield probates pursued this tactic in any given time period.

[5] The discussion relies on the statute codes (*Acts & Laws 1750*, pp. 49-54; *Acts & Laws 1796*, pp. 163-72; *Public Statutes 1821*, pp. 199-213); Charles M. Andrews, *The Connecticut Intestacy Law*, Tercentenary Series, no. 2 (New Haven: Yale University Press, 1933); and the extended commentary on Connecticut law provided by Zephaniah Swift, *A System of the Laws of the State of Connecticut*, 2 vols. (Windam, Conn., 1795-96), 1: 325-31, 416-41; George L. Haskins, "The Beginnings of Partible Inheritance in the American Colonies," *Yale Law Review* 51 (May 1942): 1280-1315.

When Connecticut's early intestacy statute broke with the English common law primogeniture rule, the structure of intestate descent was profoundly altered. Because it combines birth order and gender distinctions to single out one heir, primogeniture crosscuts ties among relations of equal degrees of kinship. The brothers and sisters of an eldest son will have no interest in the parental estate so long as their brother has direct descendants. Under Connecticut's statute and others like it, all children, or all sisters and brothers, were simultaneous heirs. Thus Connecticut law reinforced the solidarity of sibling groups.

Spouses never became owners of real property, although widows were entitled to life-estates in one third of the land their husbands owned at death.[6] Widows, along with blood relations, did inherit ownership of personal property. They were entitled to one third of all personal property remaining after debts were paid, and to one half if there were no children. Besides spouses, children and their representatives[7] inherited before any other kin. Although all children participated simultaneously, a secondary birth-order distinction gave the eldest son a double share in the colonial era. Throughout the period, a gender distinction also favored sons over daughters as heirs to real property. The statute directed that sons were to take their shares in real estate and daughters in personal estate whenever possible. When there were no children or their direct descendants, the holder's siblings or their representatives became the heirs.[8] No secondary birth order or gender distinctions favored the firstborn or brothers. All brothers and sisters or their representatives received equal shares.

Varieties of Kin Recognition

Other studies of heirship have determined that the circle of recognized kin was small in seventeenth- and eighteenth-century agricultural com-

---

[6] For a detailed discussion of widows' rights, see Chapter Seven. Husbands were entitled to a life-estate in all the realty held by their wives.

[7] The direct descendants of any child "stood in" as a group for their predeceased ancestor. A typical case is as follows: A holder dies leaving two living children and the children of a predeceased child. These grandchildren take as a group whatever share their parent would have been directly entitled to had he or she outlived the holder. There are complexities that are the legal historian's delight—such as, what rules applied when no child outlived his or her parent and only grandchildren remained—but these need not concern us here.

[8] In the colonial period, the principle of representation was, among siblings, limited to children (that is, to the holder's nieces and nephews). In the 1821 code the statute was revised to permit unlimited representation of siblings.

munities.[9] Most studies use data on the overall distribution of heirs[10] simply to indicate that when children are present, heirship usually does not extend beyond the nuclear family. Jacob Whaples' will, which mentioned only his wife and children, is typical of this pattern. One can, however, also use such data to supply a preliminary view of distinctions among patrilineal, narrowly nuclear or "conjugal," and extended cognate patterns of kin selection.

Strongly patrilineal practices display generational depth in selection of heirs. They routinely include direct descendants of living heirs. Had Jacob Whaples' strategy been patrimonial, or strongly oriented to accumulation, he would have confined his son's interest to a life-estate and made his son's son(s) his eventual heir. A handful of holders did limit their sons' powers of alienation in order to ensure that their grandsons would inherit. The day after Christmas, Boxer's Day, 1770, James Moor made out a will giving his eldest son, Thomas, a right to "use and improve" his land and barn until Thomas's eldest son turned twenty-one. At that time all of Thomas's surviving sons were to inherit a share of their grandfather's estate.[11]

A few holders also took care to bolster their connections with more distant male kin. Elisha Williams was a New Light minister from Wethersfield who had also served as clerk of Connecticut's General Assembly and as rector of Yale before the college moved permanently to New Haven. After making elaborate provisions for his wife and children in his will, he also gave two of his nephews, Eliphelet and Ezekiel, one good suit apiece. Eliphelet and Ezekiel were sons of Solomon Williams, Elisha's paternal half brother (and a man well known for moderate New Light preaching during the Great Awakening). The clothes were symbolic gifts, but the brothers also consolidated their relationship through marriage: Elisha's daughter, Mary, married her cousin Eliphelet three years before her father's death.[12]

---

[9] James Deen, Jr., "Patterns of Testation: Four Tidewater Counties in Colonial Virginia," *American Journal of Legal History* 16 (1972): 154-77; Cicely Howell, "Peasant Inheritance Customs in the Midlands, 1200-1700," in *Family and Inheritance: Rural Society in Western Europe, 1200-1800*, ed. Jack Goody, Joan Thirsk, and E. P. Thompson (Cambridge, Mass.: Cambridge University Press), pp. 112-55; David Levine and Keith Wrightson, *Poverty and Piety in an English Village: Terling, 1525-1700* (New York: Academic Press, 1979). But see Richard T. Vann, "Wills and the Family in an English Town: Banbury, 1550-1800," *Journal of Family History* 4 (Winter 1979): 346-67. He found higher rates of extended kin recognition in the seventeenth century.

[10] Technically, only those who take (or would take) by intestate descent are "heirs." The term refers more broadly to all "takers" in this text.

[11] James Moor, will, Union, folio 1499, Stafford Probate District, Estate Papers.

[12] Elisha Williams, will, signed July 16, 1775, folio 6061, Hartford Probate District,

To the extent that their practices were patrilineal, Moor and Williams were unusual. It was very rare to deny a son full ownership in order to see to it that grandsons remained on the farm. In fact, as the next section demonstrates, most holders did not mention the children of living sons and daughters, or of siblings, at all, and only a few who had children made special mention of brothers or nephews.

In contemporary settings, inheritance practices are narrowly conjugal in orientation. When families do not own productive property and the life-chances of children do not depend on direct inheritance, spouses take priority. The majority of will makers today leave all their property to their spouses, bypassing children and siblings. Moreover, in the absence of spouses or children, the selection of successors becomes irregular: siblings are not routinely chosen. As Talcott Parsons puts it, "particular relationships or situations of need" determine the selection of heirs.[13]

The atypical wills of two early nineteenth-century Wethersfield men illustrate such practices. James Camp Adams, probably a cabinetmaker by trade, was childless when he died in 1820, owning only miscellaneous household goods and clothing and a one-acre homelot that had once belonged to his father's brother, Joseph. Sarah, his wife of thirty years, became the sole owner of his small estate. He did not even mention the four sisters and the many nieces and nephews who lived nearby. Neither his long-lived father nor his uncle Joseph's heirs made any recorded fuss about this unusual move.[14] John Dix, a landless, unmarried mariner, made out his will six years before his death in 1820. He did so, he said, because he was "disposed to Setout on Travils perhaps to forein Countries and Kingdoms not knowing my destiny." Disregarding his brother and sister, he gave all his belongings to his widowed mother.[15]

Adams and Dix were unusual in their poverty and in their practices.

Estate Papers; Sherman Adams and Henry Stiles, *The History of Ancient Wethersfield*, 2 vols., reprint ed. (Somersworth: New Hampshire Publishing Co., 1974), 2:806.

[13] Jeffry P. Rosenfeld, *The Legacy of Aging: Inheritance and Disinheritance in Social Perspective* (Norwood, N.J.: Ablex Publishing Corp.), pp. 8-9, 12-14, 66; Marvin B. Sussman, Judith N. Gates, and David T. Smith, *The Family and Inheritance* (New York: Russell Sage Foundation, 1970), pp. 72, 89, 119-20; Talcott Parsons, "The Kinship System of the Contemporary United States," in his *Essays in Sociological Theory*, rev. ed. (New York: Free Press, 1964), p. 184.

[14] James had no brothers. Perhaps if he had, his wife would not have inherited. But most childless holders bypassed their spouses to favor sisters as well as brothers. James Camp Adams, will, signed November 11, 1819, Wethersfield, Hartford Probate District, Estate Papers.

[15] John Dix, will, signed, October 19, 1814, Wethersfield, Hartford Probate District, Estate Papers.

As the following data show, spouses were usually rejected as main heirs to land, and a high degree of orderliness existed in the selection of heirs.

Practices: All Heirs

A clearly circumscribed and narrow circle of kin became heirs to these estates. Table 3.1 shows everyone who shared any interest whatsoever in a decedent's property. Major heirs such as Waitstill Whaples and Sarah Adams are represented, but so are those who received only small, symbolic gifts—a treasured silk dress, perhaps, or a handsome pocket watch. It includes those who, like Jacob Whaples' wife, inherited only use-rights in property, as well as owner-heirs. Widows and the occasional widower always appeared in substantial numbers, in part because the law usually ensured that they received at least use-rights in land and ownership of some personal property. Spouses aside, the takers were always overwhelmingly blood relations. In this population of approximately 1,020 heirs, only twenty were in-laws. Very few unrelated persons participated. Since four of the six unidentifiable takers were, judging by surnames, male relatives, there were at most four non-kin takers, including a servant couple recognized for their honorable service (columns 1 and 8).

TABLE 3.1

INDIVIDUAL HEIRS: RELATIONSHIP TO ESTATE HOLDERS

	Unknown (N)	Known (N)	Spouse (%)	Chld. & Rep. (%)	Sibs. & Rep. (%)	In-Laws (%)	Par-ents (%)	Non-kin (%)	Grandchild, Niece, Nephew All (%)	Parent Alive (%)
	(1)	(2)	(3)	(4)	(5)	(6)	(7)	(8)	(9)	(10)
1750s										
Wethersfield	2	203	10.5	74.9	10.3	0.5	0.5	0	(15.9)	3.0
Upland	0	139	10.1	74.1	7.2	2.2	0.7	0	(21.6)	5.6
1770s										
Wethersfield	2	188	11.8	79.0	5.9	1.6	0	1.1	(18.8)	0.5
Upland	0	146	10.5	81.1	0	2.1	0	0	(15.4)	6.3
1820s										
Wethersfield	2	164	11.1	53.7	31.7	2.5	0.6	0	(30.3)	0.6
Upland	0	178	10.1	73.6	11.2	3.4	0	0	(21.4)	1.7

Note: Heirs who took by representation were sometimes referred to as a group, for example, "Samuel's children." When biographical information did not supply the exact number, an average was calculated on the basis of those children or siblings from each area and time for whom the number of descendants is known.

In addition, there were three charitable bequests. Two childless women created trusts for their town ministries—one each from the upland and from Wethersfield in the 1820s, and Elisha Williams, a trustee over funds given him by English friends for "promoting the Instruction of Indian Children," passed this responsibility on to his second wife, Elizabeth Scott Williams.[16]

Even among blood relations, the scope of kin recognition was narrow, largely confined to children, siblings, and their representatives. Children and their representatives clearly dominated (column 4), and they dominated in proportion to the percentage of probates with children in each area and time period.[17] Spouses aside, siblings and their representatives followed as the second largest group of takers; their presence rose and fell in inverse relation to that of children and children's descendants (column 5). Parents were excluded (column 7), reflecting not only the normal rhythm of aging and death, but a more general avoidance of ascending generations. Grandparents and kin related by common descent from grandparents—aunts, uncles, and cousins—never participated.

The scope of kin recognition was not only narrow, it was also shallow in generational depth. Descendants of siblings and children were always a substantial minority of takers (column 9).[18] But, unlike James Moor's grandsons, most "stood in the place" of dead parents. Very few grandchildren or nieces and nephews shared an interest in these estates while their own parents were still alive. Such heirs accounted for no more than 6 percent of the takers in any time or area (column 10). Once again, then, a primary feature of patrilineal practices is largely missing. When family standing and honor is associated with the preservation of an ancestral estate, estate holders will make provisions, that, in effect, treat children and grandchildren (or siblings and nieces and nephews) as co-heirs. They will attempt to regulate the order of succession for future generations.

Of course, the exceptional practices of a few families may have skewed the overall pattern of heirship. But an examination of takers by families confirms the pattern just described. First, few holders mentioned grandchildren or nieces and nephews when they had living parents. Only 12 of the 154 decedents for whom there were estate distributions did so, and five of them, including the Reverend Williams,

---

[16] Elisha Williams, will, signed July 16, 1755, folio 6061, Hartford Probate District, Estate Papers; Francis Parsons, "Elisha Williams: Minister, Soldier, President of Yale," *Papers of the New Haven Colony Historical Society* 7 (1908): 188-217.

[17] See Appendix B, Table B.2. Unless the text clearly indicates otherwise, the decedent is the reference for all kin terms throughout this study.

[18] Table 3.1, column 9, includes the two references to children of spouses' siblings.

granted only token or "symbolic" inheritances. The cases were widely scattered. Again, kin recognition lacked the patrilineal attribute of generational depth.

Second, the scope of kin recognition was very narrow when holders had children or grandchildren. Only rarely did any person apart from spouses and children or their direct descendants share any interest in decedents' property (Table 3.2). Furthermore, when holders who had children did include others, the great majority gave property to sons- and daughters-in-law, not to siblings (nine of twelve estates; see Table 3.2, columns 4-5). Thus even the exceptions followed a cognate principle of assimilation of spouses, not a patrilineal preference for male blood kin. Third, in the absence of surviving children or their descendants, siblings were the preferred heirs (spouses' coparticipation aside); siblings were the main heirs in twenty-six of thirty-two such cases. Thus the selection of kin groups followed a clear order: direct descendants took first; siblings and their children took next (spouses' coparticipation aside).

The reader may have noticed that in three cases other kin deprived all children of any share in their parents' estates (Table 3.2, column 2). Two cases occurred through the mechanism of debt and with the active cooperation of the children themselves. For example, when Thomas Lawson's administrators, his brother Robert and his only child's hus-

TABLE 3.2

THE SCOPE OF HEIRSHIP WHEN ESTATE HOLDERS HAVE CHILDREN

	Usable Estates[a] (N)	Children Do Not Inherit (%)	Only Children Inherit[b] (%)	Only Children and Their Spouses Inherit[b] (%)	Children and Other Kin Inherit[b] (%)
	(1)	(2)	(3)	(4)	(5)
1750s					
Wethersfield	25	0	96	0	4
Upland	18	6	83	11	0
1770s					
Wethersfield	25	0	92	4	4
Upland	18	0	83	11	6
1820s					
Wethersfield	16	6	81	13	0
Upland	20	5	85	10	0

[a] Estate is solvent and distribution beyond spouse is known, or potential heirs got property during the holder's lifetime.
[b] Disregards coparticipation by decedent's spouse and children's representatives.

band, were empowered by the probate court to sell the land of Thomas's insolvent estate in 1820, they sold it to a male blood relation (probably Robert's son). In this way Lawson's land remained in the "line" rather than falling into the hands of strangers or a female descendant.[19] One more case of "disinheritance" was the result of poverty combined with a very early death. A Coventry man, two months before he died in 1755, sold his entire landed holding of eleven acres and his house to the brother with whom he, his new wife, and infant son lived. Although he died a creditor to his brother as a result of this transaction, his net estate, composed entirely of personal property, was worth less than seventy pounds lawful money. It went to his widow, who was until 1760 responsible for raising their only child.[20]

Practices: Owners Only

Holders were especially selective in their choice of kin when designating those who would become owners of their property.[21] The lion's share of these estates went to children and their direct descendants. They inherited almost 85 percent of all property in the 1750s (Table 3.3). As expected, the percentage of property passing to other heirs dropped in the 1770s when all but four holders had children, and rose in the early nineteenth century when very few had children. At all times, children took more property than their sheer numbers would dictate, primarily because heads of families generally had larger estates than did childless probates. As befits family-farm communities, true succession—succession to heritable rights—was overwhelmingly confined to direct descendants.

One other aspect of these figures should be noted. Widows' rights to ownership of one third to one half the value of net personal estates could not be overridden by wills. Nevertheless, the proportion of total property passing outside the line of direct descent was very low. That

[19] Thomas Lawson, administrator's account, signed December 21, 1820, Union, folio 333, Stafford Probate District, Estate Papers. Also see Thomas Bunce, Administrator's Note, signed July 25, 1822, Wethersfield, Hartford Probate District, Estate Papers; Wethersfield Land Records, 16: 30, deed, signed May 1771.

[20] Ebenezer Lamb, inventory, taken January 28, 1755, folio 2344, Windham Probate District, Estate Papers; Windham Probate Court, Record Book, 3; Coventry Land Records, 4: 283, deed, signed January 4, 1755.

[21] As used in this text (unless context indicates a narrower meaning) an owner is anyone who has an estate of inheritance. Life-estates (for example, dower) and lesser interests are, therefore, not included. The term does include those who own property in which others have lesser interests (use-rights, for example), those whose ownership is subject to a condition (for example, obligations to care for parents), and even those whose estates are restricted to a certain class of heirs (as in fee-tails).

TABLE 3.3

PROPORTION OF PROPERTY INHERITED BY CHILDREN AND OTHERS

		Heirs		Property Given to:	
	(N)	Children* (%)	Others (%)	Children* (%)	Others (%)
1750s					
Wethersfield	165	78	22	84.2	15.8
Upland	110	77	21	84.2	15.8
1770s					
Wethersfield	141	85	15	92.6	7.4
Upland	97	94	6	96.7	3.2
1820s					
Wethersfield	122	59	41	76.7	23.3
Upland	125	70	30	84.1	15.9

Note: Percentage of property taken is based on the monetary value of goods as established by the inventory appraisals. In the case of real property, where the value was missing but quantity known, value was estimated from the average value of inventoried acres for the given area and time.
* Children or direct descendants.

this was so indicates both the low value of personal property relative to real property in most of these estates and the inroads made on personal property by the rules of debt payment that dictated that liabilities were first to be paid out of movable goods.[22]

The pattern of favoring one's children, then siblings, emerges starkly in arrangements concerning ownership of inherited real property in the eighteenth century. Not even spouses emerged as claimants, except in very small numbers. When children or their descendants were present, no one else was given heritable rights in any portion of real property in 73 to 100 percent of the cases (Table 3.4). The scattered exceptions, besides the three cases of "disinheritance" of children just discussed, involved small shares of land given to widows or children's spouses. In five families, sons-in-law inherited land: in one of these, a son-in-law, by agreement with his wife and the widow, inherited jointly with his wife, the holder's only child; in the remaining four, the holders had inheriting sons. Thus, holders were not creating substitute heirs; they were reinforcing alliances with affines. Moreover, in all but one of these families, estate holders also gave their daughters fee-simple interests in land.

On the whole, heir selection was narrow and orderly when no chil-

---

[22] Chapter Eight contains an extensive discussion of indebted and landless estates.

TABLE 3.4
OWNERSHIP OF REAL PROPERTY: THE EXTENT OF KIN INCLUSION

	Landed Holders: Children Present					Landed Holders: No Children			
	Landed[a] (N)	Missing[b] (N)	Chldrn Excluded (%)	Chldrn Only (%)	Chldrn & Others (%)	Landed[a] (N)	Missing[b] (N)	Sibs. Only (%)	Others Only (%)
1750s									
Wethersfield	23	0	0	96	4	5	0	100	0
Upland	16	1	7	73	20	1	0	100	0
1770s									
Wethersfield	24	0	0	100	0	2	0	100	0
Upland	16	0	0	87	13	1	1	—	—
1820s									
Wethersfield	17	1	6	87	6	14	1	69	31
Upland	16	0	6	87	6	5	0	80	20

[a] Holders had net distributable real estate or passed land to heirs during their lifetimes.
[b] Net estate may or may not have included realty.

dren were present. In twenty-one of twenty-six such estates, siblings or
their descendants inherited all the land. But a study of Table 3.4 suggests that childless holders were becoming less orderly in their choice of
heirs in the 1820s, especially in Wethersfield. Two wives and one husband inherited all of their spouses' land in Wethersfield, and an unmarried Wethersfield woman gave her land in trust to her minister rather
than to her brothers or sisters. In the upland during the same time, one
widow gave all of her land to her husband's brother.

CONCLUSION

A striking pattern of sibling group selection and distinction character-
ized the prevailing order of succession both in Wethersfield and in the
upland communities. Property first passed to children. When there
were no children or grandchildren of either sex, property passed to the
holder's siblings. Although blood kin dominated as heirs, the preliminary evidence indicates that the pattern of succession was not lineal.
Practices lacked generational depth, a key aspect of strongly patrilineal
inheritance patterns. In addition, gender distinctions favoring males
were infrequently used as a primary principle of selection: more distant
male blood relatives never displaced nearer female blood kin.[23]

    Coupled with the absence of unigeniture, these data indicate that in-

[23] The one "disinheritance" of a daughter in favor of a nephew via a real estate sale
excluded.

heritance practices in both Wethersfield and the upland reinforced cognate rather than lineal kin ties. As discussed in the last chapter, in cognate systems, the strongest ties, when not limited to the conjugal family alone, occur within generations of siblings. Since females and their descendants are not "lost" as relations, no primary gender distinction cuts through the solidarity of sibling groups, and the double tracing of descent loosens ties among those related only by one ancestor.

Moreover, the treatment of spouses is the first indication that inheritance practices did, indeed, display the tension between unity and provision characteristic of producers elsewhere. Succession to real property was especially orderly, and spouses were almost universally rejected as owners of land when children were present, as is typical of farm families when the life-chances of children depend on inheritance. Practices were cognate, but not narrowly conjugal as are modern share-and-share-alike provisioning strategies.

Among the holders studied here, even the exceptions to the pattern of sibling group selection and distinction suggest a cognate rather than lineal kin orientation. The minority practice of including in-laws as heirs to realty suggests that assimilation of affines, a form of extended cognate kin recognition, had made inroads even in the sphere of property relations where blood ties are especially likely to dominate.

The blending of sibling relations and marriage ties is illustrated in the sphere of sentiment through a series of letters exchanged between an engaged Wethersfield couple. Lucy Williams (who figures in this study as an heir to a share in her younger brother's intestate estate in the 1820s) remained at Wethersfield while her future husband, Comfort Williams,[24] searched for a permanent position as a minister in Vermont and New York. In an otherwise chatty letter—Lucy not only sends news of her own parents, paternal grandparents, a maternal aunt, and, especially, sisters, but also of visits to his sisters and mother—she gratefully acknowledges his request that she unburden herself concerning the "troubles that oppress my mind." She responds with the source of her deepest anxieties:

> What shall I tell you, My friend knows from what source they arise, but am I at liberty to speak of the faults of a parent. Many times I have wished to converse with you on this subject but something within has sealed my lips. . . . Could I see my father exhibiting before his family a good example conscientious in the dis-

---

[24] There was a pale shadow of a patrilineal strategy of consolidation of property through cousin marriage: their respective paternal great-grandfathers were brothers.

charge of duty—as a parent, as a member of society & as an accountable being.[25]

To her professed hesitancy and residual feelings of disloyalty, Comfort responds that there can be "no evil to arise" from her confidence because, he writes, "You ought to consider me as near to you as a brother if not any nearer. What you would communicate to a tender brother, communicate to me without reserve."[26] His phrase "if not any nearer" expresses a hope that there is a degree of intimacy beyond that of brother and sister, but he feels himself on surer ground in using the imagery of sibling bonds to justify deep confidence. The bond between brother and sister could even legitimate the open declaration of filial discontent, anger, and shame.[27] (In the same letter Comfort reports that he has visited another of *her* mother's sisters, who had recently emigrated to Vermont upon her second marriage. An easy mingling of references to each other's maternal and paternal kin is common in their letters throughout the history of their marriage.) Lucy picks up his circuitously expressed hope and, somewhat formally, reassures him of the special closeness of their relationship: "I will venture to tell you that you are much nearer & dearer [than a brother]." But when she wished to tease him—she had sent two letters to his one—she reverts quite easily to sibling imagery: "Now Sir when you have read this consider the relationship between us of brother and sister that I may be satisfied with myself that I have written before you have answered my last.[28] There is humor in that "Sir"; they usually call each other friend. Not only the distinctive intimacy of marriage, but its assimilation to the affectionate, informal relations between siblings justifies the lack of ceremony.

In the pattern of heirship, the few cases available hint at a breakdown in the orderly choice of heirs in the 1820s. A few childless holders be-

---

[25] Lucy Williams to Comfort Williams, December 15, 1810, Papers of Comfort Williams, 1806-1840, RG 69: 8, The Connecticut State Library, Hartford (all materials cited about Lucy and Comfort Williams can be found at the same location). It is unclear whether her father suffered from madness or from some unnamed "depravity." In a series of comments in letters and diaries, she writes that her father had fallen severely ill and had "lost his reason" (Lucy Williams to Comfort Williams, August 27, 1811; Lucy Williams, Journal, May 22, 1811). Thus his "decaying" and "loss of reason" may have been the "fits" and dementia that so often were described as accompanying a "hard" illness and dying in this period. Her father recovered, though, and elsewhere she accuses him of complete neglect of his children and his recently widowed mother; see Journal, October 29 and November 21, 1811.

[26] Comfort Williams to Lucy Williams, January 14, 1811.

[27] In her diary, Lucy writes, "I sometimes feel not the least glimpse of filial affection for him"; see Lucy Williams, Journal, October 29, 1811.

[28] Lucy Williams to Comfort Williams, February 15, 1811.

gan to prefer spouses (or others, if unmarried) to siblings, especially in Wethersfield, but the prevailing pattern among probates in both areas was an orderly succession of sibling groups. The position of widows will be thoroughly explored in Chapter Seven, but even if disparities in the treatment of widows emerge, this should not obscure the main finding here. Any variation in inheritance patterns took place within a fundamentally cognate structure of kin recognition.

CHAPTER FOUR

EQUALITY AND INEQUALITY
AMONG CHILDREN

Who gets what? The aspect of inheritance that first captures the imagination is the distribution of property among heirs. It seems to evoke dramatically the issue of equality and inequality. Most sixteenth-century jurists praised and promoted primogeniture as the only sound policy for great landed families and stable monarchies, while a few condemned it on behalf of outcast younger sons. Seventeenth- and eighteenth-century radical republicans used primogeniture as a symbol of an oppressive aristocratic order. Jean Yver, who has analyzed the patchwork of inheritance rules that applied to commoners in sixteenth-century France, supposes that the strictly partible customs then prevailing in western France are traceable to the originally free status of its peasantry. He highlights a persistent theme: the association of partibility with a free peasantry and impartibility with heavily manorialized regions and a dependent population.[1] Another recurring theme in inheritance studies, the subordinate position of spouses and daughters, is also basic to the question of "who gets what."

When land tenures and inheritance rules allowed it, European producers tended to settle on impartibility or preferential partibility as a solution to the tension between unity and provision. These practices distinguished land from other property, reserving land for one or some but not all children. Such distribution schemes are an important feature of the "favored heir plus burdens" pattern. Some American studies have also found that northern rural property holders heavily favored sons over daughters and some sons over others. Philip Greven's study of Andover, for example, establishes a relationship between heightened local population pressure on land and increased inequality in the distribution of land among sons.[2]

[1] Emmanuel Le Roy Ladurie, "Inheritance Customs in Sixteenth-Century France," pp. 37-70, and Joan Thirsk, "The Debate about Inheritance," pp. 177-91, in *Family and Inheritance: Rural Society in Western Europe, 1200-1800,* ed. Jack Goody, Joan Thirsk, and E. P. Thompson (Cambridge, Mass.: Cambridge University Press, 1976).

[2] Philip J. Greven, Jr., *Four Generations: Population, Land, and Family in Colonial Andover, Massachusetts* (Ithaca, N.Y.: Cornell University Press, 1972); Christopher M. Jedrey, *The World of John Cleaveland: Family and Community in Eighteenth-Century New England* (New York: Norton, 1979); Daniel Snydacker, "Kinship and Community

The dilemma posed by the need to provide for heirs while preserving viable enterprises is sharpest when the fates of children, rather than collateral kin, hang on its resolution. To recall the expectations outlined in Chapter Two, practices ought to be fairly homogeneous and stable in the upland subsistence-plus communities. The comparative economic autarky of the upland towns made their residents highly dependent on local land. Under these conditions, inheritance practices ought to display the inequalities that are the result of a careful juggling of the tension between unity and provision.

Since commercialization encourages several potential alternatives to preferential partibility, the practices of Wethersfield holders should show more variation. Market-oriented agriculture puts a greater premium on efficient production. So long as they still want to maintain viable farms, smaller holders should be under added pressure not to divide their land. The extent of partitioning in Wethersfield should therefore be more closely correlated with holding size than in the upland. Furthermore, when commercialization generates opportunities for nonlanded employment, as it did in Wethersfield, it should in the long run loosen the connection between inheritance and life-chances. Two different partitioning strategies may result. First, holders may switch to egalitarian share-and-share-alike strategies, dispersing property that merely supplements children's resources; all property is treated simply as a provisioning fund. Second, holders may attempt to maximize the success of family-held economic enterprises by reserving all rights and claims in them for one or a few heirs. These property owners need not stretch family resources to secure the futures of all. They have the luxury of selecting those whose fortunes will be linked to a direct inheritance and those whose welfare will depend on success in negotiating developing labor markets.

In sum, in the absence of commercialization, inheritance practices should display a sharp tension between unity and provision. The "favored heir plus burdens pattern" ought to be the rule. In particular, some form of preferential partibility should prevail. As I will argue later, this is an anti-exceptionalist position. Advocates of the American exceptionalism thesis contend that regional conditions diminished the connection between family property and life-chances and produced distinctive, modern family relations. To argue that individualist or egalitarian treatments of property should prevail only as town life becomes commercialized is to reject this view.

in Rural Pennsylvania, 1749-1820," *Journal of Interdisciplinary History* 8 (Summer 1982): 41-61; John Waters, "Patrimony, Succession, and Social Stability: Guilford, Connecticut, in the Eighteenth Century," *Perspectives in American History* 10 (1976): 131-60.

PARTITIONING AND INEQUALITY

The New England colonies are well known for their egalitarian intestacy statutes. Indeed, these statutes were a touchstone for Revolutionary-era republicans from jurisdictions in which primogeniture prevailed. But two inegalitarian aspects of the intestacy law in Connecticut deserve mention. First, the eldest son or his representatives received a double share until 1792, when the legislature abolished it because it was inconsistent with the republican principles motivating legislators in several other states to abolish primogeniture and entail at about the same time.[3]

The legislators did not, however, remove a second inegalitarian element of the statute. Daughters and younger sons, or their representatives, were to inherit equal shares of their parent's property. However, the statute dictated that sons were to have as much of their shares in real estate as the estate permitted.[4] Thus, shares were equivalent in value, but the law in principle sharply distinguished between land and movables, intending the land to be a male preserve. That this was the intent is clear from the wording of a postcolonial amendment giving the courts discretionary powers in this respect: "Whenever the court shall find, that it will best accommodate the heirs . . . , to distribute part of the personal estate to the male heirs, and part of the real estate to the female heirs, such court shall order such distribution."[5] The amendment was an acknowledgment that the legislature's original intention was unrealistic. Most estates did not have enough personal property to provide daughters with shares that did not include land. In this study, for example, daughters of landed intestates always inherited real property from their parents.

These two aspects of the law contributed directly to inequality in inheritance patterns. The double share for the eldest son contributed to inequalities among sons and to inequalities between daughters and sons. The distinction between real and movable property created inequalities between sons and daughters in the allocation of real estate. Once again, it is emphasized that the inheritance patterns, as analyzed in this study, were the combined result of direct decisions made by holders in deeds and wills, by heirs in heir agreements, and by the courts as they applied the law of intestacy. (However, most landed

---

[3] On Revolutionary-era ideology and reform of inheritance statutes in other jurisdictions, see the important piece by Stanley N. Katz, "Republicanism and the Law of Inheritance in the American Revolutionary Era," *Michigan Law Review* 76 (November 1977): 1-29. Also see Michael Bruce Levy, "Liberalism and Inherited Wealth," Ph.D. dissertation (Rutgers, The State University of New Jersey, 1979).

[4] *Acts & Laws 1750*, p. 52; *Public Statutes 1821*, p. 207.

[5] Ibid.

holders who had children did allocate at least some of their property through wills or deeds: about 80 percent did so in the 1770s and the 1820s, but fewer did so in the 1750s—no doubt because holders at mid-century were comparatively young when they died.)[6]

We know that both upland and Wethersfield probates shunned unigeniture. In fact, partitioning was extraordinarily extensive. Three quarters of the children of probated landholders were given ownership of some land in both Wethersfield and the upland in the 1750s. The great majority also got some land on the eve of the Revolution: 71 percent in Wethersfield, 75 percent in the upland. Access to some parental land was as widespread in the early nineteenth century. In Wethersfield, again, 76 percent of the children of probated landholders inherited. Upland children did even better: 83 percent of such children got some real estate in the 1820s.

The data are consistent with the general proposition, established by prior inheritance studies, that when tenure rights are secure and there is no direct threat of fragmentation, the practices of landed producers are partible.[7] Compared with areas of permissive inheritance in Europe, however, the sheer extent of partitioning was distinctive, and it is probably correct to attribute this to comparative land abundance in the context of widespread land ownership. It is noted now, though, that pressure on local land was increasing in both the upland communities and Wethersfield between mid-century and the eve of the Revolution. Wethersfield's population increased by almost 50 percent between 1756 and 1774, while the populations of the four upland towns grew by over one third.[8] These conditions, however, were not associated with any tendency to exclude more children altogether in either area, which may have been because possibilities for emigration were decreasing at the same time. By the Revolutionary era, the internal settlement of Connecticut was largely complete, and it was explicit British policy to discourage westward emigration. There were fewer places for excluded children to go.

However, extensive partitioning is not necessarily the equivalent of egalitarian share-and-share-alike practices. In the next sections I analyze two facets of inequalities among children: the fates of daughters relative to sons, and inequalities among sons. I consider not only exclu-

[6] Rates of "informal testacy" (holders used wills or deeds or both) in Wethersfield and the upland, respectively, were 61 percent and 71 percent in the 1750s, 79 percent and 87 percent in the 1770s, 80 percent and 80 percent in the 1820s.

[7] See the following articles in *Family and Inheritance*: Jack Goody, "Introduction," pp. 2-3; Cicely Howell, "Peasant Inheritance Customs in the Midlands, 1280-1700," pp. 114-17; E. P. Thompson, "The Grid of Inheritance: A Comment," pp. 344-46.

[8] See Table 1.1.

sion from ownership of land, but also the inequalities among those who are allotted land and other property. One can state firmly at this point, however, that the sheer extent of partitioning is incompatible with inheritance strategies aiming at intergenerational consolidation and accumulation of holdings. Strongly patrilineal practices were not, on this evidence, the norm.

THE COLONIAL ERA

Inequalities between Sons and Daughters

Inequalities between sons and daughters were typically created in one of two basic ways. First, holders could simply exclude all daughters and members of daughters' families from heritable rights in land and confine their share of property to personalty.[9] Holders who did so thus made a radical distinction between real and movable property and, with respect to real property, used gender as a primary principle of heir selection. To achieve this result, decedents either had to transfer all their land during their lifetimes or leave a will. Intestate distributions of land never resulted in the exclusion of all daughters.

The use of gender distinctions to exclude daughters emerges with particular clarity when estate holders made provisions for unborn children. The poignancy of Thomas Kingsbery's case, for example, lay not only in the fact that he died leaving an eight-year-old son and a four-year-old daughter, Samuel and Anna, as well as a young wife, but also in the very specific and alternative futures that he mapped for his unborn child in his will of May 29, 1754. If the child was born a son, he and Samuel would split their father's Coventry farm on condition that they each pay to Anna a cash legacy one fifth the value of their respective shares when they became twenty-one.[10] If either boy died before reaching twenty-one, the other was to get the entire farm and the added obligation to his sister. If, however, the child was born a daughter, Samuel got the whole farm and each daughter a legacy one-sixth the value of the whole farm.

The inference is clear. Boys were entitled to equal standing within their father's home community, and this result was best and most eq-

[9] References to property taken by sons or daughters in the rest of this chapter include property going to them, their direct descendants, and, unless otherwise noted, to their spouses. The comparison is really one of sons and their families (actual or potential) with daughters and their families.

[10] Thomas Kingsbery, folio 238, Windham Probate District, Estate Papers. In the case of instructions for afterborns, in the quantitative analyses that follow, coding was done according to instructions for the event that actually occurred. Thomas Kingsbery's youngest was a boy.

uitably obtained by giving them each equal shares of land. Not only was it unnecessary to give daughters direct access to productive property, but it seems their futures cost less than those of sons. Either that or it was tempting to cut corners on daughters. The reduction of legacies in the event that there were two daughters shows that the latter was probably the case. Apparently this was done in order not to double the already considerable but short-term burden on Samuel represented by the payment of sizable lump sums to his sisters.

The second form of gender-based inequality occurred when daughters or members of their families became owners of real property but found themselves with smaller shares than their brothers. This often occurred as a direct result of estate holders' explicit instructions. These instructions could get quite elaborate, as they did in John Morton's will. He gave his two sons an equal share of his real estate: "Except one-fifth Part of s^d. Estate to each of my Daughters—that is to say I will that Each of my Sons shall have five Parts and each of my Daughters one—or least I should be mistaken I add that my five Daughters . . . shall have as much as one of my sons."[11] Though we may have trouble following the calculation, the distributors of his estate did not. Each son took one third of the estate and the daughters as a group were left with the remaining third, to be divided among them. Each daughter, then, was left with 6.67 percent of the real estate, a share one fifth of that taken by each of their brothers.

This second form of gender-based inequality, however, was not necessarily the result of such direct calculations. It could and often did occur as a result of the cumulative impact of decisions made over the holder's life span. For example, a father might make out a perfectly egalitarian will, but if he had also given land to married sons during his lifetime, the overall result would be a decided preference for sons over daughters. When such holders were intestate, the results were the same unless they designated lifetime transfers to sons as advances. Finally, some preference for sons was the automatic result of intestate deaths.

Extensive partitioning did not in fact preclude notable gender distinctions. Daughters everywhere bore a disproportionately heavy burden of exclusion from land (Table 4.1, columns 5-6). In the 1750s about twice as many daughters as sons failed to inherit land in both Wethersfield and the upland. Their disadvantage was heaviest in the 1770s: over 40 percent of the daughters, but fewer than 15 percent of the sons, were excluded in each area. Gender distinctions also affected the relative fates of those sons and daughters who did become owners

---

[11] John Morton, will, signed November 1, 1773, Wethersfield, folio 3833, Hartford Probate District, Estate Papers.

TABLE 4.1
INHERITANCE OF REAL PROPERTY BY THE CHILDREN OF LANDED HOLDERS

	Number			Percentage Inheriting No Realty			Dtrs.' Average Share ÷ Sons' Average Share*
	Estates	Sons	Dtrs.	All Children	Sons	Dtrs.	
	(1)	(2)	(3)	(4)	(5)	(6)	(7)
1750s							
Wethersfield	23	62	69	24	15	33	.65
Upland	14	36	35	24	19	34	.50
1770s							
Wethersfield	24	72	75	29	13	45	.33
Upland	16	44	48	25	7	42	.29
1820s							
Wethersfield	15	43	46	24	14	33	.76
Upland	15	41	43	17	10	23	.24

Note: Figures include children capable of inheriting through their representatives.

* Daughters' average shares as a proportion of sons' average shares: total real estate at appraised value passing to daughters divided by the number of daughters taking real estate in that time and area as a proportion of the same figure for sons.

of real property. Colonial daughters who inherited real estate took an average share that was considerably less valuable than that taken by sons (column 7). In the 1750s Wethersfield daughters who did inherit acquired land or buildings worth about two thirds of the value of the average inheritances of sons, while upland daughters received shares about one half the value of sons' shares. In the 1770s the average allotment given to daughters was very small in both areas (in Wethersfield, one third of that going to sons; in the upland, 29 percent of that going to sons). Holders in both areas seemed to respond to local land shortages not by excluding more children altogether, but by concentrating their resources on their sons and the sons' families.

The disparities between sons and daughters did not result from the unusual practices of a few holders. Sons were heavily preferred heirs in most colonial families (Table 4.2). Both the method of excluding all daughters and the method of giving them small shares were common. Like Thomas Kingsbery, who gave his daughter only a cash legacy, a substantial minority of colonial estate holders in both areas simply excluded all their daughters from ownership of any portion of their real property (Table 4.2, column 2). They were especially apt to do so on the eve of the Revolution. Furthermore, even when colonial daughters

TABLE 4.2

LAND AND INEGALITARIAN TREATMENT OF DAUGHTERS

	Estates (N)	All Dtrs. Excluded (%)	Inegal. DAS* (%)	All Excluded or Inegal. DAS* (%)
	(1)	(2)	(3)	(4)
1750s				
Wethersfield	21	29	38	67
Upland	11	36	27	64
1770s				
Wethersfield	21	48	38	86
Upland	14	43	43	86
1820s				
Wethersfield	12	33	08	42
Upland	13	15	54	69

Note: For landed families with daughters and sons only.
* Daughters' Average Share of real estate was one half or less than that of Sons' Average Share. When estate holders did not directly express daughters' shares as a proportion of sons' shares, DAS/SAS was calculated within families.

did get real estate, they typically received average shares that were no more than half the value of average shares inherited by their brothers (column 3). The combined result of the practice of excluding daughters and of giving them small shares when they did get real estate was that only a minority, and by the 1770s a very small minority, of colonial families in either area placed daughters on anything resembling an equal footing with sons (column 4).

The heavy and increased favoring of sons was not due to the direct threat of fragmentation. When families in the 1770s are ranked within each area by the total acreage given to children, holders who were in the bottom half of these rankings were not much more likely to exclude their daughters than were holders in the top half.[12] It is plausible, however, that holders were responding not to immediate threats to the viability of their particular holdings, but to the greater land shortages generally and to the closure of foreseeable options for expansion just before the Revolution. Almost all sons got a foothold on land. In fact, in the 1770s, the period of greatest pressure on land, sons were least likely to be excluded (Table 4.1, column 5). But pressure did mean that

[12] All daughters were excluded from 50 percent of those estates that fell into the bottom half of these rankings in both areas. All daughters were excluded from 30 percent of the estates that were in the top half of the upland ranking; the comparable figure for Wethersfield was 36 percent. Ranking includes only those holders who had both sons and daughters.

greater efforts to secure the position of sons occurred at the expense of daughters.

Factors special to commercial and subsistence-plus towns did not influence the extent of partitioning or inequalities among sons and daughters during the colonial period. Judging from these data, "asymmetric" or preferential partibility was the rule in both areas. When it was time to pass on their land and its attached buildings, most colonial holders heavily favored those whom they expected to become independent members of their communities, the sons who were the rising generation's new heads of households. The egalitarian thrust, represented by the very high degree of partitioning generally, was "familistic," not individualized, and hence compatible with curtailing women's claims to a direct share in productive property.

It is reasonable to wonder why daughters inherited land at all, since most who did so got only small shares. A large part of the answer is that most landed holders had comparatively little personal property. When Capt. Caleb Griswald, of Wethersfield, died in 1754 he left behind four sons and four daughters ranging in age from fifteen to twenty-four. He died a fairly prosperous farmer, having managed to amass through inheritance and purchase land worth over 550 pounds lawful money. His gross personal estate was worth only 132 pounds, however. Miscellaneous debts and probate fees consumed over 50 pounds of it, and when his wife took her thirds, including most of his livestock, there was very little personal property left.[13]

Among landed holders, gross personal estates were, on the average, about one third the value of total estates held at death during each time and in each area. The proportion of net personal to total net estate was in every case less, and often it was reduced to trivial amounts or to nothing by debt payments. If there was any net personal estate at all, the widow, when there was one, usually took a third (or more) of what remained. Among landed families, personal property from estates held at death could operate, therefore, only as very partial compensation for heavily favoring sons' access to real estate. Hence, fragmentary shares of real estate went to daughters when holders died intestate or decided not to burden favored sons with payment of legacies.

When personal property was available, colonial daughters did get the largest share. The distributors of Martha Robbins's intestate estate, for example, gave her only son, John, his double share entirely in land; he got twenty-six acres (worth 862 pounds old tenor). They divided the

[13] Caleb Griswald, inventory, taken February 11, 1755, administrator's account, exhibited February 3, 1756, and estate distribution, made March 5, 1756, folio 2419, Hartford Probate District, Estate Papers.

entire net movable estate worth 1,035 pounds among her six daughters. Since it did not stretch far enough to make up their six single shares, the daughters also carried away between three and nine acres of land each.[14]

Among colonial families who had both sons and daughters, daughters' average shares of personal property were greater in value by at least 50 percent than the average shares going to sons.[15] Actually, this is a conservative estimate of the relative value of personal property taken by daughters since we do not have a complete record of the personal property given to daughters when they married during the holders' lifetimes. Still, the pattern in the colonial period is unmistakable: a mirror image treatment of personal and real property prevailed. Land, the most fundamental form of productive property, was treated primarily as the reserve of sons, while personal property went principally to daughters.[16]

Inequalities among Sons

The last two sections compared the fates of colonial daughters as a group with that of sons. But within these groups there was, of course, room for variation in the treatment of each member. Daughters, in fact, did not receive individualized treatment. For example, either every daughter got land or none at all got land in all but four colonial families.[17] In the great majority of families, daughters were also given inheritances that were equal or nearly equal in value. In sum, within a given family, the average inheritance share taken by daughters was, or was close to, the actual value of shares taken by each daughter. In light of this fact, it is reasonable to focus on inequalities among sons.

Egalitarian share-and-share-alike strategies were not characteristic of colonial families in either Wethersfield or the upland. Favored sons got shares at least twice the value of those given their least favored

[14] Martha Robbins, estate distribution, made November 6, 1754, Wethersfield, folio 4554, Hartford Probate District, Estate Papers.

[15] In Wethersfield in the 1750s, daughters' average share was 2.1 times the value of sons' average share; in the upland at the same date, 1.5 times the value. The figures in the 1770s were 1.6 and 1.5 in Wethersfield and the upland, respectively.

[16] Some suggest that women, when they can, resist this pattern by using egalitarian or compensatory inheritance strategies. See, for example, John Waters. "The Traditional World of the New England Peasant: A View from Seventeenth Century Barnstable," *New England Historical and Genealogical Register* 30 (January 1976): 18. There are very few landed women in this study. Of those who do have both sons and daughters, two do include only daughters, but the other two favor sons. The cases are scattered.

[17] In the entire period, 1750-1820, there were only eight cases in which some, but not all, daughters got heritable rights in land.

brothers in two thirds or more of those landed families that had more than one son. Thus, for example, Jeheil Rose of Coventry willed three pieces of outlying land and buildings worth about 430 pounds lawful money to Jeheil, Jr. He also gave his namesake his silver shoe buckles. But his only other son, Timothy, was certainly the favored heir. He got land evaluated at about 890 pounds lawful money. He also inherited 150 pounds worth of notes due to his father's estate and two thirds of his father's "Creatures" and "Husbandry Tools." (His mother took the other one third free and clear, that is, in fee-simple.)[18]

Some families gave one or two sons direct access to land and left the others legacies or bequests large enough to put them on a par with their landed brothers. Therefore, Table 4.3 is based on the value of the total inheritance of each son. It is still the case that most colonial families short-changed some sons. They did so somewhat more frequently in the upland, and holders in both areas were particularly prone to do so just before the Revolution. In the 1770s, over half the Wethersfield

TABLE 4.3

INEQUALITIES AMONG SONS IN LANDED FAMILIES WITH AT LEAST TWO SONS

	All Estates		All Could Get 20 Acres			Not All Could Get 20 Acres	
	(N)	SLF/SMF Unequal* (%)	(N)	SLF/SMF Unequal* (%)	Not All Get 20 Acres (%)	(N)	SLF/SMF Unequal* (%)
	(1)	(2)	(3)	(4)	(5)	(6)	(7)
1750s							
Wethersfield	17	41ns	7	71	14	10	20
Upland	9	55	6	83	31	3	0
1770s							
Wethersfield	21	57ns	12	67	17	9	44
Upland	13	77	12	75	33	1	100
1820s							
Wethersfield	13	15††	6	29	0	6	0
Upland	11	54	9	67	11	3	0

ns Chi-square not significant.

* Share of the Least Favored son divided by the Share of the Most Favored son is one half or less. Shares based on the appraised value of all property inherited by each son.

†† Chi-square significant at .05 level. Based on two column tables (SLF/SMF was/was not one half or less), by community type.

[18] Jeheil Rose, will, signed April 7, 1773, and inventory, taken June 1773, folio 3271, Windham Probate District, Estate Papers.

holders gave favored sons shares at least twice the value of those received by least-favored sons. Three quarters of the upland holders did so at the same date (Table 4.3, column 2). In the colonial period, then, a pattern of preferential partibility operated at the expense of some sons as well as daughters.

The meaning of inequalities among sons, however, depends in part on the wealth of holders and the number of their sons. Small holders who skimped on the inheritances of some were preventing excessive fragmentation. They were trying to avoid the loss of their families' independent standing within the community by guaranteeing the life-chances of at least one son. In this sense inequalities were forced. To use a principle of absolute parity under such circumstances was instead to opt for a small headstart for each son. In contrast, a holder in a position to set up every son who, nevertheless, heavily favored one or two sons truly chose an inegalitarian route.

The large majority of colonial families in a position to provide each son with at least twenty acres of land or its cash equivalent[19] chose to concentrate their resources on some sons at the expense of others. From 67 to 83 percent of such colonial families did so (Table 4.3, column 4).[20] Although these relatively fortunate families did favor some sons, most still gave each son at least the minimal twenty-acre basis for independent standing in their home communities (column 5). Setting-up as many sons as possible outweighed the desire for accumulation in all but a few families.

Although the data are only suggestive because the upland cases are so few, it is interesting to note that most colonial families who could not give all sons twenty acres were egalitarian (column 7). However, only one third of such families pressed equality of treatment so far as to deny every son a twenty-acre threshold (not shown). These pursued a provisioning or head-start strategy at the expense of generational continuity. The rest, whether egalitarian or not, saw to it that inheritance provided at least one son with a minimum holding.

The Colonial Era: Parallel Practices

Before turning to an analysis of inheritance practices in the 1820s, it is best to consolidate the findings on the colonial era. The property arrangements made by Coventry's Wilson family are a good place to begin because they embody most aspects of the prevailing colonial norm

---

[19] At local land prices as established by the average value of an acre of land in each area and time at inventory evaluations.

[20] In each area a majority of those families fortunate enough to be able to provide each son with at least forty acres were inegalitarian.

of preferential partibility. When John Wilson died in 1773, he owned a house and barn on forty-seven acres of land. When one takes into account the other ninety-four acres he had already given away, he was, by second-generation Coventry standards, a well-off middling farmer. Judging from the personal estate he left behind, worth just over 100 pounds before debts were paid, he practiced diversified agriculture with some concentration on dairying and wool production—enough to supply him with a small cash income.[21]

Like most colonial holders, John Wilson made a sharp distinction between land and movables. His only daughter, Abigail Herrick, got what he called her full share of his estate, all in movables, when she married. By excluding his daughter from land, John Wilson was in a position to give each of his three sons just about enough land to make up a small working farm. Instead, he cut corners on two sons to give a more substantial holding to the third. When his eldest son, William, married in 1749, John gave him thirty-four acres of land lying at the outermost corner of his home farm. He also gave twenty acres of land to his youngest son, Joseph, sometime later.

His middle son, Francis, was John's main heir, however. Francis also received thirty acres when he married, but his land adjoined his father's home lot, and ten years later, in 1767, he was given ten more acres. Shortly after the last transaction, Francis died. The premature death of his son must have been a severe blow to John, especially since Francis and his family lived and worked on John's farm. Evidently the father very much wanted Francis's family to continue the arrangement. Prompted by his son's death to make out his will in 1768, John gave the use of half his house and barn to his own wife, Dorothy, and the other half to his son's widow, Abigail. In addition to the property already belonging to their father, Francis's two sons inherited the forty-seven acres that remained of their grandfather's home lot (possession pending the death of their grandmother), in return for which they were to pay small legacies to their four sisters.[22]

In short, John was quite willing to divide his farm among several heirs, but he still had to make hard choices. He confined women to use-rights, personal property, and legacies. Two sons got enough land to become family heads, but one, William, would have to accumulate

[21] His inventory carefully listed his five cows, one bull, and his flock of ten sheep as well as his stored animal feed and cheese. Although cloth production was ordinarily women's work, John also died owning the household's two spinning wheels and loom. John Wilson, inventory taken September 28, 1733, folio 4219, Windham Probate District, Estate Papers.

[22] Wilson, will, signed May 21, 1768; Coventry Land Records, 3: 197, 612, 4: 437, 5: 315, deeds, signed February 1749/50, February 1758, and April 1764.

property on his own if he were to have more than a very small farm, and a third was likely to remain single for the rest of his life. Only the son chosen, or willing, to remain with his parents got a substantial farm. John Wilson's policy was not one of intergenerational accumulation, however. The eighty-seven-acre portion of his home farm allotted to Francis's family would be divided soon enough.

Like John Wilson, most families put less emphasis on intergenerational accumulation than on efforts to set up as many children as possible in the communities of their birth. Inheritance patterns were extensively partible in both the upland and Wethersfield, but the allocation of land did not follow a share-and-share-alike pattern of dispersion. Rather, preferential partibility prevailed. Families also allocated real and personal property differently. Their use of gender distinctions heavily favored sons' direct access to land, and some sons were advantaged over others in most families. Finally, the more crowded conditions of the 1770s were associated with sharpened and more widespread inequalities among sons and between sons and daughters.

Colonial inheritance practices were similar in Wethersfield and the upland. Judging from these communities, differences in local opportunities for nonlanded employment and in agricultural practices were not associated with different patterns of partitioning or degrees of inequality. Wethersfield's more specialized artisanal and mercantile trades were, for example, not attractive enough to persuade greater numbers of Wethersfield holders to consolidate their estates by denying some sons a meaningful inheritance. Neither were market-induced pressures for more efficient production.

As noted earlier, it is probably correct to attribute the sheer extent of partitioning to comparative land abundance and widespread farm ownership. But similar practices in the upland and in Wethersfield were not necessarily the result of precisely similar mechanisms. The upland communities were less densely settled than Wethersfield. They also had the advantage of more recent distributions of large quantities of proprietors' land. In short, person-land ratios were lower in the upland. But Wethersfield, far more densely settled and with far fewer reserves of unallocated land in its recent past, had the offsetting advantage of comparatively intensive agriculture.[23] Thus similar rates of partition-

[23] Most of Wethersfield's undivided land was distributed in the late seventeenth century, although comparatively small allotments were periodically made throughout the first half of the eighteenth century. The upland residents did not begin settling and distributing the land in their towns until the period 1712 to 1734. Bruce Daniels, *The Connecticut Town: Growth and Development, 1635-1790* (Middletown, Conn.: Wesleyan University Press, 1979); Sherman Adams and Henry Stiles, *The History of Ancient Weth-*

ing could certainly have been encouraged by different sets of local conditions.

It is also true that the same inheritance practices can have different consequences in different demographic and economic contexts.[24] Although the asymmetries in allocation of property were more exaggerated in the 1770s in both areas, the rather resolute continuance of partitioning indicates the stability of the desire to secure the independent status of as many children as possible. Such partitioning may have encouraged the crystallization of the economic differences that increasingly differentiated upland from river-valley communities. Thus partitioning may help to account for both the upland's greater receptivity (or vulnerability) to rural industry in the early nineteenth century and Wethersfield's continued intensification of agricultural production.

The research strategy used in this study cannot pinpoint the causal dynamics of which these inheritance practices were a part, but the analysis of equality and inequality among children does establish a very important basic point. None of the features distinctive to the northern countryside as a whole—comparative land abundance, a nonseigneurial social structure, and widespread land ownership—diluted the importance of direct inheritance enough to eliminate the tension between unity and provision. The colonial pattern of preferential partibility, with its systematic asymmetries in the treatment of children, attests to this tension. Further, this pattern has little resemblance to modern share-and-share-alike provisioning strategies. Finally, the colonial pattern of preferential partibility common to upland and Wethersfield holders is a baseline for evaluating inheritance practices in the 1820s.

EQUALITY AND INEQUALITY IN THE 1820s

The overall picture of inheritance is one of divergent rather than parallel practices in the 1820s. The percentages of children excluded from ownership of land fell modestly (24 percent in Wethersfield, 17 percent in the upland), giving the impression of eased conditions in both areas (Table 4.1, column 4). The inter-area difference in the percentage of children excluded was due largely to differences in the treatment of daughters: a third were excluded in Wethersfield, and 23 percent in the uplands (Table 4.1, column 6).

ersfield, 2 vols., reprint ed. (Somersworth: New Hampshire Publishing Co., 1974), 1: 91-117, 785.

[24] Lutz Berkner and Franklin Mendels, "Inheritance Systems, Family Structure, and Demographic Patterns in Western Europe, 1700-1900" in *Historical Studies of Changing Fertility*, ed. Charles Tilly (Princeton, N.J.: Princeton University Press, 1978), pp. 209-25.

These figures are misleading, however. Upland holders were some-what more prone to extend partitioning to daughters than their Weth-ersfield counterparts: eleven of the thirteen landed families with sons and daughters did so (compared with eight of twelve such families in Wethersfield). But upland daughters who inherited land received token shares, just as they had before the Revolution. Their average share of realty was only one quarter the value of their brothers' average share (Table 4.1, column 7). Sons were still the heavily preferred heirs in most upland families. Altogether, two thirds of the upland families either ex-cluded their daughters entirely or included them only to give them shares that were no more than half the average shares given to their sons (Table 4.2, column 4).

In striking contrast, when Wethersfield daughters inherited land, they received an average share that was almost the same as that re-ceived by sons (just over three quarters the size of sons'; see Table 4.1, column 7). Thus, though more Wethersfield than upland families used a primary gender distinction to exclude all daughters, for the first time only a minority of families (42 percent) heavily favored sons' access to land (Table 4.2, column 4).[25] In fact, Wethersfield holders displayed a sharply polarized use of gender distinctions. Daughters were excluded only from estates that were in the bottom 50 percent of landed es-tates.[26] All the larger holders included all of their daughters, and all but one put their daughters on a footing basically on a par with their sons.

The pattern of diverging practices was maintained in the distribution of personal property. In six of fourteen upland families who had per-sonal property and sons and daughters, daughters got larger shares of personal property than their brothers. This was true of only one of ten such Wethersfield families.[27] All told, upland daughters took average shares that were 1.2 times the value of the average shares taken by sons. In Wethersfield, sons now had the favored edge. They took average shares of personal property that were twice the value of shares taken by daughters. In short, upland practices closely resembled the colonial pattern, while Wethersfield holders virtually abandoned the mirror-im-age treatment of personalty and realty.

[25] Examining only those estates in which daughters did get land (N = 19), the chi-square for inegalitarian treatment (daughters' average share was/was not one-half or less than sons' average share) by community type is significant at .05 level in the 1820s.

[26] In fact, all but one child excluded from land—son or daughter—were excluded from such estates. In the upland of the 1820s, 36 percent of the excluded children came from those estates falling into the top half of the ranked upland estates.

[27] The chi-square based on a two-column table (daughters' average share was/was not greater than sons' average share) by community type was significant at the .10 level in the 1820s (N = 24). The chi-square were not significant in the 1770s (N = 28) or the 1750s (N = 29).

The picture of inter-area divergence is the same when one turns to inequalities among sons. Once again, the practices of upland holders more closely resembled the practices of their colonial forebears than those of their Wethersfield contemporaries. Just over half of the landed upland families were still cutting sharp corners on the inheritance of one or more sons (Table 4.3, column 2); but the percentage of Wethersfield families that did so plummeted to 15 percent. Those who could give each son at least a twenty-acre minimum (or its equivalent) were now pursuing different strategies in Wethersfield and in the upland. Two thirds of such upland families still chose to concentrate their resources on some sons at the expense of others, while in Wethersfield less than a third did so (Table 4.3, column 4).

In sum, in the 1820s preferential partibility still prevailed among upland holders, as it had among colonial probates in both areas. Daughters and some sons had limited access to productive property. Preferential partibility was not, however, primarily the result of excluding children altogether from land, but of endowing some favored children with larger shares than others. Recall that in the early nineteenth century, the upland communities were beginning to concentrate more of their total resources on nonagricultural production. The resolute continuance of partitioning, despite the upland's (modestly) increased population density, extensive agriculture, and worn soils, is consistent with the literature that suggests that local sources of by-employment form an important part of the "grid of inheritance." They allow for continued partitioning by relieving pressure on the customary margins over subsistence.[28]

That these holders did not simply turn to share-and-share-alike strategies, however, suggests that the basic tension between unity and provision still guided inheritance practices in the upland. *Preferential* partibility suggests that these holders did not intend to supply their children with a mere head start. They wanted to guarantee the status of freeholder (or marriage to a freeholder) to as many children as possible without ruining the chances of all. Although by-employment helped to expand the limits within which the tension between unity and provision could be resolved, neither the still new sources of local employment nor the increased opportunities for emigration and resettlement in the early nineteenth century eradicated the basic tension.

In Wethersfield, the pattern of preferential partibility broke down. For the first time, notably more Wethersfield than upland children were excluded from ownership of land, primarily because fewer daughters

[28] Thompson, "Grid of Inheritance," p. 342; David Levine, *Family Formation in an Age of Nascent Capitalism* (New York: Academic Press, 1977), p. 13.

obtained land. But exclusion of children was more closely related to levels of economic well-being than it was in the upland. Agriculture oriented toward extra-local markets put more pressure on small holders than on large to emphasize unity at the expense of equality of access. The larger holders in this community of intensive agriculture could afford to be more generous.

Still, it is surprising to see daughters gaining direct access to so much land. After all, the holders still owned viable productive enterprises, and one might expect that an orientation toward cash returns would encourage less partitioning in the interests of efficiency. This is especially likely when a high degree of occupational specialization and opportunities for emigration provide alternatives for excluded children.[29] Yet even the holders who could provide substantial inheritances for daughters without giving them productive property failed to make the distinction between productive and other property.

Joseph Bulkley, a merchant with shipping interests both at home and in New York City as well as an owner of three hundred acres (either held at death or deeded to sons during his lifetime), is a clear illustration of a holder who had ceased to make distinctions according to property type. He not only stated in his will that all lifetime gifts in land and cash were to be calculated as advances, but also that it did not matter who got real or personal property, so long as the value of the shares taken were as stipulated: ". . . for the More Easy Setteling of said Estate there Shall be No distinction betwen Real or personal Estate in said Settlement so that any or Either of my Sons or dathers May have Real or Moveable Estate as Shall be Most Convenient."[30] The result was that sons and daughters alike took prime meadow land and personal property, including stocks and debts receivable.[31]

Several factors could have encouraged the decline of distinctions between land and movables and greater equality between sons and daughters. First, as already noted, more intensive agriculture permitted continued partitioning. In addition, the abandonment of gender distinctions when providing direct access to land was connected to patterns of rights creation, as analyzed in the next chapter. In all probabil-

---

[29] Colin Creighton, "Family, Property and Relations of Production in Western Europe," *Economy and Society* 9 (May 1980): 154-56; Howell, "Inheritance in the Midlands," pp. 153-55; Michel Verdon, "The Stem Family: Toward a General Theory," *Journal of Interdisciplinary History* 10 (Summer 1979): 87-105.

[30] Joseph Bulkley, will, signed November 9, 1818, Wethersfield, Hartford Probate District, Estate Papers.

[31] The distributors of Bulkley's estate, presumably in cooperation with his executors (his wife and three of his five sons), did reserve his store located on the Rocky Hill wharf (worth $750) for two sons.

ity, this was not simply because these holders were more egalitarian, but because their practices were more individualized. They precluded the imposition of indirect claims on productive property or its takers: it was ownership or no claims at all (the widow's dower excepted). Second, as the Bulkley example indicates, it seems that practices were oriented toward the market value of property, not toward its particular use. One did not so much set-up children with a direct inheritance of a particular form of productive property as give them a potential cash fund.[32] Whatever the precise mechanism, the pattern of preferential partibility had been undermined in commercialized Wethersfield.

CONCLUSION

A close analysis of the inheritance shares of children has established a picture of first parallel, then diverging practices. Within an overall context of extensive partitioning, the colonial norm was one of preferential partibility. Sons were heavily favored over daughters in access to land, while personal property was used to compensate daughters. In addition, in most landed families some sons were favored over others. The pattern of preferential partibility was also the norm among upland holders in the 1820s, but by then it had sharply eroded in Wethersfield.

The way in which northern economic development affected rural social relations is contested, specifically in the area of family behavior and sentiments. Some historians hold that economic development itself was part and parcel of general conditions—lack of a seigneurial social structure, widespread family farm ownership, land abundance, high geographic mobility—that encouraged advancement by dint of individual effort and entrepreneurial and individualist values. Property arrangements creating or reinforcing extended kin ties, patriarchal authority, sharp inequalities, or claims that curbed liquidity and circulation were neither encouraged by such conditions nor compatible with such methods of advancement and values. In an extreme version of this position, inheritance as a means of directly guaranteeing the life-chances of offspring is held to have been a peripheral phenomenon.[33]

[32] To be sure, none of these holders went so far as did some of the later nineteenth-century New Jersey testators studied by Lawrence M. Friedman. These requested that their executors simply liquidate their holdings and disperse the cash proceeds; see "Patterns of Testation in the Nineteenth Century: A Study of Essex County Wills," *American Journal of Legal History* 8 (1964): 50.

[33] See, for example, Charles S. Grant, *Democracy in the Connecticut Frontier Town of Kent* (New York: Columbia University Press, 1961); Jackson Turner Main, *The Social Structure of Revolutionary America* (Princeton, N.J.: Princeton University Press, 1975), pp. 219-20.

Others argue that market development was segmented. Growth in the volume of intercolonial and export trade and consolidation of the mercantile networks supporting this trade did not immediately disrupt the largely self-supporting nature of production and exchange within rural subsistence-plus communities. These self-enclosed communities fostered familistic, patriarchal values. Household heads sought to anchor each family member to the community through property arrangements that reinforced patriarchal authority within households and strong ties among households related by kinship. The primacy of the connection between family standing and viable farm holding precluded arrangements that simply dispersed property among kin.[34]

The sheer extent of partitioning in the upland and in Wethersfield seems to support those who argue that conditions distinctive to the American North encouraged special orientations toward the use of land. The extensive partitioning has struck observers from Tocqueville to present-day social historians as exceptional, and it has even been used to make the claim that under these unique conditions, a direct inheritance was not important in securing the life-chances of children. Yet the European literature on peasants and yeomen strongly supports the idea that highly inegalitarian inheritance practices were forced by threats to viability rather than motivated by the goal of accumulation. In light of this view, one could argue the extensive partitioning found in the American North was only the fulfillment of the yeoman's egalitarian program under particularly hospitable conditions. It is, of course, a form of counterfactual speculation to suppose that had European owner-producers been faced with similar person-land ratios, they, too, would have practiced more extensive partitioning.

But the outcome of European-American comparisons need not rest on the sheer extent to which children were included or excluded from land. A further exploration of American partitioning moves us away from counterfactual argument. The majority of colonial holders in both Wethersfield and the upland clearly practiced preferential partibility, as did early nineteenth-century upland probates. Further, in both areas the response to the relatively closed environment of the early 1770s was an increase in the incidence of preferential treatment. This is exactly what one would expect of inheritance strategies aiming to resolve tensions between unity and provision. When inheritance is meant to secure directly the social standing of children, one expects the claims of some to be subordinated to others for the sake of maximizing the chances that inheritance will achieve the intended result for at least

[34] James Henretta, "Families and Farms: 'Mentalité' in Pre-Industrial America," *William and Mary Quarterly*, 3rd ser., 35 (January 1978): 22, 24-26; Waters, "Patrimony."

some heirs. These systematic preferences are not the attributes of the egalitarian share-and-share-alike practices that indicate a breakdown in the connection between direct inheritance and life-chances. Indeed, these systematic preferences more closely resembled the inequalities typical of European producers pursuing a "favored heir plus burdens" strategy.

Finally, the pattern of preferential partibility gave way only in Wethersfield and only as this community became highly dependent on extra-local markets both in its agricultural production and in the structure of occupations serving extra-local trade. It appears, then, that not factors unique to the region, but rather those entailed in a high degree of commercialization of rural life were associated with shifts in inheritance practices.

The upland and colonial pattern of preferential partibility may have more closely resembled the European "favored heir plus burdens" strategy than it did modern share-and-share-alike practices, but the "favored heir plus burdens" strategy does not simply make distinctions among heirs by allocating unequal shares of property. It indirectly recognizes the claims of excluded and less-favored heirs to property through overlapping rights that impose burdens on favored takers. It remains to be seen whether preferential partibility was accompanied by such overlapping rights and whether the picture of parallel, then diverging practices holds up in the patterns of rights-creation established by these holders. Only then will it be possible to evaluate fully the issue of American exceptionalism as it bears on inheritance.

CHAPTER FIVE

INHERITED OBLIGATIONS AND KINSHIP TIES

Although inequality among heirs is perhaps the issue one first associates with inheritance, the pattern of rights-creation is more important in shaping kin ties. The types of rights created in property affect the number and strength of obligations among blood and conjugal kin, among members of living, past, and future generations, and between families and outsiders. The network of relations thus established may not correspond to the boundaries of the family defined as a unit of consumption or socialization, but it can be very important when kin rely on family-held productive property.[1] Indeed, at least one historian argues that among landed families, family structures ought to be distinguished by the nature of property rights held by various family members, not by differences in household composition or some other aspect of family organization. Thus Colin Creighton makes the very strong claim that property rights and the inheritance strategies crucial in creating them are the primary dimension of family structure in landed societies.[2]

When European producers gave favored sons access to land, they also required them to meet obligations to other family members. The burdens imposed on main heirs were at the same time created on behalf of others—rights and obligations that gave a characteristic cast to kin ties. European producers underscored relations between parents and adult children and among siblings when they apportioned use-rights in the same piece of land to several family members, and when they required favored heirs to care for aged kin or to pay legacies out of future revenues.

I have called these "extended cognate" inheritance practices in part to distinguish them from strongly patrilineal strategies. The latter promote intergenerational accumulation not only by heavily restricting the extent of partitioning, but by imposing restraints on alienation that en-

[1] For a particularly rigorous elaboration of the principle that the boundaries of the family shift depending upon the set of activities analyzed, see Michel Verdon, "Shaking Off the Domestic Yoke, or the Sociological Significance of Residence," *Comparative Studies in Society and History* 22 (January 1980): 123-25.

[2] Colin Creighton, "Family, Property, and Relations of Production in Western Europe," *Economy and Society* 9 (May 1980): 137-39.

dure to the third generation. But extended cognate inheritance strategies are also unlike share-and-share-alike inheritance practices that
simply disperse family property. The obligations created by extended
cognate practices attest to a vision of family property as an ongoing
concern that must supply the needs of all family members.[3]

Colonial and early nineteenth-century upland holders practiced preferential partibility. It remains to be seen whether they also used overlapping rights to create ties among kin. So long as family property must
be made to provide for the new generation, holders should impose obligations to other family members on main heirs. To the extent that
market penetration, rather than regionwide factors such as land abundance and possibilities for emigration, is related to a diminished relationship between inheritance and life-chances, extended cognate practices ought to decline only in Wethersfield. Upland holders should
continue to use patterns of rights creation that resemble those of European producers in permissive inheritance areas.

RIGHTS AND OBLIGATIONS

When estate holders excluded daughters from land, they commonly required their sons to pay legacies to excluded daughters in virtue of the
land they took. Thomas Fuller of Willington, a self-identified husband-
man and weaver, pursued this strategy in his 1754 will. His two living
sons, David and Solomon, split the ownership of his buildings and
eighty-two-acre farm. Each was required to pay one of the decedent's
two married daughters, Mehetabel and Ester, forty-six (Spanish) dollars "or Public Bills Equivalent" in seven-dollar annual installments.
Solomon, however, was only a minor. Ester, therefore, had to wait for
her first payment until Solomon was twenty-three, while David, who
had just married in 1753, was allowed the "use and Improvement" of
his brother's share until Solomon came of age.[4] Thus, with respect to

---

[3] Good discussions of burdens occur in Lutz Berkner and Franklin Mendels, "Inherit-
ance Systems, Family Structure, and Demographic Patterns In Western Europe, 1700-
1900," in *Historical Studies of Changing Fertility*, ed. Charles Tilly (Princeton, N.J.:
Princeton University Press, 1978), pp. 213-14; Margaret Spufford, "Peasant Inheritance
Customs and Land Distribution in Cambridgeshire from the Sixteenth to the Eighteenth
Centuries," in *Family and Inheritance*, ed. Jack Goody, Joan Thirsk, and E. P. Thompson
(Cambridge, Eng.: Cambridge University Press, 1976), pp. 156-76. See also David P. Ga-
gan, "The Indivisibility of Land: A Microanalysis of the System of Inheritance in Nine-
teenth Century Ontario," *Journal of Economic History* 36 (March 1976): 128-32, 138-
39; Daniel Snydacker, "Kinship and Community in Rural Pennsylvania, 1749-1820,"
Journal of Interdisciplinary History 8 (Summer 1982): 50-51, 55-59.

[4] Thomas Fuller, will, signed March 4, 1754, folio 2091, Hartford Probate District,
Estate Papers; Willington Land Records, C: 72, deed, signed November 30, 1748.

ownership and management of land, Thomas made a radical distinction between sons and daughters, but entitled the latter to claims upon the future revenues from the land, and practiced absolute equality among children of the same sex.

Unmarried children who did not inherit ownership of the holder's house often received specified use-rights in it. Martin Kellogg's will, for example, says: "I give to My sᵈ Daughters Mary and Sarah the Use and Improvement of the one half of my Dwelling House during the Time They Shall remain Unmarried and to each of them during the Term of their continuing Unmarried."[5] It did not take a will to create use-rights for minors or single adults. For example, although the distributors of Thomas Robbins's intestate estate gave ownership of his house and other buildings to his only son, they allowed his minor daughters "the Privilege of Solely Improving and peaceably Enjoying the East Chamber of Said Dwelling House for the Term of Seven Years . . . if they or Either of them shall need and require the Same for their own personal uses."[6]

The Fuller case illustrates an obligation typically created between favored sons and less-favored daughters, while the Kellogg and Robbins cases illustrate obligations that could be created when the child-rearing phase of the family cycle was disrupted by the death of the head of the household. The rights and duties created in retirement-contract arrangements established another common obligation. There were two basic variations, both designed to transform sons' expectations into guaranteed inheritances while also ensuring that the holder's subsistence needs would be met. In the first arrangement, holders passed ownership to their sons, while reserving for themselves life-estates in a portion of the property transferred. Holders thus relinquished their powers of alienation and testamentary control to their sons but retained the managerial powers essential to their continued effectiveness as farmers. A second arrangement was the retirement contract proper.[7] Here both ownership and use were transferred to the son, but on condition that he fulfill specified obligations to the grantor (or the grantor and grantor's spouse) for maintenance and care.

---

[5] Martin Kellogg, will, signed October 7, 1753, Wethersfield, folio 3148, Hartford Probate District, Estate Papers.

[6] Thomas Robbins, estate distribution, made April 1, 1763, Wethersfield, folio 4566, Hartford Probate District, Estate Papers.

[7] For similar practices in Europe, see Lutz Berkner, "The Stem Family and the Developmental Cycle of the Peasant Household: An Eighteenth Century Austrian Example," *American Historical Review* 77 (April 1972): 398-418. Also see Jack Goody, "Introduction," pp. 28-29; Berkner, "Inheritance, Land Tenure, and Peasant Family Structure: A German Regional Comparison," pp. 78, 93-94; Cicely Howell, "Peasant Inheritance Customs in the Midlands, 1280-1700," in *Inheritance in Western Europe*, pp. 143-45; Spufford, "Inheritance in Cambridgeshire," pp. 173-74.

An unusually complex agreement negotiated in mid-eighteenth-century Willington combines features of both arrangements. John Poole, Sr., gave ownership of one half of his farm to his son John, Jr., who then leased back his share to his father for his father's natural life. In return, John, Jr., got the use of all of his father's farmland and a use-right in a room in the house (still owned by the father). But he only got these uses so long as he (1) worked the whole farm according to "Good Husbandry"; (2) bore half the cost of maintaining the husbandry tools and fences; (3) paid half the taxes; (4) delivered to his father half "the improvements in produce of the whole sd farm"; and (5) allowed his father and one of his younger brothers to work on the farm "During Ye pleasure of the sd John Poole sr."[8]

Occasionally uses and legacies got quite complex, extending strong ties through the third generation. This was true of Joseph Woodhouse's will, which gave land to three of his sons, John, Samuel, and Daniel, and to three grandsons. Daniel, the only unmarried son, received half the home lot and a quarter of the pasture land as a life-estate that was then to pass to "the Heirs of his Body lawfully to be begotten." But if Daniel died childless, John, who got ownership of the other half of his father's home lot and one quarter of the pasture land, was to inherit Daniel's share of the home lot. In that event, also, Samuel was to split Daniel's pasture land with Lemuel, the decedent's grandson by a fourth son, William.

Samuel also received ownership of half the land already occupied by the predeceased son William's family. Title to the other half together with its house and barn passed to William's only son, Lemuel. Lemuel's portion was burdened by a use-right in one third of all property to his mother during her widowhood, and by use-rights in the house to his two unmarried sisters. He was also required, in virtue of ownership of eight acres of extra-local land, to pay legacies to his sisters. If he refused, they were to receive ownership of the land. Samuel, too, received extra-local land in return for which he was expected to pay legacies to his three married sisters and the daughter of one more predeceased sister. If he failed to do so, this land was to go to his sisters and sister's child. Finally, the eldest sons of both Samuel and John, along with Lemuel, inherited a twelve-acre meadow lot.[9]

Several aspects of the Woodhouse arrangement were unusual. Very few of the many holders who required landed heirs to pay legacies enforced these obligations by specifying that the would-be recipients of

[8] Willington Land Records, D: 132, deed of indenture (lease), signed May 28, 1763. (John Poole, Sr.'s estate entered probate in 1773.)

[9] Joseph Woodhouse, will, signed June 24, 1774, Wethersfield, folio 6236, Hartford Probate District, Estate Papers.

the legacies were to get the land should the favored takers fail to meet their obligations ("executory" devises). Note that Joseph Woodhouse closely identified extra-local land—a most "peripheral" form of holding—with cash. Only a small minority of estate holders had extra-local land, but most used it in a similar way: as a functional equivalent of legacies for less-favored heirs. For such holders the purchase of extra-local land appears to have been not so much "speculation" as a form of petty savings in a world without local banks. It was not so unusual to settle sons on land without even giving them use-rights at first. Sons in this position had only the expectation that the land would become theirs at the death of their parents.[10]

As Chapter Three showed in detail, only a small minority of holders gave grandchildren or nieces and nephews even token gifts when their parents were still alive. Woodhouse, in contrast, singled out all his sons' eldest sons for special gifts of land; unlike most others, he followed a deliberate policy of generational extension. More important, only four other holders used entails or other arrangements limiting their children (or siblings) to life-estates while giving heritable estates to childrens' (or siblings') heirs.[11] Only six holders attempted to regulate in any way relations between living heirs and their own offspring. Woodhouse, then, was one of the very few to use patterns of rights-creation that had a dynastic or strongly patrilineal tinge.

Even in this relatively complex case, most of the ties created were, literally or by proxy, mutual obligations among siblings or two-generation parent-child ties. Lemuel, for example, simply replaced his father. His obligations to his sisters were similar to Samuel's obligations to his sisters, or the Fuller sons' to theirs. That his grandfather created them was the accident of his father's early death. That Samuel divided certain lots with his nephew rather than with his brother was a similar accident, as was his paying a legacy to his dead sister's daughter. Apart from the restrictions imposed on Daniel, the ties enforced by the crea-

[10] One finds evidence of this arrangement when the grantor or testator mentioned that the property transferred was land on which the grantee or devisee already lived. An unknown proportion of such arrangements go undetected. For example, one can only guess that perhaps Samuel and John, both married before their father's death, already lived on the land they eventually inherited.

[11] Connecticut law diverged from English law in its interpretation of such devises. Statutory reforms of 1784 and 1821 confirmed earlier colonial court rulings that a grant or devise "to X for life, then to the heirs of his or her body" conferred a life estate on the first taker and a fee-simple estate in the first taker's heirs. *Welles et Ux. v. Olcott*, 1 Kirby 118 (Conn. Super. Ct. 1786); *Public Statutes 1821*, pp. 301, 310; Zephaniah Swift, *A System of the Laws of the State of Connecticut*, 2 vols. (Windham, Conn., 1795-96), 1: 247-50, 267. Also see Richard R. Powell and Patrick J. Rohan, *Powell on Property*, one-vol. ed. (New York: Mathew Bender, 1968), pp. 47-79, 456-60.

tion of overlapping rights were extensive and complex, but they were the lateral and parent-child bonds characteristic of "extended cognate" strategies.[12] And, in Daniel's case, the restrictions did not appear to be in the service of accumulation so much as an effort to induce Daniel to marry.

Rights Creation: The Inter-Area Comparison

So that we can get an overall picture of estate holders' proclivities to create overlapping claims in property, I make a distinction between "light" and "heavy" obligations.[13] "Heavy" obligations are ownership of property expressed in conditional or contingent form; entail and entail-like settlements; prior informal uses by the eventual owner; substantial use-rights reserved for the decedent or created for some other party (apart from the dower right);[14] and obligations to pay legacies and annuities, or to care for others backed by the conditional transfer of property. "Light" burdens are obligations to provide care and to pay legacies or portions attached to the taking of property but not backed by conditional transfers; uses carved out of less than a quarter of the value of property transferred; and authority to redeem property from other heirs.[15] The following analysis is limited solely to landed holders, since only one landless decedent created overlapping rights in property. It is also limited to those burdens created in virtue of the taking of real

[12] No holder ever created obligations between an heir and the heir's niece or nephew when the parent (related by blood to the decedent) was still alive. Of the forty-two families in which children of predeceased heirs participated, just under a quarter of the holders created ties between at least one of their own children or siblings and these children of predeceased heirs. There was virtually no inter-area variation in this respect until the 1820s. Holders created these ties in three of the seven such upland families. These ties were not created on behalf of any of the children from the ten such Wethersfield families in the 1820s.

[13] The ties discussed here, with the exception of use-rights, required positive action by decedents in wills or deeds. In all but four cases, failure to use deeds or make out wills meant that ties were not created. Rates of total intestacy (no wills or deeds) among landed families were virtually identical in the two areas in the 1750s, slightly lower in the upland of the 1770s (12.5 percent versus 21 percent) and the 1820s (25 percent versus 35 percent) than in Wethersfield.

[14] I do not include life-estates reserved for widows here since this was an obligation imposed by law. I do, however, include services, payments, and uses to widows that substitute for or exceed their legal right to life-estates in a third of their husbands' lands (held at death). I discuss widows' inheritance in detail in Chapter Seven.

[15] Redemption schemes force takers to sell their inherited property to specified parties at the latters' option. Three holders gave their sons the option to buy their sisters' land. Instead of requiring their sons to pay legacies, the decedents left it to their sons to choose between a "favored heir plus burdens" arrangement or a division of land extending to females.

property. Overlapping rights were created in personal property by only three landed holders. These holders also created heavy obligations attached to possession of real property.

Inter-area variation in the pattern of rights-creation was similar overall to variation in the pattern of land distribution (Table 5.1). Whether all burdens or only the heaviest are considered, the percentage of colonial estate holders who used them rose in both areas (columns 3 and 4, 8 and 9). Thus the creation of overlapping claims in real property or its revenues was most widespread in the same period that rates of exclusion from ownership of real property and inequalities in the value of shares taken were at their height.[16] In the colonial era, extended cognate practices were typical of both upland and valley holders.

Examination of the data from the perspective of children who inherited real estate (Table 5.2) shows a trend toward concentration of burdens in the colonial era. Among sons, the percentage of owner-takers who were burdened decreased, but the number of parties dependent on them increased, as did the density of ties among these sons and their dependents. The percentage of daughters who were burdened was small, reflecting their subordinate position with respect to ownership of real property, and the parties dependent on them were few.

The picture in the 1820s is one of dramatically diverging practices (see Table 5.1). Only two of Wethersfield's twenty-nine landed estate holders created substantial (or "heavy") obligations when they transferred real property, while 38 percent of the upland estate holders did so (Table 5.1, column 4). Among those with children, only one used such obligations in Wethersfield, while half of the upland holders with children did so (Column 9). In the latter area, although the percentage of sons burdened had declined (see Table 5.2), the number of persons to whom on average each son was obligated was far closer to the figures for the pre-Revolutionary period than it was to those for contemporary Wethersfield.

In Wethersfield, then, almost all holders simply abandoned the use of overlapping rights either to enforce the claims of less favored heirs or to provide security for the older generation's retirement. Although cash legacies, marriage portions, and bequests of personal property to those excluded may have constituted an economic burden on these estates, property was retained and transferred in discrete bundles, with all the attributes of ownership intact. Family bonds were no longer reinforced

[16] Not all excluded or less-favored heirs were given claims on favored heirs or their property; but in all periods, all such claims were created on behalf of less-favored takers or retired parents, and all but one such claim fell on the shoulders of favored sons or brothers.

TABLE 5.1

CREATION OF OBLIGATIONS IN LANDED FAMILIES

	All Landed Families					Landed Families with Children				
	Missing (N)	Usable Estates (N)	Any Obligs. (%)	Heavy Obligs. (%)	No Obligs. (%)	Missing (N)	Usable Estates (N)	Any Obligs. (%)	Heavy Obligs. (%)	No Obligs. (%)
	(1)	(2)	(3)	(4)	(5)	(6)	(7)	(8)	(9)	(10)
1750s										
Wethersfield	0	28	43[ns]	(32)[ns]	57	0	23	48[ns]	(39)[ns]	52
Upland	1	16	56	(56)	44	1	14	50	(50)	50
1770s										
Wethersfield	0	26	62[ns]	(46)[ns]	38	0	24	63[ns]	(46)[ns]	37
Upland	1	16	69	(63)	31	0	16	69	(63)	31
1820s										
Wethersfield	2	29	17[††]	(7)[†††]	83	1	15	20[†]	(7)[†††]	80
Upland	1	21	48	(38)	52	1	15	53	(53)	47

Note: These figures do not include widow's dower.

[ns] Chi-square not significant.

[†] Chi-square significant at .10 level. Based on two-column tables (presence/absence "any obligations"; presence/absence "heavy obligations") by community type.

[††] Chi-square significant at .05 level.

[†††] Significant at .01 level.

TABLE 5.2

ALLOCATION OF BURDENS AMONG ADULT CHILDREN INHERITING REALTY

	Adult Sons (N)	Sons Burdened (%)	Distinct Parties to Whom Sons Linked (N)	Mean Ties per Burdened Son (N)	Adult Dtrs. (N)	Dtrs. Burdened (%)	Distinct Parties to Whom Dtrs. Linked (N)	Mean Ties per Burdened Dtrs. (N)
1750s								
Wethersfield	31	52[ns]	14	1.3	33	6	1	1.0
Upland	14	57	15	2.0	11	27	2	1.0
1770s								
Wethersfield	45	47[ns]	43	2.1	28	18	5	1.8
Upland	30	43	37	2.8	21	5	1	1.0
1820s								
Wethersfield	30	13[†]	6	1.5	24	4	1	1.0
Upland	36	33	25	2.2	31	16	1	1.0

Note: These figures include only those adult sons and daughters who took ownership of real property directly (not through their representatives or spouses). Widow's dower excluded. Indirect ties created between owners because they had obligations to the same dependent are not counted.
[ns] Chi-square not significant.
[†] Chi-square significant at the .10 level. Based on two-column tables (sons were/were not burdened), by community type.

by the pattern of rights created when property was transferred to family members.

The divergence in inheritance patterns in the 1820s speaks to the alternative paths pursued by families as zones of specialization developed. In Wethersfield, intensive agriculture allowed for continued and extensive partitioning of land by middling and larger holders. Neither small nor large holders, however, burdened takers of productive property with obligations to others. The lack of property ties between holder and heirs, and among heirs, is consistent with the literature suggesting that in commercially oriented agriculture zones, market-induced concern for flexibility of enterprise boundaries leads to a collapse of complex, cooperative inheritance practices.[17] By failing to reinforce family ties, these individualized property arrangements played a part in narrowing effective kin reference to conjugal families.

Joint Ownership

The preceding discussion did not mention ties created by joint ownership arrangements. This is, in part, because the ties just discussed could not be broken by the unilateral action of the burdened heir. Such heirs could not rid themselves of their obligations (to pay legacies, care for parents, stand aside while users enjoyed "peaceable possession") except by also renouncing their rights to the property, or, as in the case of uses, finding a buyer willing to take the encumbered property.

In contrast, all the forms of joint ownership—coparcenary, tenancy in common, joint tenancy—and the cooperative relations they involved could be nullified by the unilateral action of one of the tenants.[18] Under each of these arrangements, a single tenant not only could convey his or her interest by deed, but could compel a court-supervised partition of the co-owned property.[19] In fact, early eighteenth-century Connecticut legislators assumed that a failure to divide land so held was ordinarily an accident. This can be seen in the wording of the preamble to

---

[17] Creighton, "Family and Production," pp. 154-59; Howell, "Inheritance in the Midlands," pp. 149-55. But see Gagan, "Inheritance in Ontario," who reports the imposition of burdens on heavily favored heirs in a late nineteenth-century wheat-exporting area.

[18] Unless the person(s) who conveyed the property explicitly stipulated otherwise. The extent to which the law would allow such restrictions is not relevant here because no estate holder in this study ever imposed them when creating such tenures.

[19] The Connecticut statute explicitly acknowledged English common law on this point. "All Persons . . . hold[ing] . . . as Coparceners, Joynt-Tenants, or Tenants in Common, may be Compelled by Writ of Partition to Divide . . . where the Partners cannot Agree to make Partition among themselves." See *Acts & Laws 1750*, p. 144; also see *Public Statutes 1821*, p. 303 and *Powell on Real Property*, pp. 264-67, 604-608, 614-15.

a statute that allowed (or forced) guardians to participate in such partitions on behalf of their minor charges:

> Whereas there are many Parcels of Land . . . held by several Persons in Partnership, or as Tenants in Common, or in Joint-Tenancy: And it hath often so fallen out, that One of the Partners or Tenants have Died before any Division hath been made, and their Heirs left to Inherit such Lands being Minors; whereby the surviving Partners, or Tenants are hindered in their Improvement.[20]

The words "before any Division hath been made" suggest that legislators assumed that premature death often interfered with partitions that tenants, in due time, would otherwise have made. But whether or not legislators read the minds of most colonial landholders accurately, it is of primary interest here that any individual tenant could unilaterally insist on abolishing the arrangement.

Given that these forms of tenure imposed only weak restraints on an individual's power to alienate land and to name successors, the line between co-tenant and independent owner was very blurred indeed. When, for example, Ebenezer Skinner created a joint tenancy in his house, ironworks, two smith shops, and sixty-five acre main lot for his two sons, he may have hoped both that they would work it cooperatively and that it would remain undivided. But within a little over a year one son exchanged his patrimony for land acquired by his brother.[21] The farm did remain intact but each son apparently went his own way.

The line between co-ownership and independent ownership of subdivided lots or buildings is not only blurred conceptually, but it is sometimes hard to tell when co-ownership has been created and when heirs have been given independent shares. For example, Thomas Stoddard's will stated only that the residue and remainder of his estate (including his entire 130-acre main farm) was to be "equally divided" between three sons, Eli, Elisha, and Benjamin, to be held by them and "their Heirs and Assigns for ever." A statute of the period anticipated such devises. When the will did not appoint a person to make the stated division (and heirs did not submit agreements actually partitioning the land), the court was to appoint distributors to partition the land among the devisees in such proportions as the will directed.[22] Stoddard's will, as so many others, was not accompanied by an estate distribution.

Additional evidence shows that it is not always accurate to assume

---

[20] *Acts & Laws 1750*, p. 113, and *Public Statutes 1821*, p. 263. The statute was enacted in 1720.

[21] Bolton Land Records, 2: 445, 511, deeds, signed November 15, 1745, and February 28, 1746/47.

[22] *Acts & Laws 1750*, p. 110; *Public Statutes 1821*, p. 208.

that heirs took independent ownership of subdivided shares in such cases. But the same evidence also shows that there was very little difference between the situations of co-tenants and independent owners. The evidence comes from a petition signed in 1785 by the two surviving brothers, Elisha and Benjamin; Abigail Buck, the remarried former wife of Eli; and Abigail's new husband. The petition asks the legislature to empower Abigail, the mother and guardian of Eli's heirs, to make deeds on behalf of her minor charges.

This document is worth citing at length. The petitioners state that the three brothers had been "living in perfect Harmony, wrought together & carried on their Business jointly with a view not to break their father's Estate but to purchase one or more settlement that finally the homestead might not go out of the family." From their "joint Earnings" they "jointly" purchased about eighty-five more acres from four neighbors, intending these purchases to be a settlement for Eli since "Eli . . . was a married Man & had a family." Eli entered into "possession" of the purchased lands and continued to "occupy" them until his death. The petitioners go on to state that the brothers had agreed that Eli would quitclaim his inherited "title" to his father's 130 acres; in turn, Elisha and Benjamin would quitclaim their right to the jointly purchased land. Indeed, the deeds were drawn up, ". . . but thro' inadvertence they were never executed until s^d. Eli was taken ill with the small pox, when they could not converse with each other & there was no justice of the Peace in Town [whom they knew to have] had the small pox & in hopes that he might recover nothing was done." Eli did not recover. The result was that the surviving brothers held both the "paternal Inheritance" and the purchased lands "in common & undivided" with the heirs of their brother Eli. This despite the fact that they had "improved in severalty both before & since the decease of s^d Eli." They close by pleading that they were "very unwilling to divide the homestead left them by s^d Thomas into three parts which would ruin the whole." The legislature approved the request.[23]

Notice that the problem the jointly held land created supports the legislature's view that joint ownership was normally meant to be only a temporary arrangement and that premature death could be severely disruptive. In addition, unless the petitioners were in error, the clause in their father's will, in the absence of an heir agreement or distribution, created a tenancy in common. But it is equally clear that it did not matter whether these brothers inherited their father's farm as tenants in

---

[23] Thomas Stoddard, will, signed August 24, 1772, folio 5277, Hartford Probate District, Estate Papers; "Connecticut Archives," Estates of Deceased Persons, vol. 19, doc. nos. 167a-b, 168a-b, petition and resolve.

common or as independent owners of subdivided thirds. Until Eli married, they worked cooperatively. Their joint "possession" was both a legal status and a mutually established part of their daily, routine management of the farm, but the latter could have been as easily accomplished had they been independent owners. Then, at some point after Eli did marry, he ceased entirely to behave as if he had possession. So long as he retained an interest in his paternal inheritance, either as a cotenant or as an independent owner, his legal status was incongruent. His sudden death would have been equally disruptive had he been an independent owner.

The petition, if it is truthful, also provides evidence of actions and motives that are a vivid example of extended cognate bonds in the service of balancing the tension between unity and provision. The brothers wished to keep their father's farm intact and "within the family." Though we may doubt that dispersion through excessive partitioning was an immediate threat, they clearly feared the centrifugal force of subdivision.

Equally, the brothers wished to make this farm directly provide an independent settlement for each new head of household. They clearly thought this goal was best achieved through cooperative working of the whole farm, rather than through subdivision and subsequent individual efforts to expand.[24] An independent settlement was not an iron-clad prerequisite for marriage; Eli married in 1770, and, therefore, had as a married man worked in cooperation with his brothers for a few years before occupying the newly purchased land. But Eli's independence was a goal to which all three brothers directed their immediate attention—after all, Eli already had a family, they said. It may simply have been a coincidence that Benjamin never married and that Elisha married very late (at the age of thirty-nine) but shortly after Eli had been settled. Benjamin may have found bachelorhood congenial, and perhaps it was not for lack of trying that Elisha did not marry sooner. But the result was that the paternal farm never had more than one new conjugal unit to sustain.

Unity was preserved without unigeniture and with no subordination of one son's rights to property in favor of another. In addition, the balance between unity and provision achieved in this family did not accomplish absolute equality of standing: one son did not become head of a new family. Preferential succession, the colonial norm, prevailed in

---

[24] Note also that the original inheritance, together with the added holdings its revenues provided, gave each brother an interest in between sixty-five to eighty-five acres, just about the range estimated by colonial historians as necessary to establish a "comfortable" family farm.

the end, but it resulted from decisions reached by men,[25] each of whom had been given by their father equal authority over the "ancestral" property. Though absolute parity among males was not achieved, their father's property provided all sons with secure landed status in the community of their birth.

The Incidence of Joint Ownership

The line between joint and independent owners was very blurred under Connecticut law, but the reader may be curious about the incidence of joint ownership. Disregarding those instances where decedents or distributors simply referred to the "heirs of" a predeceased child or sibling,[26] joint inheritance of real property occurred in twenty-two landed estates. Only eight estate holders deliberately created joint tenures through deeds or wills; they did not cluster in any time period or in either Wethersfield or the upland. Estate distributors were responsible for the other jointly inherited estates, and these cases did cluster. In the 1820s court-appointed distributors created joint tenures in ten Wethersfield estates (38 percent),[27] while joint inheritance played a role in no more than 15 percent of the colonial or early nineteenth-century upland estates.

Once again, inheritance patterns in Wethersfield showed the greatest discontinuity. But in this case, the meaning of the discontinuity is not immediately clear. In part, it may have been a new response to poverty. Wethersfield distributors handled seven estates totaling less than thirty acres in the 1820s. In every case they created tenancies in common in at least 50 percent of the land. In the seven other estates—all but one of which were quite large—they distributed, they partitioned all the property or subjected no more than 25 percent of the total real estate to joint tenures. But the new response cannot be explained fully by reference to an old problem (poverty), a problem faced by earlier generations.

The type of realty subject to joint arrangements provides another clue. Most joint arrangements, whether created by decedents or distributors, were established in "business" buildings (sawmills, ironworks, etc.) or in peripheral lots in the colonial era. Only an occasional home

---

[25] Thomas excluded his three daughters from a share in land.

[26] The reason for ignoring these twelve instances is that the group takers were simply stand-ins for children or siblings who were given separate shares.

[27] Not all of these were intestate cases. In two, distributors allocated property according to wills that were not specific about what particular property should constitute a given share. There was no change in the statute law to account for the switch in distribution methods, and the research uncovered no Hartford District Probate Court directives ordering joint arrangements.

lot or main lot was jointly owned, and they were never held by more than two co-tenants. But in Wethersfield in the 1820s, over half the joint arrangements were created in core holdings. At that time, Wethersfield distributors allocated the home lot in eight cases. In all but two, they distributed it to three or more heirs to "hold in common & undivided." Rather than partition immediately, they left the decision to the heirs.

As the following section shows, Wethersfield will makers were also prone to allocate their main lots to several heirs in the 1820s (though they did not also create joint ownership when they did so). But this was not a trait they shared with many of their upland contemporaries or colonial forbears. Thus it is the new approach to the distribution of the home lot that accounts for the "bulge" in the incidence of joint ownership. So let us take a closer look at practices concerning core holdings.

THE HOME LOT OR HOME FARM: A FAMILY RESERVE?

In towns all over New England, lots still bear the names of the families who first built their houses and barns on them. The buildings together with the land called the "Goodrich lot" may have been sold eventually to the Kelloggs, and then to others, but the name still endures to mark the place of the first founder. Many associate "lineal" inheritance strategies with a distinctive, especially inegalitarian treatment of core buildings. To single out a son or a brother to inherit a home lot touches on more than an estate holder's concern to maintain the economic integrity of the working enterprise. It can symbolize an outlook that identifies family standing with intergenerational continuity on particular holdings. To John Waters, for example, the practice of limiting succession to the home lot or homestead to one or two males is a primary piece of evidence that the mentality of eighteenth-century Guilford, Connecticut, farmers was "traditional, marked by strong patrilineal, English peasant mores."[28] Their "passion for land," he writes, arose "because they saw their 'noble image' in their sons who would continue their names and lineage."[29]

Were the core lots of the estates in this study singled out for special treatment? The distributors of Thomas Robbins's intestate Wethersfield estate reserved his home lot for his only son, although all his daughters got other land, and you may recall that Joseph Woodhouse

---

[28] "Patrimony, Succession, and Social Stability: Guilford, Connecticut, in the Eighteenth Century," *Perspectives in American History* 10 (1976): 139-40, 149-50.
[29] Ibid., p. 160.

reserved his own home lot for two of his four sons. How frequently did this restrictive treatment occur?

Some estate holders with complete working farms—land holdings composed of a house, barn (and often other buildings), and its complement of plowland, meadow and pasture, and, possibly, woodland—made no distinction at all between their home lot, or the main lot on which the house was located, and other property. Joseph Bulkley's will, for example, stated only what relative shares his children were to receive and explicitly stated that it did not matter who got real property, let alone who got his Wethersfield home lot. Distributors were usually more specific. When decedents had distinct lots with buildings, estate distributions regularly mentioned them, and, although the law of intestacy determined the relative value of shares taken, distributors could restrict the heirs to particular plots. They could often exercise considerable discretion even when the distribution backed a will. In fact, Joseph Bulkley's will was accompanied by an estate distribution that gave the portion of his home lot not distributed as dower to one of his five sons.[30]

Table 5.3 shows the distribution of home lots or home farms. Note that in the upland there were always several estates in which neither holders nor distributors bothered to distinguish the "core" holding from other land (column 3). In all such cases the land was passed to more than two heirs. But before one concludes that this indicates relatively little concern for continuity, one must take into account the different institutional matrices within which practices regarding the "core" developed.

Because of different patterns of initial settlement and methods of distributing town-held or proprietary land, the meaning of the core holding was not the same in the two areas.[31] In Wethersfield, the land containing the dwelling house, along with the garden plot and other farm buildings, was normally a lot with boundaries clearly marked off from the greater portion of the farm's plow land and pasture. (The latter was often held in scattered lots, even in the nineteenth century.) In the upland, the original grants were continuous large blocks that usually contained the main farmland as well as the buildings. The "natural" dis-

[30] Joseph Bulkley, will, signed November 9, 1818, and estate distribution, returned to court August 15, 1835, Wethersfield, Hartford Probate District, Estate Papers.

[31] For detailed discussions of the contrasts between the seventeenth-century nucleated village-settlement pattern and the "block" pattern characteristic of a large part of the eastern upland, see Richard Bushman, *From Puritan to Yankee: Character and the Social Order in Connecticut, 1690-1765* (New York: Norton, 1970), pp. 41-53, 73-103; Dorothy Deming, *The Settlement of the Connecticut Towns*, Tercentenary Series, no. 6 (New Haven: Yale University Press, 1933).

TABLE 5.3

THE DISTRIBUTION OF HOMESTEADS: ESTATES WITH HOUSES AND LAND

| | Home Lots Distinguished | | | Distinguished Home Lots: Distribution Strategy | | | | | |
| | | | | All Holders | | | Holders with Children | | |
	Estates (N)	Yes (%)	No (%)	(N)	Lineal* (%)	Other (%)	(N)	Lineal* (%)	Other (%)
	(1)	(2)	(3)	(4)	(5)	(6)	(7)	(8)	(9)
1750s									
Wethersfield	22	95	5	21	67[ns]	33	19	74[ns]	26
Upland	15	61	29	11	64	36	10	60	40
1770s									
Wethersfield	23	95	5	22	77[ns]	23	21	76[ns]	24
Upland	14	86	14	13	77	23	13	77	23
1820s									
Wethersfield	21	100	0	21	29[tt]	71	12	42[t]	58
Upland	16	86	14	14	71	29	12	75	25

[ns] Chi-square not significant.
* Eighty percent or more of the main lot or home lot is passed to one or two male blood kin.
[t] Chi-square significant at .10 level. Based on two-column tables ("lineal"/ other treatment of home lot or main lot) by community type.
[tt] Chi-square significant at .05 level.

tinction was between the main lot or home farm and outlying, added lots. There was, then, no core in the sense of Wethersfield's small home lot, although there could clearly be peripheral parts of the holding. In this respect, Wethersfield's institutional legacy was more conducive to policies oriented to the intergenerational retention of some part of the farm—the home lots that, often literally, carried the family name.

Once holders and distributors did bother to distinguish a home lot or main lot from other land, colonial practices were quite restrictive. The large majority of colonial holders and distributors singled out the land on which the decedent's house stood in order to pass it to one or two male blood kin (Table 5.3, column 5). In this respect there was a certain convergence among those holders who had children. In Wethersfield, one or two sons got the home lot in about 75 percent of these families in both the 1750s and the 1770s, while in the upland a "lineal" distribution occurred more frequently on the eve of the Revolution than earlier (column 8). It is noteworthy that upland holders and distributors normally had to overlook the conventional boundaries of the lots when they wished to single out a special section for treatment as a family reserve.

In the 1820s upland home lots were treated no differently. Three quarters of the holders and distributors who distinguished home lots reserved them for the "line." But in Wethersfield the situation was reversed. The holders' home lots went to several heirs, to women, to affines, or, in one instance, even to a friend in over 70 percent of the estates (58 percent when the lot went to children). A subportion of the farm that already had precise boundaries and contained the holder's house and other buildings was specifically mentioned but was then allocated in a nonlineal fashion.[32] The home lot no longer represented continuity or a family seat.

With the exception of early nineteenth-century Wethersfield, families distinguished a main lot in order to treat it both as a male reserve and as an "island" to be passed intact or to two heirs. This was not the universal practice, but it was the colonial norm and continued to be so in the upland of the 1820s. The evidence adds strength to the generalization that holders were oriented to the qualitative features of their holdings, not simply to their market value. This orientation was characteristic of both valley and upland in the colonial era but appeared to weaken in postcolonial Wethersfield.

Can one conclude that this aspect of inheritance was strongly patrilineal, as John Waters, for example, argues? The answer is a qualified "yes," because the clear preference for male kin and the sharp limitations on the number of successors to land are two essential aspects of patrilineal practices. The qualification, however—and it is a major one—is that estate holders' attempts at preservation were limited in extent. Only a handful restricted their heirs' powers of alienation (as the evidence on rights-creation has shown). The language of life-estates was second nature to these estate holders since it was fundamental to property relations between husbands and wives and widely used in retirement contracts. But they did not use such devices to protect the core of their holdings from leaving their families. The small number of heirs admitted indicates that these holders wanted to treat their homesteads as family reserves, but they did so by entrusting their preservation to the judgment of their sons and brothers, not by limiting the independent control of these male household heads.

CONCLUSION

This chapter and Chapter Four examined several basic facets of inheritance strategies. Extended cognate practices prevailed in the colonial

---

[32] As was the case in Reverend Marsh's Wethersfield estate. His will of April 1809 said that his "dwelling house, and lands and buildings about it" were to be divided among his four children. Hartford Probate District, Estate Papers, 1821.

period, a pattern sustained in the upland in the 1820s, but not in Wethersfield. In Wethersfield a few of the poorer landed families still practiced a heavily gender-based form of preferential partibility, and a minority still disadvantaged some sons, but partitioning was rarely
accompanied by creation of overlapping rights in property. Holders no
longer used inheritance transfers to reinforce bonds among heirs or between holders and heirs. Strategies imposing burdens on favored heirs
collapsed. The practice of limiting ownership of the home lot to one or
two male heirs, a widespread feature of preferential partibility in the
colonial period, also declined in Wethersfield, as did the differential
treatment of land and personal property more generally. Fewer families
seemed to identify social standing with maintaining intergenerational
continuity on a given land holding.

It would appear, then, that in postcolonial Wethersfield the connection between inheritance and life-chances was loosening. The town's
comparatively specialized agriculture and its more specialized occupational structure were associated with inheritance practices that resembled individualistic, even share-and-share alike, modern practices more
than they did the practices of contemporary uplanders.

The colonial pattern was quite similar to the practices of those European peasants who held land under heritable tenures and flexible inheritance rules. At the core of the "favored heir plus burdens" strategy
is the ongoing effort to guard against fragmentation while recognizing
and protecting the claims of each heir to family property.[33] Conditions
special to the northern countryside, such as widespread family-farm
ownership in a context of land abundance, did encourage extensive
partitioning. But they did not in themselves loosen the fundamental
connection between direct inheritance of family property and life-
chances. The characteristic solutions to the unity-provision problem in
the colonial era were similar to those in unspecialized agricultural communities overseas.[34]

---

[33] Lutz Berkner and Franklin Mendels, "Inheritance Systems, Family Structure, and
Demographic Patterns in Western Europe, 1700-1900," in *Historical Studies of Changing Fertility*, ed. Charles Tilly (Princeton, N.J.: Princeton University Press, 1978), pp.
213-14; Berkner, "Inheritance, Tenure, and Family"; Howell, "Inheritance in the Midlands"; Spufford, "Inheritance and Land in Cambridgeshire."

[34] For practices that seem most closely to resemble the pattern found here (extensive
partitioning and obligations), see Linda Auwers on late seventeenth- and early eighteenth-century Windsor, a Connecticut River valley town whose early history and later
development resembled Wethersfield's; Jedrey on Chebacco village in eighteenth-century
Massachusetts, an old seacoast town which he describes as semicommercial, but which,
on his evidence, more closely resembled the upland communities studied here than Wethersfield; Snydacker on the practices of Moravian and Lutheran farmers in late eight-
eenth- and early nineteenth-century Pennsylvania: Auwers, "Fathers, Sons, and Wealth

Inheritance practices diverged only when an unevenly expanding market system produced sharply distinct economies in the upland and valley. Major shifts in orientation toward family-held productive property accompanied the commercialization of the countryside. In short, within the sphere to which inheritance practices most directly speak, the evidence supports an anti-exceptionalist position. The timing and nature of variation in strategies for managing productive property and setting-up children had dynamics similar to those in family-farm regions of western Europe.

Still, inheritance practices were not identical in the Old World and in the New. American subsistence-plus farmers were not "peasants," at least not of the same type as their European cousins. This dissimilarity is not surprising. The economy of the American North bore the fundamental impress of its colonial status. Its growth and structure were symbiotically related to the European economy; its family-farm areas did not precisely duplicate any of those in Europe.

In the spirit of recognizing that resemblance is not identity, certain aspects of the position I took in the opening pages of this study need modification. I had argued that to the extent that the practices of European peasants were not oriented toward accumulation, they were also extended cognate practices. But it may be a form of conceptual stretching[35] to embrace in the term "extended cognate" both the inheritance practices found here and those found in European regions of impartibility. Land shortages and customary law combined to make inheritance by one son or brother the norm in many areas of England and the Continent. Brothers did not normally share the same fates, and women inherited land only in the absence of males of the same degree of kinship—if even then. Although these were not dynastic practices, they did to some extent reinforce lineal kin ties. One might, therefore, want a language that preserves the difference between partible and impartible versions of the "favored heir plus burdens" strategy.[36]

---

in Colonial Windsor, Connecticut," *Journal of Family History* 3 (Summer 1978): 136-49; Christopher Jedrey, *The World of John Cleaveland: Family and Community in Eighteenth-Century New England* (New York: Norton, 1979), pp. 58-94; Snydacker, "Kinship and Community in Pennsylvania."

[35] Giovanni Sartori, "Concept Misinformation in Comparative Politics," *American Political Science Review* 64 (December 1970): 1033-53.

[36] For areas in early modern Europe where the typical practice was to pass all land to one heir or to pass all but small fragments to one heir, see Spufford, "Inheritance and Land in Cambridgeshire," pp. 158-60; Berkner, "Inheritance, Tenure, and Family," pp. 77-81; Berkner, "Stem Family and the Peasant Household," p. 399; Ladurie, "Family and Inheritance Customs." For impartible or near impartible practices in subsistence-plus, diversified farming areas elsewhere, see Michel Verdon, "The Stem Family: Toward

It does not necessarily follow from cross-Atlantic differences, though, that the actions and orientations of most early Americans were entrepreneurial, individualist, or, as some would have it, modern. The logic "America was different, therefore its values were modern," rests on a suppressed Gemeinschaft-Gesellschaft premise. At the core of this logic is the assumption that there is essentially only one form of community life common to the preindustrial Atlantic community. The absence of this "traditional" form must mean that its modern successor has replaced it. The logic is faulty, and, in the arena of inheritance at least, early American values and actions did not in fact resemble those of a later period. Extensive partitioning and the absence of complex restraints on alienation do indicate that American property orientations were not patrimonial or patrilineal. But colonial practices created complex ties between adult children and parents, among siblings, and even among in-laws. Indeed, the construct "extended cognate" was developed because it indicates that the practices it describes were not patrilineal, without implying that they were similar to the share-and-share-alike practices that dominate today.

a General Theory," *Journal of Interdisciplinary History* 10 (Summer 1979): 87-105; Conrad M. Arensberg and Solon T. Kimball, *Family and Community in Ireland* (Cambridge, Mass.: Harvard University Press), pp. 6-7, 63; John W. Cole and Eric R. Wolf, *The Hidden Frontier: Ecology and Ethnicity in an Alpine Valley* (New York: Academic Press, 1974), pp. 158-59, 206.

CHAPTER SIX

PARENTAL POWER, MARRIAGE, AND THE
TIMING OF INHERITANCE

In December 1747, Samuel and Lucy Robbins, a couple in their sixties, deeded over what remained of their landed holdings, more than ninety acres including the home lot, to their two youngest sons, Josiah and Elisha. Each of the boys immediately and surely inherited his future standing as an independent landed man; the deeds were in fee-simple with no conditions attached. Although the sons' independent standing was immediately guaranteed, it was also postponed: when the couple made out the deeds, they reserved the *use* of the entire estate for themselves while Samuel still lived, and a third for Lucy's dower in the event that she should outlive her husband.[1] Thus these conveyances allowed the father to retain managerial powers over the land and provided for the mother's maintenance, while they transformed the sons' expectations into guaranteed futures. Normally, holders using this type of transaction reserved uses for just part of the land they deeded over. But these two sons were young and could afford to wait: Elisha was eighteen, and Josiah had just turned twenty-four. Indeed, Josiah married two years later, one speculates, on the strength of his inheritance.

Joseph Woodhouse, you may recall, used a different strategy. He retained title to all his land until he died, but at least one of his sons married and built a house on Joseph's land.[2] This informal or de facto transfer of possession created a patriarchal family compound. It allowed Joseph's son, William, and his wife to live under their own roof. Yet William, who predeceased his father, never became an owner-producer. In this respect he died his father's dependent.

As these two examples suggest, lifetime transfers can reveal a good deal about the use of parental property at such critical junctures as marriage and retirement. Although this entire study rests on transactions made by holders during their lifetimes as well as on those taking place at their deaths, we have yet to take a close look at inter-area variation in the timing of transmission.

---

[1] Samuel Robbins, Wethersfield, folio 4561, Hartford Probate District, Estate Papers; Wethersfield Land Records, 9: 421, 437, deeds, signed and acknowledged December 23, 1747. The transactions occurred six years before Samuel died.

[2] Joseph Woodhouse, will, signed June 24, 1774, Wethersfield, folio 6236, Hartford Probate District, Estate Papers.

Philip Greven's analysis of inheritance in *Four Generations* emphasizes variation in the timing of inheritance transfers. Writing about seventeenth- and eighteenth-century Massachusetts men, he argues that extensive partitioning coupled with late transfers fostered patriarchal families and dense local kin networks. Partibility encouraged sons to stay put, while late transfers left many of them dependent on fathers well into adulthood. Conversely, the growing use of lifetime transfers coupled with less partitioning meant earlier independence, more geographic mobility, and more nuclear families among fourth-generation Andover sons.[3]

In focusing on the tie between father and adult son, and the issue of independence, Greven follows a lead George Homans established in the form, virtually, of an axiom for medieval peasants. Regarding the link between timing of transmission and parental control over marriage among thirteenth-century English villagers, Homans writes: "Our conclusion must also be that the son and heir did not marry until he had the land, either after his father died or after his father made over the land to him."[4] He follows with this caveat, which nonetheless underscores the rule: "We must not take the rule of *no land, no marriage* to have been a strict one."[5] He goes on to write that the excluded sons were very likely never to marry or to emigrate because of the difficulty in acquiring land. His analysis of the particular phenomenon, rates of marriage,[6] is of less interest here than the underlying assumption that life-chances were heavily dependent on inherited land.

The argument that the late transfer of land is an exercise of patriarchal power assumes that the larger context is one in which direct inheritance is a central determinant of life-chances. When this assumption is correct, whatever decision the head of household makes about the timing or the form of transfer is fraught with significance. The head of household has extensive control over the fates of children regardless of

[3] Philip J. Greven, Jr., *Four Generations: Population, Land, and Family in Colonial Andover, Massachusetts* (Ithaca, N.Y.: Cornell University Press, 1972), pp. 131, 146-50, 229-30. Also see discussion of lifetime transfers in Barry Levy, " 'Tender Plants': Quaker Farmers and Children in the Delaware Valley, 1681-1735," *Journal of Family History* 3 (Summer 1978): 116-55. For the classic discussion of the relation between partibility and mobility, see H. J. Habbakuk, "Family Structure and Economic Change in Nineteenth-Century Europe," *Journal of Economic History* 15 (1955): 1-12.

[4] George C. Homans, *English Villagers of the Thirteenth Century* (New York: Norton, 1975), p. 152.

[5] Ibid., p. 158 (emphasis added).

[6] See, for example, J. Hajnal's criticism of Homans's inferring from the rule "no land, no marriage" that marriage age must have been late in the medieval English upland: "European Marriage Patterns in Perspective," in *Population in History*, ed. D. V. Glass and D.E.C. Eversley (London: Edward Arnold, 1974), pp. 123-24.

the particular manner in which it is exercised. In a different context, say one in which the life-chances of children are determined by their labor-market positions, late transmission of property merely indicates how little this property counts in guaranteeing the social standing of off-spring. In such contexts, one must examine aspects of family life other than property management to determine whether fathers wield patriarchal authority in the much-reduced sphere still subject to their direct control.

In partial contrast to Greven, then, this study views lifetime transfers to potential heirs—be they informal settlements, retirement contracts, transfers of title with uses reserved, or even straightforward lifetime gifts—as signs that inherited property was still important. Correspondingly, the failure to transfer property before death is not by itself a good indication of patriarchal authority. It is too ambiguous when the extent of individually achievable social mobility is debated. Retention may identify patriarchal fathers and dependent children, but it is more likely to mean that the fates of children are only weakly connected to the use and inheritance of parental property. A better measure of patriarchal authority is the extent of the rights retained by the grantor when transferring property to heirs.

PARENTAL POWER AND LIFETIME
TRANSFERS OF REAL PROPERTY

The picture of parallel, then diverging inter-area practices is as marked for lifetime transfers of land as it is for patterns of rights-creation. Table 6.1 does not include holders who had only minor children at the time of their deaths, but it does include all others who held land at some point prior to their deaths, even if they died landless.[7] All of those included had the option to make use of lifetime transfers. The use of lifetime transfers in both areas was at its height in the 1770s partly because the probate population was older on the eve of the Revolution than at any other time. Colonial practices did not differ greatly in the upland and valley, although Wethersfield holders were somewhat less likely to relinquish control over significant portions of their land in the 1770s. About half of them did so (compared to two thirds of their upland contemporaries; see Table 6.1, columns 3 and 8). The gap widened markedly in the 1820s. The large majority of Wethersfield holders, including those who had children, now retained all or nearly all their property

---

[7] Only two of the fourteen landed women used deeds to transfer land to potential heirs. Of the five who had children, only one used deeds.

TABLE 6.1

USE OF LIFETIME LAND TRANSFERS

| | All Landed Holders | | | | | Landed Holders with Adult Children | | | |
| | Lifetime Transfer | | Age at Death | | | Lifetime Transfer | | Age at Death | |
(N)	Do Use[a] (%)	Exclude Trivial[b] (%)	Age Known (N)	Over 60 (%)	(N)	Do Use[a] (%)	Exclude Trivial[b] (%)	Age Known (N)	Over 60 (%)
	(2)	(3)	(4)	(5)	(6)	(7)	(8)	(9)	(10)
1750s									
Wethersfield 27	41	37ns	24	42	19	47	42ns	17	59
Upland 14	50	43	14	43	13	46	38	13	46
1770s									
Wethersfield 27	56	48ns	27	78	23	61	52ns	23	83
Upland 16	63	63	14	64	15	67	67	13	69
1820s									
Wethersfield 31	19	13††	28	58	15	40	20†	14	79
Upland 24	42	38	22	55	17	59	53	17	59

Note: Excludes those who died leaving only minor children.

[a] Includes de facto transfers of possession. In only four cases was this the only type of lifetime transfer used.

[b] Transfer must be under 15 acres, less than 15 percent of the total real estate transferred, and not include house or other buildings on main lot.

ns Chi-square not significant.

[†] Chi-square is significant at .10 level. Based on two-column tables (did/did not use "substantial" lifetime transfers) by community type.

[††] Chi-square is significant at .05 level.

until they died, while about half the upland parents still gave away substantial portions of their land.

Finally, the inter-area divergence cannot be reduced to differences in the age structure of the decedent populations in each area. Those who lived longest were more likely to make lifetime transfers than those who died young. After 1750, however, more Wethersfield than upland holders were over sixty when they died. Had age differences been at work, Wethersfield holders should have had a greater, not lesser, rate of lifetime transfers.

For the purpose of discussing lifetime transfers and shared power over land, Table 6.2 shows more detailed data on landed holders who had adult children. Holders who used deeds only as will substitutes are treated as if they had not made lifetime transfers.[8] Again, I emphasize

---

[8] Deeds as will substitutes (purely testamentary transfers) were used when all lifetime

TABLE 6.2
TYPE OF LIFETIME LAND TRANSFERS USED BY HOLDERS
WITH ADULT CHILDREN

	Landed Holders (N)	Holders Retain All Property* (%)	Holders Use Over- lapping Rights (%)	Holders Use Only Clean Breaks (%)
	(1)	(2)	(3)	(4)
1750s				
Wethersfield	19	53	32	16
Upland	13	54	15	31
1770s				
Wethersfield	23	39	26	35
Upland	15	33	33	33
1820s				
Wethersfield	15	67	20	13
Upland	17	47	41	12

* Holders who use lifetime transfers only as substitutes for wills (all transfers to potential heirs occur within two years of holder's death *and* holder dies landless) are counted among those who retain all property.

that with respect to the basic question—how many relinquished control over real property before their deaths?—the pattern of parallel, then diverging practices is quite clear. A majority or close to a majority of heads of households did so in both areas in the colonial period. In the 1820s only one third of Wethersfield family heads relinquished control before their deaths, while a majority of upland holders still did so (see Table 6.2, columns 3 and 4). In one respect, however, practices were uniform: holders rarely gave daughters land during their lifetimes. Only seven scattered holders did so.[9]

When holders did use lifetime transfers, they could decide to retain some interest in the property transferred or to make title contingent on services to themselves. Holders could create strong ties between parent(s) and adult children. Conversely, the transfer could be a clean break: a gift or purchase of unencumbered property.[10] A steadily de-

---

transfers to potential heirs occurred within two years of the holder's death and the holder died landless.

[9] These seven holders transferred land to seven daughters (all of whom were married) and to five sons-in-law. Figures do not include daughters participating in the two purely testamentary transfers.

[10] In both areas after the 1750s, a substantial minority of holders with children did sell some of their land to heirs (in the 1770s, 22 percent in Wethersfield, 27 percent in the upland; in the 1820s, 20 percent in Wethersfield, 29 percent in the upland). But these

clining percentage of holders with adult children created ongoing recip-
rocal arrangements in Wethersfield, while a steadily increasing percentage did so in the uplands (Table 6.2, column 3). By the 1820s
Wethersfield holders were giving up arrangements involving both re-
ciprocal obligations and clean breaks in favor of holding onto their
land. By contrast, upland holders, who used lifetime transfers almost
as frequently as before, now favored shared interest arrangements at
the expense of clean breaks.

Most of the shared power transfers involved either the retirement
contract proper or uses reserved for parents. These gave either secure
title to the grantee, or title subject to defeat only if the grantee failed to
provide agreed-upon services. In other words, few of the shared power
arrangements had a strongly patriarchal tinge. Holders did not with-
hold title or retain the right to revoke it unilaterally. But at least eight
men, including Joseph Woodhouse, did involve at least eleven sons in
informal settlements, subsequently ratified in deeds or wills. In such
cases fathers met an immediate need (the sons were all married) by using family resources to provide a son and his family with a livelihood.
Although the holder gave up use of the land that was informally transferred, he retained the power to allocate it among his heirs or to alienate it at any time. In fact, in the Woodhouse case, for example, William's children did not receive all the land that he had occupied. His son
split it with William's brother.[11]

In such situations, the father's authority clearly did stretch to the

---

were usually purchases made by heirs who also received gifts. Only 5 to 17 percent of the
holders in any given area and time relied solely on sales to any given recipient. Furthermore, there was no rising trend in either area after the Revolutionary period. Among
these probates the purchase was an unpopular and supplementary device.

[11] It is usually assumed that a son, informally settled, had no legal claims at all—only
an expectation that he would eventually inherit. The Statute of Frauds, which declared
that oral agreements did not create a legally valid interest in land, and the colonial statutes, which clearly stated that a recorded deed gave the most secure claim to title, do indicate that William would probably have been out in the cold against the claims of anyone who had a recorded deed from his father. *Acts & Laws 1750*, pp. 108-109, 120-21;
Public Statutes 1821, pp. 301-303. Also see Lawrence M. Friedman, *A History of American Law* (New York: Simon and Schuster, Touchstone, 1973), pp. 55-57. It does not
follow that William had no claims on his father. His continuous occupation and improvement of the land (building a house, raising a barn, tilling the soil) in full view of the community and with the active cooperation of his father, especially if coupled with evidence
that his father intended to pass this land to William, may have given William some re-
dress against his father. See William E. Nelson, *Americanization of the Common Law:
The Impact of Legal Change on Massachusetts Society, 1760-1830* (Cambridge, Mass.:
Harvard University Press, 1975), pp. 49, 121-22. Also see Zephaniah Swift, *A System of
the Laws of the State of Connecticut*, 2 vols. (Windham, Conn., 1795-96), 1: 338, 2:
443-47, who writes that equity can enforce oral agreements to transfer land if there is
"execution" of the agreement.

households of adult sons. The father's property arrangements reinforced an extended-family structure, if not an extended household. One speculates that two houses minimized daily friction and gave the son and his wife greater autonomy in the rearing of children than a stem household would have done. But still, William was more dependent on his father than he would have been had he lived under the same roof with secure title to his portion of the paternal farm. It is precisely on such grounds that some consider the arrangement of property rights a more important feature of family organization than household composition in family-farm areas.[12]

Holders could refuse to transfer title to sons already settled on the land because they wanted to retain the flexibility necessary to handle future contingencies, such as an unexpected change in the marital status of one of the heirs or a sudden need for credit. Occasionally there is evidence that holders made such arrangements simply to control filial behavior. This was clearly Elisha Williams's intention when he settled his son on a separate house on his home lot, but later stipulated in his will that his son was to inherit ownership of the whole home lot only if he and his children continued to live there while Elisha's widow still lived. In the event that his son "should Remove & Dwell elsewhere," the widow was to receive ownership of the home lot.

Elisha Williams's case is interesting not only because so few fathers used conditional transfers to regulate the behavior of adult sons, but because elsewhere he states abstract views that stress equality and autonomy. In his polemic against the anti-itinerancy laws aimed at evangelical New Light ministers, Williams paraphrased (actually cribbed from) Locke:

> Reason teaches us that all Men are naturally equal in Respect of Jurisdiction or Dominion over one another. . . . Altho' true it is that Children are not born in this full State of Equality, yet they are born to it. Their Parents have a Sort of Rule & Jurisdiction over them when they come into the World and for some Time after: . . . 'till Reason shall take its Place . . . when he comes to such a State of Reason as made the Father free, the same must make the Son free too.[13]

Let us set aside, as the deeply imbedded norm (and no misinterpretation of Locke), the easy transition from references to children to a discussion limited to sons. Williams used Lockean logic to argue that the

[12] Greven, *Four Generations*, pp. 14-16; Colin Creighton, "Family, Property, and Relations of Production in Western Europe," *Economy and Society* 9 (May 1980): 129-58.

[13] Philalethes [Elisha Williams], *The Essential Rights and Liberties of Protestants . . .* (Boston, 1744).

legislation illegitimately encroached on "natural liberty." It was also an easy matter to equate the "natural reason" on which this liberty and equality rested with the widely used language of "Christian conscience." Once done, Williams could move on to his controversial proposals for increased religious toleration. But Lockean logic did not produce any malaise about prolonged tutelage with respect to parental property. When it came to the filial responsibilities dictated by natural reason, there was no harm in giving conscience a firm, legally reinforced nudge. Pressed, he might have pointed out that his use of property to regulate the behavior of his son was not an illegitimate exercise of patriarchal power since his son's subjection was formally voluntary.[14]

Lockean logic should have been harder to square with his ownership of a slave, but it certainly was not incompatible with his houseful of apprentices, Indian servants, and their children.[15] It is not surprising, then, that his more conservative successor to the ministry of Wethersfield's first society church was able to call Williams an enthusiastic advocate of strict family governance. As corrosive as a Lockean argument could sometimes be in the public sphere, it was no threat to the internal domestic organization of even the more patriarchal households of American freemen.

But again, the conditional clause in Williams's will was unusual, and the incidence of discovered informal settlements was low. When interpreting the data on lifetime transfers, however, one is immediately confronted with a problem. The number of informal settlements discovered was low in comparison with lifetime transfers of secure title. One may conclude that holders generally preferred the less "patriarchal" forms of lifetime transfers. But how many holders actually created informal settlements without leaving evidence of their actions?

The fact is, one does not know. But again nothing is solved by simply asserting that those who retained title to their property were, like Williams, patriarchal. These may have been families in which sons made their own way, receiving their late inheritance as a "dividend." One could assume that as the incidence of discoverable lifetime transfers rises, so does the rate of undiscovered informal arrangements. On this assumption, many of the colonial and later upland "retainers" were pa-

---

[14] John Locke, *Two Treatises of Government*, rev. ed., ed. Peter Laslett (Cambridge, Eng.: Cambridge University Press, 1960).

[15] He had one slave, two apprentices, two Indian "maidservants" or "girls"—one of whom had two children—and a Negro servant. The legal statuses of the latter and of the Indian women are unclear from the will. Their services and/or their persons were carefully divided among Elisha's two children and his wife. See Elisha Williams, will, signed July 16, 1755, Wethersfield, folio 6061, Hartford Probate District, Estate Papers.

triarchs who postponed their sons' independence. But this assumption also strengthens the case that property arrangements were no longer closely tied to marriage and retirement in early nineteenth-century Wethersfield, since the incidence of discovered lifetime transfers was comparatively low there.

MARRIAGE AND LIFETIME TRANSFERS

Sons and Real Property

When lifetime transfers of land are examined from the perspective of sons' needs, an interesting pattern emerges (see Table 6.3). In the colonial period, between 44 and 61 percent of the adult sons of landed holders received all or part of their inheritance in the form of lifetime transfers (column 2).[16] In the 1820s the percentages dropped sharply in both areas, but for rather different reasons. Among the handful of Wethersfield families that did use lifetime transfers, there was a slight increase in the average number of sons receiving such transfers (from 1.9 in the 1770s to 2.2 in the 1820s). But overall, few sons got lifetime grants because so few holders used them. In the upland, however, lifetime transfers declined largely because the majority who used them had become more selective in designating grantees (the average number of sons receiving grants, among those families using them, dropped from 2.9 to 1.3). In the upland a form of stem arrangement developed with

TABLE 6.3

LIFETIME TRANSFERS OF LAND TO ADULT SONS OF LANDED HOLDERS

	All Adult Sons (N)	Receiving Lifetime Transfers* (%)	Known Married Sons (N)	Receiving Lifetime Transfers* (%)	Known Single Sons (N)	Receiving Lifetime Transfers* (%)
	(1)	(2)	(3)	(4)	(5)	(6)
1750s						
Wethersfield	35	49	8	89	13	38
Upland	27	44	15	60	5	0
1770s						
Wethersfield	59	44	33	52	12	33
Upland	33	61	20	65	4	25
1820s						
Wethersfield	42	26	26	35	12	17
Upland	33	36	16	65	12	25

* Those who inherit property only by will substitutes are not included.

[16] Excluding the sons participating in the two testamentary substitutes.

respect to lifetime transfers: only a minority of grants went to sons who did not have obligations to the grantor.

Table 6.3 also gives data for lifetime transfers to sons whose marital status is known. With the exception of Wethersfield in the 1820s, a majority of married sons received property in their fathers' lifetimes (column 4). When compared with their unmarried brothers (column 6), married sons were heavily overrepresented as recipients of lifetime transfers, particularly in the upland. Moreover, the percentage of married sons receiving lifetime gifts was nearly constant in the upland (at 60 to 65 percent), while it steadily dropped in Wethersfield. Further, three quarters of the married sons who inherited land during their fathers' lifetimes got at least some of their land before they married or within two years of their marriages (not shown).[17]

Although one cannot say that the marriages occurred because the sons received property ("no land, no marriage"), these data certainly indicate that there was a close connection between rearrangements of rights in parental property and marriage. With the exception of those raised in early nineteenth-century Wethersfield, these young men grew up in communities in which it was the norm for married sons to receive some portion of their inheritance in advance. It is an open question whether parental resources were simply mobilized in response to the needs created by new or likely marriages or whether such transfers were intended as, and were effective as, incentives to marry.[18]

Daughters and Personal Property

Daughters' marriage portions were customarily made up of movables or cash. As we have seen, holders rarely transferred land to their daughters during their lifetimes. The brief references to lifetime transfers to daughters found in wills and in distributors' notations are too scanty to tell us much about the composition of these marriage portions. But something of the flavor of these transactions comes to us from the correspondence of a bride, Lucy Williams, who did not receive what she clearly regarded as the standard portion. Once again Comfort Wil-

---

[17] In each time period, this was true for at least 60 percent of all married sons in both areas.

[18] See Daniel Scott Smith, "Parental Power and Marriage Patterns: An Analysis of Historical Trends in Hingham, Massachusetts," *Journal of Marriage and the Family* 35 (August 1973): 419-28, who uses a variety of indicators to show that parental control over marriage diminished after 1780 in Hingham, Massachusetts. He offers his data as indirect evidence that property and marriage were no longer intimately connected. The timing of the shifts he found—bunched in the late eighteenth and early nineteenth centuries—is compatible with the data on Wethersfield.

liams's arduous search for a permanent position as a minister provides the occasion for the following exchange. Lucy, still in Wethersfield in the summer of 1811, was preparing to meet her husband, who had finally obtained a solid prospect for a permanent position in Ogdensburgh, New York. She writes:

> I thank you for your advice about furniture—but my dear friend I dont know that I shall have any—at least, it will be so trifling that it will be next to nothing—But very little besides beds and linen. . . . My father has not yet regain'd his reason—nor do I think he ever will—this makes it more difficult to obtain any thing than it would be if he had the exercise of his rational powers—I am sorry for you—I am sorry for myself—we both want to live genteelly. . . . I ought to have every thing to furnish our house when we have one—instead of which I shall have but verry little—verry little indeed. It gives me some uneasiness—but I suffer it to trouble me as little as possible. . . . I wont be verry unhappy if I live virtuously—and I wont suffer trifles to make me so.[19]

Comfort replied gallantly enough that to imagine he was troubled because she was "not possessed of a fortune is to impeach my love. You are mine and I am satisfied, furniture, or no furniture, money or no money. I did not marry you for property." He did think, however, that she might find the sentiment an insufficient answer to her questions about Ogdensburgh. He went on to write that people of the "first class," those he wished her to visit on her arrival, did indeed "live very genteelly. Their houses are handsomely furnished. . . ." Just as theirs would be, he assured her, with or without her family's assistance.[20]

[19] Lucy Williams to Comfort Williams, August 27, 1811, folder 1, box 1, Papers of Comfort Williams, 1806-40, RG 69: 8, Hartford, The Connecticut State Library. Ogdensburgh was in fact a particularly unfortunate choice for setting up a household; it suffered heavily in the opening hostilities of the War of 1812. Lucy had arrived in February, but was forced to evacuate with her infant son by October, as were all other women and children. She and Williams never returned, and they were not to settle for more than a few months in any one place until the spring of 1816, when they set up housekeeping in Utica, New York.

[20] Comfort Williams to Lucy Williams, September 7, 1811. Lucy had also hoped, in the early letters, that they would by their own efforts achieve the social standing to which they felt entitled. In fact, their status did depend less on direct inheritance than on influence networks that extended from the minister of Wethersfield's first society church to those who taught Comfort at Dartmouth College. In this case, the couple's efforts to obtain a house of their own, let alone gentility, were frustrated because Comfort's network was only good enough to get him trial positions in poor, newly settled towns that typically provided their ministers with a grudging pittance. Worse, he was sent to towns riven by religious conflict. In such communities it could take up to a decade to settle on a minister whose doctrine and, most particularly, oratorical style were to everyone's liking.

Lucy clearly felt that the marriage portion was her right and her father's obligation. Its lack compromised her position with her husband and was a primary manifestation of her father's disgrace. (Remember that her father was not only ill, but, according to her, "depraved," failing to meet his minimal obligations as a family head.)[21] A generous marriage portion in early nineteenth-century Wethersfield evidently included purchased, not homemade, furniture or cash substitutes. But linen and bedding were at the core of the expected portion. In fact, bedding and linen usually overwhelmed in value any other category of household goods including furniture, clothing, and kitchen equipment in the inventories of all but the wealthiest holders.

Evidence of lifetime gifts to daughters is erratic. Neither the wills mentioning prior transfers nor the distributors' notations provide systematic evidence about the frequency of such gifts. Such references occurred only when it was necessary to make up for disparities created by slightly different marriage portions or by the presence of unportioned single daughters. Thus there is likely to be no evidence about marriage in the following situations: when all daughters were married at the holder's death; when a married daughter was the only daughter; and when the estate was both insolvent and intestate. Basically, then, one cannot determine the actual rates of marriage portions given to daughters with these data. One can only establish a minimum incidence.

Lifetime transfers to daughters appear to have been more uniform than transfers to sons. There is positive evidence that only one estate holder gave lifetime gifts to unmarried daughters.[22] Also, when there is evidence that holders gave lifetime gifts to married daughters, in every case all married daughters got one—not at all true when it came to lifetime transfers of land to sons. Once again, daughters' treatment was not individualized. Within a given family, there was a uniform policy toward daughters.

All told, there were 198 daughters, from seventy-nine families, definitely known to be married.[23] At first glance, Table 6.4 shows a pattern of converging, then parallel practices. On the eve of the Revolution, two thirds, or close to two thirds, of the married daughters in each area definitely got marriage portions. In the 1820s the figures drop to one third in the upland and just over one third in Wethersfield (column 2).

[21] Journal of Lucy Williams, November 8, 1811.

[22] When there was no independent evidence from vital records or genealogies, I assumed that a daughter who had the same last name as the estate holder was single. Because there was some marriage between cousins, a small number of adult daughters classified as single were probably actually married.

[23] Fourteen more families had only single adult daughters. The marital statuses of the adult daughters could not be determined in two families.

TABLE 6.4
MARRIED DAUGHTERS AND LIFETIME TRANSFERS

	Known Married (N)	Receiving Lifetime Transfers (%)	No Evidence of Receiving	
			Evidence Unlikely* (%)	Remaining (%)
	(1)	(2)	(3)	(4)
1750s				
Wethersfield	31	65	35	0
Upland	26	46	38	15
1770s				
Wethersfield	41	61	34	5
Upland	30	67	30	3
1820s				
Wethersfield	34	38	56	6
Upland	36	33	64	3

* Daughter is only daughter, all sisters are married, parents' estate is insolvent and intestate.

Except for the uplands in the 1750s, however, virtually all the remaining married daughters came from families in which the wills and estate distributions were unlikely to mention marriage portions. Again, one can surely establish only a minimum incidence with these data. It is quite possible that married daughters universally received some movables or cash during their parents' lifetimes.

A few families certainly deviated from the practice of giving lifetime gifts to married daughters and compensations to those unmarried at the holder's death. In seven estates, ten married daughters received inheritance shares that equaled those received by their unmarried sisters. Either the married daughters had not gotten marriage portions, or they were, in virtue of their inheritances, deliberately advantaged over their single sisters. The same is true of the married daughters of four insolvent and intestate holders, except that if the married daughters had received lifetime gifts, their advantage was unintentional.

CONCLUSION

Where the evidence is strongest, the pattern of parallel, then diverging practices holds. Colonial and early nineteenth-century upland holders used lifetime transfers of land to make arrangements for their retirement or to smooth the way for sons who married. But in the large majority of early nineteenth-century Wethersfield families, marriage and retirement took place without reordering family property relations.

Land came to heirs as an unpredictable dividend, its timing depending on only one critical event: the deaths of holders.

The evidence on lifetime transfers makes sense. Extended cognate practices were attempts to balance a tension between unity and provision, a tension that persisted only when at least two generations depended on family property. It is not surprising that holders used their property to help set up new households or to reinforce the new division of labor created when parents retired. The use of lifetime transfers attests to the importance of family property to both generations. The collapse of preferential partibility and the declining use of overlapping rights, by contrast, signals the disappearance of the tension between unity and provision. Children depended less and less on parental property. One further consequence was that share-and-share-alike practices dispersed property only at the deaths of holders.

There is one probable exception to the pattern of parallel, then diverging practices. Holders almost never gave daughters land while they lived, and it is probable that the marriage portion composed of movable property was the norm in both areas throughout the late eighteenth and early nineteenth centuries. A daughter's portion was never meant to guarantee her social standing directly. Rather, it was meant to secure her a more or less advantageous position on marriage markets. Here, there was no inter-area variation. There was one difference, however: when extended cognate strategies dominated, few daughters ever got much land. In contrast, many early nineteenth-century Wethersfield daughters eventually received nearly as much land as their brothers—not because they continued to marry and care for aged kin, although they probably did so, but because their parents pursued egalitarian practices at their deaths.

While analyzing the practices of these holders, I was struck by an incipient, recurring theme: the nature of "independence" in these communities. It emerges here, and in the work of others, in the twinning of marriage and the status of independent householder. Think only of the Stoddard brothers, who went to court because smallpox had intervened to stall the paperwork necessary to carry out their stricken brother's intentions. All assumed that when a brother married he ought to own his own land. Their feelings echoed the apparent sentiments of fathers who made lifetime transfers of land. Most did not deny title to married sons or to sons who shouldered the responsibility of caring for aged parents. Holders passed on the powers inherent in ownership, granting sons the independence that went with it.

The theme of independence also emerges in the central fact that holders did not seek to extend their authority over property to unborn generations or even to set up systematic relations of super- and subordination among male heirs. This emphasis on independence makes sense in communities founded on family farming. Widespread ownership of middling farms establishes a fundamental parity among producers, and ownership confers autonomy as well.

Some have equated this independence with the "rugged individualism" and competitive ethos of Social Darwinism and the Gilded Age.[24] But, at least insofar as inheritance practices shed light on it, the prism of later nineteenth-century ideology cannot produce an accurate view of the particular qualities of independence in the colonial period and, in the subsistence-plus communities, well beyond. For one thing, the status "independent householder" was a goal, not an easily attainable given. Those who did not inherit this status (directly through ownership of productive property, or vicariously, through marriage to one who did) were severely handicapped. In most families it took cooperation and sharp calculations about the allocation of property to assure intergenerational renewal of this status. Independence was closely associated with active kin networks and careful calibration of family obligations. Also, as others have found, the social hierarchy of these communities was age-stratified; they were gerontocracies. Even favored sons from families of the "better sort" did not escape service in a series of lesser local offices before taking their place in especially honorable and locally powerful positions.[25] This was not the independence of youth striking out on its own or the independence associated with the prerogatives of high birth; it was a status that became one's due only after a prolonged period of apprenticeship, literal or figurative.

Moreover, the isolated family farm was not a self-subsisting unit in the subsistence-plus communities. These families were enmeshed in local exchanges of land, labor, and produce, in a web of local offices, and in complex personal credit networks. To become an independent householder was not to "do for oneself" in the ordinary sense of "by oneself." Rather, it was to enter directly into this web of relations, not merely indirectly through "virtual representation" by a father or mas-

---

[24] See Charles S. Grant, *Democracy in the Connecticut Frontier Town of Kent* (New York: Columbia University Press, 1961), pp. 31-54; Louis Hartz, *The Liberal Tradition in America* (New York: Harvest-Harcourt Brace, 1955), pp. 59-66, 74-78, 89-91; James T. Lemon, *The Best Poor Man's Country: A Geographical Study of Early Southeastern Pennsylvania* (Baltimore: Johns Hopkins University Press, 1972), p. vi; and Seymour Martin Lipset, *The First New Nation: The United States in Historical and Comparative Perspective* (Garden City, N.Y.: Doubleday-Anchor, 1967), pp. 125-31.

[25] Edward M. Cook, Jr., *The Fathers of the Towns: Leadership and Community Structure in Eighteenth Century New England* (Baltimore: Johns Hopkins University Press, 1976), pp. 81-94; James Henretta, "Families and Farms: 'Mentalité' in Pre-Industrial America," *William and Mary Quarterly*, 3rd ser., 35 (January 1978): 6-18; J. Main, *Connecticut Society*, pp. 9-12.

ter. Thus independence was hardly monadic individualism; it was itself a condition relating one to others. It described one who had entered as an equal into relations with others who were similarly independent.

Finally, independence was so much a relational condition that to be independent was normally to have dependents. The independent man organized the labor of others and spoke for them in arenas outside the household. Independence simultaneously described families, "independent households," and a certain group of individuals—family heads—but it was certainly not the abstract autonomy of persons. Independence did not blur certain types of authority relations. Rather, for the man who stood as master to his servant, apprentice, or even slave, and as patriarch to his wife and children, independence was founded on hierarchical relations within households.

Thus "independence" may have had special characteristics in the early American North, but to read into it the seeds of "Lockean individualism" or to make "doing for oneself" evoke Robinson Crusoe imagery is once again to impose a dichotomous framework of understandings on the study of preindustrial agrarian communities. It hampers efforts to clarify the structure of early American towns and to place them in relation to agrarian communities elsewhere, and it mistakenly cuts off discussion of significant regional variation and qualitative historical change.

CHAPTER SEVEN

PATRIARCHAL HOUSEHOLDS AND
INHERITANCE BY WOMEN

Extended cognate practices embodied a fine balance: when passing on their land, fathers relinquished authority over sons, only so that sons, in turn, could become householders able to exercise the authority that ownership of significant productive property conferred. But quite obviously the independence of sons and the authority of household heads did not extend to women. Women, for the most part, were household dependents. Although we have already looked at daughters' inheritances, we did so largely to assess property holders' priorities in setting-up the households of sons and of daughters. In this chapter we will examine inheritance by widows for the first time and reassess the data on daughters' shares. To concentrate on women and inheritance is really to consider more closely the authority relations within households.

Many have described northern colonial households as patriarchal. Patriarchy can refer narrowly to paternal authority over children or broadly to all forms of male dominance over women. "Patriarchal household" connotes authority relations wider than the former and more specific than the latter. Household authority relations are patriarchal under two conditions. First, a household head is a patriarch when he, and not others within the household, is the ultimate arbiter of decisions concerning the internal organization of the household. Second, a household head is a patriarch only to the extent that he has the power to speak on behalf of his dependents in matters dealing with the larger community. To put it another way, the larger community reaches others indirectly through the mediation of household heads.[1]

The colonial North may have been uniquely hospitable to the formation of patriarchal households. Family-based enterprise, congregational forms of worship, and a decentralized political administration

---

[1] On household patriarchy in seventeenth-century England, see Lawrence Stone on the "restricted patriarchal nuclear family" in *The Family, Sex, and Marriage in England, 1500-1800* (New York: Harper Colophon, 1979). See also Linda Auwers, "Fathers, Sons, and Wealth in Colonial Windsor, Connecticut," *Journal of Family History* 3 (1978): 136-39, who extends Stone's formulation and applies it to New England towns. See also the excellent discussion in Mary P. Ryan, *Cradle of the Middle Class: The Family in Oneida County, New York, 1790-1865* (Cambridge, Eng.: Cambridge University Press, 1981), pp. 22-25, 31-34.

combined to make the household itself a "master" social institution, particularly in the comparatively self-reliant subsistence-plus areas.[2] One starts with the fundamental fact of the household as the locus of production. Family members also supplied most of the necessary labor themselves. When they did not, family relations served as the model for relations between masters and servants, and masters and apprentices (not only because so much of the training and labor took place within households, but because Americans, particularly rural Americans, lacked the guild structure that would have given these relations a distinctive cast). Primary education and the care of the poor were also primarily household functions. The local congregations were often little more than clusters of households; even the ministers were in principle no more than first among equals in matters spiritual. Finally, the town meeting had the power to make most of the political and economic decisions that immediately affected the daily lives of members of the community.

Even when the centrality of the household began to give way under the impact of commercialization, and as the locus of politics slowly shifted to state and national arenas after the Revolution, new institutions would at first model themselves after households. Manufacturers initially tried to assimilate relations between employers and wage laborers to those of master and apprentice, parents and children. The first prisons and poorhouses, in retrospect clear signals that a social order based on households was waning, were also organized like households.[3] In short, the rural American North was, for a long time, a world in which the household was the center.

Correspondingly, it was a world that put large powers in the hands of heads of households. Perhaps nothing so neatly captures the household patriarch's two-sided authority as mediator and ultimate arbiter as visions of civil order that assigned the heads of households the role of "governors."

> As the Civil State, as well as the *Churches of Christ*, is furnished with Members from private Families: if the Governors of these little Communities were faithful to the great Trust reposed in them, and Family-Religion & Discipline were thoroughly . . . maintained . . . the Civil State, would prosper and flourish from Generation to Generation.[4]

[2] John Demos, *A Little Commonwealth: Family Life in Plymouth Colony* (Oxford: Oxford University Press, 1971), pp. 182-86; Auwers, "Fathers, Sons, and Wealth."

[3] David Rothman, *The Discovery of the Asylum* (Boston: Little, Brown, 1971), pp. 3-56.

[4] James Lockwood, *Religion the highest Interest of a civil Community and the surest Means of its Prosperity: An Election Sermon* (New London, 1754), p. 33.

When Reverend Lockwood (whose estate figures in this study) invoked this familiar imagery in his sermon before the General Assembly as it convened in 1754, he combined it with an emphasis on the "necessary subordination of Persons" and on superior and inferior stations.[5] He would repeat this imagery of heads of households as "governors" before his Wethersfield congregation in a eulogy to his predecessor Elisha Williams. Though Williams was far less conservative politically, Lockwood claimed confidently, and with justification, that orderly family government had also been one of Williams's first priorities.[6] Although ministers of different theological persuasions might differ as to the legitimate extent and limits of patriarchal authority,[7] they generally found it useful to argue that the best guarantee of orderly rule at home was proper religious observance. They did so because they viewed heads of households as crucial intermediaries between home and meetinghouse, just as legislators saw them as magistrates who were responsible for education, care, and social comportment of children, aged parents, wives, and idiots.

Note, however, that patriarchal household organization does not preclude public supervision of relations between household heads and their dependents. Selectmen, ministers, deacons, and legislators all helped to define and enforce the rights and obligations of both household heads and their dependents. They did so in part because they saw in the household heads' orderly rule the foundations of social and political order. But they also did so because they saw in the authority of the father and husband a power potentially excessive unless disciplined by the laws of God and legislators. In short, they linked communal order to the exercise of a superior but bounded male authority, seeking to identify the point at which legitimate authority became a tyrannical abuse of power.

To be sure, at mid-century, republican conceptions of civil order were already beginning to compete with the conservative imagery of superior and inferior "stations." In the Revolutionary era and thereafter,

[5] Ibid., p. 14.

[6] Lockwood, *Man mortal: God everlasting, and the sure, unfailing Refuge and Felicity of his faithful People, in all Generations, A Funeral Sermon* (New Haven, 1756). Elisha Williams is known for his anonymous authorship of a pamphlet that opposed the anti-itinerancy laws. In it he makes the classic Christian-conscience argument for toleration and begins to argue for disestablishment. His rather cerebral New Light position helped keep Wethersfield from experiencing any great turmoil during the height of the Great Awakening. See references to Williams in Richard Bushman, *From Puritan to Yankee: Character and the Social Order in Connecticut, 1690-1765* (New York: Norton, 1970), pp. 227-30, 240-41, 277.

[7] See Philip J. Greven, Jr., *The Protestant Temperament: Patterns of Child-Rearing, Religious Experience, and the Self in Early America* (New York: Knopf, 1977).

the strand of Revolutionary ideology that stressed good character as the foundation of civil order did much to modify the imagery of household heads as civil magistrates. It also contributed mightily to the new conceptions of the domain of married women and family privacy that would crystallize in the second quarter of the nineteenth century. But for the moment, the law regulating women's control over property reinforced patriarchal household relations. Until the mid-nineteenth century spate of married women's property acts, the statutory laws embodied the imagery of "little governments," the ideology of dependency and protection that had dominated at their enactment.

DEPENDENCY AND PROTECTION: THE LAW

The Proprietary Capacities of Married Women

Under the common law married women lost all rights to most forms of personal property, which would become the property of their husbands. When married women did possess estates of inheritance (in real property), they retained only the negative attributes of ownership. A husband had extensive managerial powers over his wife's realty, although he could not permanently alienate it without her explicit consent (in this basic sense she owned the property and he did not).[8] Because of her husband's managerial rights and her inability to make contracts, a married women could not dispose of her own property unilaterally. While her husband was alive, a married woman retained no positive rights to alienate or manage her realty. In addition, married women were not definitively granted the ability to make wills until the statute of 1809.[9] For them, the inheritance system was not permissive. They could not choose their successors; their heirs-at-law automatically inherited.

[8] He was sole "administrator" of her real property, entitled to its income and profits without any duty to account to her for these. See Richard Morris, *Studies in the History of American Law*, 2nd ed. (New York: Octagon Books, 1964), p. 135. Connecticut law protected all estates of inheritance (in real property) coming to women, either before or during marriage, by "descent or otherwise." It required private examination of the wife whenever she gave her consent to deeds alienating her property to ensure that her consent was freely given. See *Acts & Laws 1750*, p. 119; *Public Statutes 1821*, p. 304. On similar consent provisions elsewhere, and their sometimes lax administration, see Marylynn Salmon, " 'Life, Liberty, and Dower': The Legal Status of Women after the American Revolution," in *Women, War, and Revolution*, ed. Carol R. Berkin and Clara M. Lovett (New York: Holmes & Meier, 1980), pp. 85-106; Salmon, "Equality or Submersion?: Feme Covert Status in Early Pennsylvania," in *Women of America: A History*, ed. Carol Ruth Berkin and Mary Beth Norton (Boston: Houghton Mifflin, 1979), pp. 92-113.

[9] Connecticut Archives, Civil Officers, Index, 2nd series, Estates: Laws and Statutes, p. 237, cite to Act passed, May 1809.

Such was the position of married women under the common law. In England and in the colonies that had them, equity courts mitigated the harshest effects of the common law by permitting the creation of separate estates for married women. Interested parties could make special arrangements to limit a husband's rights in his wife's property, and under certain circumstances equity procedures could give married women proprietary powers comparable to those of single and widowed women.[10]

But Connecticut, like several other colonies, had no separate equity courts. Rather, equity jurisdiction was originally held by the general assembly, which gradually conferred portions of this jurisdiction on the regular courts.[11] The Connecticut legislature and higher courts were hostile to separate estates, at least in the early national period. Zephaniah Swift—who attempted to create a Connecticut version of Blackstone's commentaries and who helped compile the 1821 code—insists that by the late eighteenth century Connecticut law was implacably opposed to several equitable arrangements for creating separate estates for married women. Marylynn Salmon finds that in a series of early decisions, Connecticut's highest courts ruled that Connecticut state law simply did not recognize equitable trust arrangements.[12] It is possible that people wishing to extend married women's property rights did not face such uniform legal opposition in the colonial period.[13] But it is probably safe to assume that attempts to create separate estates had more uncertain legal status in colonial Connecticut than in colonies that had equity courts. Certainly those who analyze married women's rights in colonies and states that did have separate equity courts conclude that when republican ideology hostile to English law and to court-made law led to abolition of equity courts, the situation of married women became more precarious until statutory reform filled the gap.[14] Connecticut's earlier rejection of equity courts and unwilling-

[10] Morris, *History of American Law*, pp. 135-38; Marylynn Salmon, *Women and the Law of Property in Early America*, pp. 101-52 (Chapel Hill: University of North Carolina Press, 1986).

[11] Zephaniah Swift, *A System of the Laws of the State of Connecticut*, 2 vols. (Windham, Conn., 1795-96), 2: 411-23.

[12] Salmon, *Women and the Law of Property*, pp. 153-78; Swift, *System of Laws*, 1: 300-22. See also the divided decision in Bacon v. Taylor, 1 Kirby 366 (1788). Connecticut did allow conventional two-party agreements between husbands and wives only so long as they were made before marriage and concerned only wives' rights after their husbands' deaths; see Swift, *System of Laws*, 1: 194, 256-57.

[13] Morris, *History of American Law*, pp. 137-49.

[14] Peggy A. Rabkin, "The Origins of Law Reform: The Social Significance of the Nineteenth-Century Codification Movement and Its Contribution to the Passage of the Early

ness to codify the position of married women until after 1820 exposed women to the rigors of the common law and to confusion over the reception of equity law for a longer period of time.

The courts' position in the area of property rights, then, appeared to be one of rueful acknowledgment of some of the illegitimate consequences of patriarchal power. This power itself, however, was seen as a basic social fact. Remedies for some of its potentially damaging consequences amounted to more careful protection of the dependent woman, not reforms that removed the dependency.[15] Thus, for instance, the courts hesitated to accept settlements giving wives the unrestricted power to transfer property because they thought women were liable to dispose of property in their husbands' interests, rather than in their own and their heirs' interests. In fact, transfers that removed property from women's heirs were suspect. They were evidence of illegitimate pressure by husbands.

The acceptance of patriarchal authority coupled with the desire to protect women and their heirs from its worst consequences is expressed clearly in a Connecticut Superior Court ruling that married women could not make wills devising real property to their husbands.

> Nor do the general reasons urged for the institution of wills seem to extend to the case of a *feme covert*. That of their use in aiding family government does not; because the government is not placed in her hands. . . . The possession of this power must be as inconvenient for *feme coverts* as it is unnecessary. It must subject . . . their heirs, and sometimes their children, to the loss of property, which the law has been studious to preserve for them: Add to which, . . . they are [exposed] to coercions . . . dangerous for them to disclose—placed in the power of a husband, whose solicitations they cannot resist, and whose commands in all things lawful, it is their duty to obey.[16]

This grim picture of coercion and danger has its incongruities when used as a rationale for circumscribing the wife's power to dispose of her own property. In the absence of such restrictions, ownership of productive property by wives could have been one key factor in equalizing authority relations within households. But rather than grant the rights in property that might have encouraged such shifts, the courts and the

---

Married Women's Property Acts," *Buffalo Law Review* 24 (Spring 1975): 683-760, on New York.

[15] See Salmon, " 'Life, Liberty and Dower,' " pp. 85-86, who makes this point strikingly in her analysis of postrevolutionary changes in South Carolina's property law.

[16] Adams v. Kellogg, 1 Kirby 195 (1786); Judge Ellsworth's Notes, 1 Kirby 438, 442-43 (n.d.).

legislature chose to protect those whom they presumed inevitably dependent.

The sharply circumscribed proprietary capacities of married women have one important consequence for the interpretation of inheritance practices. A formally identical treatment of sons and daughters (or, for that matter, sisters and brothers) had very different results for the married daughter or the daughter who subsequently married than it did for sons. Holders who gave their daughters ownership of property may have put their sons' and daughters' *families* on equal footing, but they were not giving their daughters proprietary powers equivalent to their sons'.

Very few of these estate holders attempted to enlarge the proprietary powers of their female kin. The widow Sybil Andrus was one of the few who did do so, and it is uncertain how the law would have viewed her bequest of a cow, sheep, and most of her household goods to her husband's brother's wife. She stipulated that these goods were for Nancy's "use and the use of her family exclusively and to be at her disposal without Controle from her husband or any other person to and among her Children or otherwise as she shall Judge to be most Condusive to the best interest and benifit of their family."[17] Sybil's intention is clear: Nancy was to be the sole and full owner of these goods. No other holder used such unambiguous language, however, and in only two other cases (both involving daughters) could the language be construed as intending to enlarge a woman's powers. Virtually no holder, then, did anything to dilute the paramount authority of their sons-in-law or brothers-in-law.

Widows' Rights

The law gave widows' claims special protection. Unless marriage settlements made alternative and equivalent provisions, widows were entitled to life-estates in one third of the real property owned by their husbands at their deaths.[18] The dower right took priority over the claims of creditors to estates; it was a right in one third of gross real property

[17] This was apparently solely out of respect for Nancy Andrus. It certainly had nothing to do with distrust of her husband's brother: Sybil Andrus willed all her real estate to him. Sybil Andrus, will, signed April 22, 1818, Coventry, folio 52, Andover Probate District, Estate Papers.

[18] The specific language is property "possessed in his own right." Thus, for example, an entailed estate is subject to a dower claim. The following discussion relies primarily on *Acts & Laws 1750*, pp. 43-44, 49-51; *Acts & Laws 1796*, pp. 146-48; *Public Statutes 1821*, pp. 180-82; Marylynn Salmon, "The Property Rights of Women in Early America: A Comparative Study" (Ph.D. dissertation, Bryn Mawr, 1980), pp. 255-68.

held at death. A husband's testament could not defeat it: although he could propose substitutes, a widow had the right to reject such substitutes and claim her dower.[19] Thus the law of dower imposed some limits on the husband's ability to dispose of his property, and it also restricted the use and control of property by other parties interested in a man's estate: heirs and creditors received encumbered property.

Connecticut's dower law, however, was a less imposing restriction than were dower laws elsewhere. In most other colonies and under English common law, the dower was a life interest in one third of all real property held during marriage. Hence property alienated by a husband during his lifetime was subject to the dower claim (unless the wife explicitly renounced it). The secondary literature does not discuss the motive for Connecticut's early and significant departure from this rule. Whatever the motive, the limitation of the dower to estate held at death was one statutory provision favorable to a fully developed market in land. And, in comparison with dower rules in other jurisdictions, it enhanced the private power of male heads of families relative to wives' property claims.

Since a widow did not succeed to heritable rights, she was not truly an heir to real property. Only her intestate claim to ownership of personal property (one third if there were children capable of inheriting; one half if not) put her on a footing commensurate with that of other heirs. As heir to personal property she was offered no special protection against creditors: hers was a claim in *net* personal estate. When debts threatened to consume the entire personal estate, however, the courts did reserve a small portion for widows. The bed, two spinning wheels, Bible, miscellaneous kitchen equipment, furniture, and the several barrels, hoes, ax, and a hatchet awarded to Sarah Hurlbutt of Wethersfield by court order in October of 1774 (worth a little over 11 pounds lawful money) was a typical colonial allotment of widow's "necessaries."[20] Because the allied statutes about property exempted from lifetime executions on indebted estates had gotten more specific, the distributions of "widow's necessaries" in the 1820s were more careful to include a cow and barnyard animals as well as minimal allotments of farming implements when the estate contained them.[21]

[19] In the colonial period the widow automatically came into her dower interest regardless of provisions made in wills. But by the 1821 revision she actively had to decline alternative bequests or devises before the close of probate. Failure to do so was a bar to dower.

[20] Timothy Hurlbutt, court order, October 18, 1774, folio 3023, Hartford Probate District, Estate Papers.

[21] *Acts & Laws 1750*, p. 102, referring to p. 56; *Public Statutes 1821*, p. 211, referring to p. 56.

All told, these laws aimed to secure widows' maintenance needs. The statutes protecting the dower right against creditors' claims or defeat by testament, and reserving some personal property for "widows necessaries" as against creditors, were part of a family of statutes that made care for dependent kin matters of enforceable public policy.

WOMEN AND RESOURCES

There is currently a certain shifting of perspective about the issue of women and dependency, particularly in subsistence-plus settings. The older view, which has been given sustained life by such feminist historians as Mary Ryan and Joan Wilson, is that so long as women made essential contributions to households as producers, they actually wielded considerable power.[22] The household mode of production required a certain level of cooperation and respect for the needs of women if households were to function smoothly. Thus the daily realities of production mitigated the harshest effects of the law and of a public ideology that insisted on the paramount authority of household heads.

Others are skeptical. They point out that participation in production does not necessarily confer decision-making authority on producers. Mary Beth Norton, for example, argues that there is no reason to assume that recognition of women's vital economic functions led to a significant voice in decision making. The issue, she states, is not the centrality of women's work, but their ability or inability to control the resources central to the running of the household economy. She concludes that those who imagine that colonial women had appreciable authority are perpetuating a "myth of [a] golden age."[23]

Perhaps those holding the older view are right to say that women

[22] Mary P. Ryan, *Womanhood in America from Colonial Times to the Present*, 2nd ed. (New York: Franklin Watts-New Viewpoints, 1979), pp. 3-40; Joan Hoff Wilson, "The Illusion of Change: Women and the American Revolution," in *The American Revolution: Explorations in the History of American Radicalism*, ed. Alfred F. Young (Dekalb, Ill.: Northern Illinois University Press, 1976), pp. 383-445. The older view is the "received wisdom" to its critics, the "accepted view" to Lawrence Stone, "Family History in the 1980's: Past Achievements and Future Trends," *Journal of Interdisciplinary History* 7 (Summer 1981): 65-66. Louise Tilly and Joan Scott adopt this position for the European context; see *Women, Work, and the Family* (New York: Holt, Rinehart, and Winston, 1978).

[23] Mary Beth Norton, "The Myth of the Golden Age," in *Women of America: A History*, ed. Carol Ruth Berkin and Mary Beth Norton (Boston: Houghton Mifflin, 1979), pp. 37-47. Also see Norton, *Liberty's Daughters: The Revolutionary Experience of American Women* (Boston: Little, Brown, 1980); Nancy F. Cott, *The Bonds of Womanhood: "Woman's Sphere" in New England, 1780-1835* (New Haven: Yale University Press, 1977).

were able to influence their husbands' decisions and to earn their husbands' respect in part because they were producers. There is no doubt, at any rate, that there were ideological bases for mutual respect in colonial New England households. As households rather than spiritually authoritative churches became the linchpin of Calvinist and, especially, congregational forms of worship, English and, particularly, Puritan theology put great emphasis on the sacred quality of marriage. It also insisted on affection and mutual respect as a central component of marriage.[24] But although some have thought so, such ideology was not at odds with patriarchal household organization. Influence and respect are not power. The mutual duty to respect, even the husband's duty to take his wife's counsel, were always embedded in another universal injunction: her duty to obey. A governor may respect his advisors. Indeed, he ought to do so, but his authority to act and their obligation to obey are not less for all that.

The revisionists, I think, are correct to maintain that control over resources is the crux of the matter. There was nothing in the wife's role as producer per se to dilute the husband's position as the ultimate arbiter of household business. Inheritance is, of course, one important aspect of control over resources. The issue is whether the treatment of female heirs found here suited patriarchal households. To what extent did the practices of holders perpetuate women's lack of control over resources, and, hence, the material foundations for patriarchal authority relations within households? Before assessing the issue overall, let us see how widows actually fared.

Inheritance Practices: The Treatment of Widows

The reader should keep in mind that the law defining widows' claims was designed to ensure a standard minimum participation in husbands' property. It was potentially a strong source of uniformity in practices since it curbed the testamentary freedom of the holder. Nonetheless, an estate holder was free to enlarge both his widow's rights and her share in real estate, as well as her share of personal property. Moreover, the law in Connecticut did not protect a widow's claim from lifetime transfers by her husband. Finally, a widow could agree or acquiesce to a substitute for, or a reduction of, her legally defined portion.

When Captain Martin Kellogg died in 1753 he had held a string of local offices, and had extensive landholdings and an interest in an iron-

---

[24] Stone, *Family, Sex, and Marriage*, pp. 100-103, 136-42; Edmund Morgan, *The Puritan Family: Religion and Domestic Relations in Seventeenth Century New England*, rev. ed. (New York: Harper Torchbooks, 1966), pp. 29-64.

works. His will was unremarkable, except for the provision giving his wife, Dorothy, ownership of his fifteen-acre home lot and house in addition to her thirds in the rest of his land. We can only guess at his motives. When he emigrated to Wethersfield from Deerfield, Massachusetts, shortly after 1713, he brought little except a distant connection to the Wethersfield Williams family and his recollections of a prolonged stay in captivity among the Indians in French Canada after one of several attacks on Deerfield during Queen Anne's War. His marriage into the long-established Chester family quickly integrated him into the best Wethersfield circles, and his in-laws counted particularly heavily in his land transactions and other business dealings. Their eldest son's substantial portion was, for example, Chester land purchased by Martin, and Dorothy inherited more when her only brother died a young, unmarried man.[25]

Martin may have been less likely to treat his home lot as lineal property belonging to sons because he had purchased rather than inherited his estate, and he probably had a strong sense of obligation to the Chesters. In addition, one guesses that he had an unusually healthy respect for his wife's ability to manage the property. Martin was used to negotiating with Chester women, since Dorothy and her sisters participated in most of the Chester land transactions involving Martin. In any case, when Dorothy died just a year later, she also did the unexpected. She left the home lot to her three youngest daughters, the only children still unmarried and living at home, as a reward for continuing to care for their aged (maternal) grandmother.[26]

Martin Kellogg's will was unusual. Very few widows received heritable rights in real property. In fact, only eight of the one hundred widows of landed men got ownership of any real property.[27] The ninety-three men who died leaving wives and children were almost unanimous in their refusal to give their wives the power to alienate their land. Five scattered colonial fathers, including Martin Kellogg, gave their wives small amounts of land while passing the rest on to children. No man who had children gave his wife ownership of any land in the 1820s, although Eunice Bunce of Wethersfield preempted her children at the sale

[25] Martin Kellogg, will, signed October 7, 1753, folio 3148, Hartford Probate District, Estate Papers; Sherman W. Adams and Henry R. Stiles, *The History of Ancient Wethersfield*, 2 vols., reprint ed. (Somersworth: New Hampshire Publishing Co., 1974), 1: 776-81.

[26] For land transactions, see, for example, Wethersfield Land Records, 4: 314, 5: 109, deeds, recorded November 27, 1721, and December 15, 1725. Dorothy Kellogg, will, signed September 21, 1754, folio 3142, Hartford Probate District, Estate Papers.

[27] In this context "landed men" refers to those who died owning land or who had passed land to potential heirs during their lifetimes.

of her indebted husband's estate. All told, only 6 percent of the widows of landed men who had children got ownership of any land.

This almost universal reluctance was in large part simply one more aspect of patterns of inheritance that sought to reserve land primarily for blood kin. Landed men guarded their property against alienation away from children by withholding from their wives a basic underpinning of their own authority as family heads: ownership of land. (Judging from the handful of relevant cases, widows of childless holders were preferred to siblings in, but only in, postcolonial Wethersfield: two out of three received ownership of real property. The other four childless widows of landed men in this study received only life estates.)

The other side of the refusal to give ownership to widows was the near-universality of the life-estate. Fully 92 percent of those widows of landed men who did not receive ownership received life-estates, or estates valid until remarriage, consisting of some portion of their husbands' real property.[28] Few holders substituted lump-sum payments or annuities in cash or in kind for life-estates and the powers to manage and use land that these estates conferred.[29]

As they weighed their wives' requirements for maintenance against their heirs' needs to have direct access to property, some men were comparatively generous to their wives, but others skimped. So, for example, Elizabeth Olcott, one of the few who did not receive a life-estate, apparently settled for the cow, bedding, and one hundred pounds her husband provided in lieu of her dower, even though these represented only 2 percent of the value of Deacon Timothy Olcott's Bolton estate.[30] Although most others got life-estates, some found themselves with less than their thirds because their husbands had not reserved use-rights in property deeded over to sons.

In fact, variation in the shares of land received by widows followed the by-now-familiar pattern of parallel, then diverging practices (Table 7.1).[31] Widows of landed men did not get generous shares of land in the

---

[28] Technically, an estate lasting only until a possible remarriage was a life estate with all the rights that such estates conferred. Since termination of the estate short of the holder's death was contingent on an event (remarriage) that might never happen, the interest was a life-estate. See Swift, *A System of Laws*, 1: 250-52.

[29] See, in contrast, David P. Gagan, "The Indivisibility of Land: A Microanalysis of the System of Inheritance in Nineteenth-Century Ontario," *Journal of Economic History* 36 (March 1976): 134-35. In rural Ontario most widows of willmakers were dependent on principal heirs for annuities or care.

[30] Timothy Olcott, will, signed April 20, 1753, folio 4009, Hartford Probate District, Estate Papers.

[31] A separate discussion of widows' shares in personal property is omitted because net personal property was such a small portion of these estates that one quarter of the colonial and one half of the early nineteenth-century widows in each area received only "wid-

colonial era. Certainly few received shares that exceeded their statutory thirds. The majority of Wethersfield and upland holders settled on the "thirds" as striking the appropriate balance between wives and heirs. Most of those who did deviate curtailed their widows' shares.

In the 1820s practices diverged sharply. Upland widows fared no better during this time than colonial wives: a significant minority received less than their statutory thirds, and none got more. The shift in Wethersfield was dramatic, less because so few widows received reduced shares than because, for the first time, a majority got enlarged portions (59 percent of all Wethersfield widows; 53 percent of those with children). Furthermore, generosity in early nineteenth-century Wethersfield was no more a device restricted to the well-to-do than were constricted shares in the upland a result of land hunger. In Wethersfield five of the nine married men who held over forty acres enlarged their wives' shares, while five of the eight holding under forty acres also

TABLE 7.1

SHARES OF REAL PROPERTY RECEIVED BY WIDOWS OF LANDED MEN

| | | | | Below Statutory Share | |
	Widows (N)	More Than Statutory Share[a] (%)	About Statutory Share[a] (%)	All (%)	Not Fully Compensated[b] (%)
1750s					
Wethersfield	18	17[ns]	67	17	(6)
Upland	14	14	43	43	(36)
1770s					
Wethersfield	21	10[ns]	62	29	(24)
Upland	13	8	62	31	(23)
1820s					
Wethersfield	17	59[ttt]	29	12	(6)
Upland	17	0	71	29	(24)

[a] Statutory share is one third of real property distributed (one half if decedent is childless). Distributed property includes lifetime transfers to heirs.
[b] Decreased share is not fully compensated by enlarged shares in personal property or annuities.
[ns] Chi-square not significant.
[ttt] Chi-square significant at .01 level. Based on two-column tables (did/did not receive more than statutory share) by community type.

ow's necessaries" (the portion of movables exempt from creditors' claims). In the remaining estates, no pattern to the variability in amount of personal property taken was found.

did so. In the upland two of the seven married men who held under forty acres reduced their wives' shares, but so did four of the ten who held over forty acres.

Wethersfield men still reserved the land for their direct descendants through the use of the life-estate, but commercialization of town life was associated with more generous treatment of wives after the colonial period. Commercialization could have affected this particular aspect of practices directly. Heirs who found increased portions of their land earmarked for the welfare of widows were privy to intensive agricultural techniques that made the share subject to their own immediate and sole control comparatively more productive. There was, then, less need to compromise on the security of widows. But, of course, the larger colonial holders and upland holders of the 1820s also could "afford" generous treatment of spouses without working hardship on heirs. Still, they were not generous.

This suggests that commercialization affected the position of widows indirectly. Others have shown that commercialized areas such as Wethersfield were especially receptive to new cultural conceptions of womanhood and marriage. In part because commercialization loosens the connection between household and production, it encourages ideals that place a premium on the conjugal family, motherhood, and the cultivation of emotional ties. A later section of this chapter takes up this point again, but I note now that if Wethersfield families were internalizing new ideals, these may have led to a revised cultural definition of what constituted a suitable maintenance for widows. In commercialized areas it would also have been easier to put those ideals into practice because inheritance was becoming a less important determinant of children's life-chances in families of all classes. In short, commercialization made generosity possible. Changing ideals may have made men want to be more generous.

Subsistence-Plus Settings and Patriarchal Households

On the whole, the colonial pattern of inheritance supports the revisionist position on women's dependency. Consider once again inheritance by daughters. To briefly recap, the majority of colonial daughters did inherit ownership of some land, primarily because in most cases there was too little personal property to provide even modest inheritances. But both upland and Wethersfield daughters were over three times more likely than their brothers to inherit no land at all, and most who did inherit got very small shares (see Tables 4.1 and 4.2). We have already concluded that colonial inheritance practices did reinforce the formation of patriarchal households. After all, sons—both the husbands and the would-be husbands among them—inherited much more real property than their sisters, the wives and would-be wives of the new generation.

Moreover, when holders transferred their property, they almost always gave their sons a free hand in relation to members of the sons' own immediate families. In contrast, when holders gave unencumbered fee-simple interests to their daughters (or, through intestacy, allowed the courts to do so), they ratified or acquiesced to the common law rules that sharply curtailed the proprietary capacities of married women. Holders attempted neither to enlarge their daughters' powers nor to provide additional protection for those powers married women did retain. Thus daughters who married brought comparatively little real property into their households, and they found themselves with restricted abilities to control that property, while sons who married benefited from full control over their own inheritance and from their managerial powers over their wives' inherited realty.

If a woman did not inherit land from her blood kin, she was certainly unlikely to come into ownership of land from her husband. So long as the life-chances of children depended on productive property, wives (and husbands) did not normally become their spouses' main heirs. Holders were also likely to cut corners on their wives' maintenance needs. Both law and practice combined, on the whole, to curb sharply women's control over land.

But there is another aspect of the revisionist position that needs supplementing. The life-estate was the ubiquitous method for providing for the widow's maintenance while guaranteeing the preservation of property for heirs. The life-estate indicates that although the position of wives may have been one of profound subordination when it came to control over resources, it was not one of amorphous dependence, at least not once their husbands died. Within the limitations established by the general reluctance to make widows owners of land, life estates created considerable autonomy for widows. As E. P. Thompson writes of the analogous custom of "freebench" attached to many forms of English copyhold tenure, such estates "did allow for a considerable feminine [agrarian] presence."[32] Though lacking heritable rights and allied powers of alienation and devise, the widow who had a life-estate could lease her land or use it as a lever to obtain labor from kin or neighbors.

Others do not rate the life-estate so highly. They argue that the capital sum or annuity had advantages over the conventional dower inter-

---

[32] "The Grid of Inheritance: A Comment," in *Family and Inheritance: Rural Society in Western Europe, 1200-1800*, ed. Jack Goody, Joan Thirsk, and E. P. Thompson (Cambridge, Eng.: Cambridge University Press, 1976), p. 349.

est. Alexander Keyssar argues that under American (as compared with English) conditions it was hard to rent land or find labor—comparatively hard, that is, to squeeze returns out of the life-estate. Furthermore, he assumes that when adult sons (or other kinsmen) inherited land encumbered with dower rights, widows were the passive recipients of the benefits of the sons' active management of the land. They were dependents. He and others argue that the capital sum or cash annuity represented greater freedom. The widow could at least dispose of the money as she saw fit.[33]

For middling and small holders who depended primarily on land, however, the lump sum or annuity derived from a cash principal was not a real alternative. Such sums or annuities would have required the sale of significant amounts of land, thereby jeopardizing the position of heirs. The other solution, an annuity in cash or in specified goods supplied by an heir, typically a son or the holder's brother, was a form of dependence. It is not known whether widows who held life-estates (and who were not incapacitated by old age) actually managed their land, or whether they became passive recipients of goods or income from land managed by others. But we should not assume passivity. The widow's life-estate was one widespread form of significant, formal proprietary capacity for women. In some jurisdictions its possession apparently even conferred local voting rights.[34] Moreover, if the property was rented, the widow was the lessor; if neighbors worked it, she "contracted" for their labor; and if her children worked it, this was surely the result of a not altogether one-sided dependency.

Perhaps it is no surprise that even subsistence-plus communities sheltered this persistent, well-defined proprietary capacity for widowed women. The death of husbands brought an end to patriarchal households. Women once widowed were less likely to find themselves dependent than at any other time. In the realm of control over resources, the life-estate marked the extent, as well as the limits, of their autonomy.

Commercialization and the Decline of Patriarchal Households

In 1827 the state assembly decided to locate Connecticut's state prison in Wethersfield; the town had already long had a workhouse ("asy-

---

[33] Alexander Keyssar, "Widowhood in Eighteenth-Century Massachusetts: A Problem in the History of the Family," *Perspectives in American History* 8 (1974): 83-119; Salmon, " 'Life, Liberty, and Dower'," pp. 85-106; Salmon, "Equality or Submersion?" pp. 92-113.

[34] Wilson, "Illusion of Change," pp. 417-19.

lums" for the poor).[35] Both symbolized the forces eroding the foundations of patriarchal households. State and national politics were gradually overshadowing the town meeting and the local politics so suited to reinforcing the authority of household heads. In addition, the household lost more and more of its disciplining, educational, and welfare functions to specialized institutions—institutions that were increasingly likely to be subject to the direct authority of state rather than local officials.

The late eighteenth and early nineteenth centuries have aptly been called, from the perspective of womanhood, "patriarchy in disarray."[36] At least the phrase is apt so long as we remember that the processes leading to the collapse of patriarchal households did not work evenly within the North. There is consensus among feminist scholars and family historians that the early nineteenth century was a period critical for the development of new cultural ideals about womanhood and the household division of labor.[37] Indeed, these ideological developments are linked directly to commercialization. The decline of household production for local consumption and the emergence of greater occupational specialization and centralized work places—in sum, the increased commercialization of the New England economy—were partly responsible.

The spatial segregation of the spheres of consumption, socialization, and production encouraged a sharpened distinction between public and domestic spheres of activity. Women's work had always been closely associated with the household—its interior spaces and immediate environment—and late colonial churches had taken an increasingly positive view of feminine spirituality and morality. But the hearth, nursery, and congregation became more distinctively feminine places in the nineteenth century. Although new ideals still circumscribed women's scope of action, they at least defined a sphere of comparatively autonomous action for women and a specialized defense of the "integrity and dignity" of womanhood and "women's work." Not only were women viewed as distinctively responsible for consumption and nurture, they were responsible for the moral education of children and husbands: an influence that radiated out to have its civilizing effect

[35] Adams and Stiles, *Ancient Wethersfield*, 1: 629-30.

[36] Ryan, *Womanhood in America*, p. 41.

[37] Cott, *Bonds of Womanhood*; Carl N. Degler, *At Odds: Women and the Family in America from the Revolution to the Present* (Oxford: Oxford University Press, 1981); Norton, *Liberty's Daughters*; Linda Kerber, *Women of the Republic: Intellect and Ideology in Revolutionary America* (Chapel Hill: University of North Carolina Press, 1980); Ryan, *Cradle*; Daniel Scott Smith, "Parental Power and Marriage Patterns: An Analysis of Historical Trends in Hingham, Massachusetts," *Journal of Marriage and the Family* 35 (August 1973): 419-28.

in the public domain of politics and commerce. Thus the new ideals no longer stressed the mediating function of the household head. Instead, women, through their distinctive moral functions, became the new mediators. Their moral influence gave them a public role, albeit an indirect one, in the new nation.[38]

Fully developed, this new ideology would defeminize the sphere of production. The public realm had always been associated with masculine authority and activity. As the world outside began to include the new centralized work places and mass political parties, these also became "his." The ideology, combined with new economic conditions, then, provided a new basis for legitimating women's lack of control over productive resources. But in the 1820s, especially in rural areas, the processes separating production from the household were not yet fully developed. And so in rural areas close to cities, women tended the garden crops that provided food for urban populations and cash for urban hinterlands, while young women from other areas of the countryside became the first adult recruits into the new textile mills. By the same token, the ideology that defeminized the sphere of production was not yet fully developed either.

In sum, in those areas where markets had penetrated, commercialization undermined the material foundations for patriarchally organized households and encouraged cultural ideals that valued domestic activities highly. But women were not yet shut out from the increasingly distinct world of market-oriented and specialized enterprise. If we view the early nineteenth century as a period of patriarchy "in disarray," then the data here on inheritance and women make sense. A main thrust of this study has been to show that intensive market gardening and greater local opportunities for nonlanded employment appeared to remove the constraints imposed by the older tension between unity and provision. Productive property was no longer used to set up directly some members of the next generation. It provided instead a head start in life or a dividend for all children. One suspects that the loosened tension between unity and provision and the new, more positive evaluation of women's domestic authority reinforced one another. Daughters inherited ownership of more land and widows got more generous shares of family property for their maintenance as a consequence of both.

These developments with respect to property have potentially contradictory implications for the status of women within households. Widows and daughters in commercialized family-farm areas may have had more land and other property, but the property they had played a

---

[38] Cott, *Bonds of Womanhood*, pp. 199-200.

less important role in determining the economic standing of their marital households or in structuring relations between parents and children. They had more, but it meant less.

Yet despite the more limited role of inherited property in the family economy, their larger relative shares may have given women more leverage with their husbands. Newly emerging ideals granted women increasing autonomy within those spheres culturally defined as theirs. Women's increased share of inherited property may have contributed to this enhanced power in practice, despite the fact that the material foundations for the allocation of power within households were shifting from the terrain of inherited property to that of acquired property and wages.

CHAPTER EIGHT

FAMILIES, CREDITORS, AND NEIGHBORS: ESTATE ADMINISTRATION

Inheritance addresses those aspects of family organization structured by rights in property. When the pattern of heirship is narrow, as it was among the holders in this study, analysis of inheritance focuses almost exclusively on near-kin. But the death of a property owner had an immediate impact on a larger, more complex network of relations. Surviving members of the holder's household not only had to establish new ties of authority among themselves and with other kin, but they had to modify connections with creditors and neighbors.

The court-related activities surrounding the deaths of property holders highlight this process. The probate courts closely supervised the daily management of estates during probate, the care of young children and their newly inherited property, and the payment of debts. These, together with the family disputes that occasionally arose, tell us a good deal about the public regulation of family relations, the boundaries between household and village, and networks among neighbors. We shall find that the courts reinforced the cognate structure of kinship and that, beyond the terrain of inheritance proper, the boundaries between household and village, kin and neighbors were fluid.

Finally, even when it is beyond question that inherited property is a crucial determinant of individuals' life-chances, inheritance can play no such role among propertyless or nearly propertyless families. Inheritance cannot directly speak to family authority relations or management of resources among the poorest. But by examining the impact of debt on these estates one can address the issue of family fate relative to "outsiders."

INDEBTEDNESS AND LANDLESSNESS

Probate courts allocated the property of estate holders among all competing claimants. The regulation of the claims of "outsiders" compared to those of heirs paralleled in importance the supervision of intrafamilial claims. In particular, the probate courts stabilized and regulated personal credit networks. A rough indication of the importance of this aspect of the court's work is that in 1821 thirteen of the forty-five sections of Title 32, a compilation of all statutes governing succession and estate administration, concerned the handling of debts.

Connecticut offered little protection of family claims relative to those of creditors. With the exception of spouses' rights to dower and curtesy, creditor claims were superior to those of would-be heirs. Even in the case of widows, protections were weak. Widows did have claim to small amounts of personal property unreachable by estate holders' creditors. But the need for "widow's necessaries" only indicates that the claims of creditors could be devastating to family property. The dower right was more substantial. All claims to an estate holder's real property, those of creditors and heirs alike, were subject to the encumbrance of the widow's dower.[1] Still, in Connecticut even this curb on the claims of outsiders was limited since it applied only to property held at death rather than to all land held during marriage.

Statutory distinctions between realty and other property designed to protect family land were also weak in Connecticut. For example, although all requests to sell land to cover decedents' debts had to be ratified by the legislature in the colonial era, such requests were routinely granted. In this population there was not a single exception. The petitioning process was no longer a means for balancing credit-worthiness as against family claims. Instead, it simply gave the assembly, as well as the probate courts, a routine role in supervising the orderly distribution of assets to nonheirs. After the Revolution all that remained of the distinction between real and movable property in the sphere of indebtedness was the basic rule that debts were first to be paid from movables.

The statutory provisions concerning creditors were in place by the early eighteenth century, and they were to be affirmed, subject to refinement rather than wholesale reform, in later codes. This early legislation represented the full program inherent in widespread socage tenure. By confirming and codifying the ability of landowners to use their property to establish their credit-worthiness, legislators ratified the autonomy of owner-producers. But, of course, to affirm the liberties of freeholders was to amplify the private power of the family head relative to other family members and to crystallize the legal requisites for land markets.[2]

---

[1] This is not to say that there were no changes in the apportionment of the dower interest. Marylynn Salmon and Morton J. Horwitz find that the courts, in balancing the widow's rights with those of heirs and, especially, creditors, increasingly favored apportionment designed to promote circulation and development of land; see Salmon, " 'Life, Liberty, and Dower': The Legal Status of Women after the American Revolution," in *Women, War and Revolution*, ed. Carol R. Berkin and Clara M. Lovett (New York: Holmes & Meier, 1980), pp. 92-96; Horwitz, *The Transformation of American Law* (Cambridge, Mass.: Harvard University Press, 1977), pp. 56-58.

[2] Bernard Bailyn, *The Origins of American Politics* (New York: Vintage Books, 1970),

Later, some would seize upon the land-tenure and succession statutes as the very embodiment of laissez-faire principles. So, for example, the compilers of the 1821 code congratulated their ancestors for restricting the dower to an interest in estate held at death:

> The common law gives the wife one third of the real estate, of which the husband was seised during the coverture. *But as such a lien may often be a restraint upon that free transfer of property, which the interest of the community requires*, it was a valuable improvement of the law to confine the dower . . . to lands of which the husband died possessed.[3]

Governor Wolcott, speaking before the General Assembly in 1823, could refer to Connecticut's law of succession not only as a victory for the "independence and republican equality of the people" against the "useless and burdensome encumbrances" of "hereditary ranks, privileges and orders," but as "consistent with the security of those unequal accumulations which are produced by the ever-varying activity and enterprise of individuals." In particular, not only the egalitarian law of distribution, but the "rendering of lands liable for the payment of debts" had contributed to the double triumph, "augmentation of wealth, by promoting the circulation of all property, and at the same time, . . . just and natural equalizations."[4]

Governor Wolcott supplies a buoyant justification of the difference between entrepreneurial acumen and the dynastic policies of landed grandees, the one consistent with republican virtue, the other not. Since there were, in his territory, only the ghosts of aristocratic grandees to vanquish, perhaps there was something disingenuous in his failure to acknowledge the argument that there was a conflict between the egalitarian elements of the agrarian republican program and unfettered circulation and accumulation.[5]

The law clearly viewed the death of a property holder as a key mo-

---

pp. 20-23; George L. Haskins, "The Legal Heritage of Plymouth Colony," in *American Law and the Constitutional Order: Historical Perspectives*, ed. Lawrence M. Friedman and Harry N. Scheiber (Cambridge, Mass.: Harvard University Press, 1978), p. 43; Michael Bruce Levy, "Liberalism and Inherited Wealth" (Ph.D. dissertation, Rutgers, The State University of New Jersey, 1979), pp. 26, 30.

[3] *Public Statutes 1821*, p. 180 (emphasis added).

[4] Speech, May 1823, "Reports, Resignations, and Miscellaneous," box 3, General Assembly Papers, 1823, "Connecticut Archives," RG 1, The Connecticut State Library, Hartford.

[5] On unimplemented elements of radical republican ideology bearing on inheritance, see Stanley N. Katz, "Republicanism and the Law of Inheritance in the American Revolutionary Era," *Michigan Law Review* 76 (November 1977): 1-29, and Michael Bruce Levy, "Liberalism and Inherited Wealth."

ment in the settling of accounts between estate holders and their creditors.[6] In this study, I cannot explore the probable differences in the structure of personal credit networks in subsistence-plus and commercial agriculture communities, but I can analyze the extent to which both landlessness and the priority of creditor claims affected these estates and the heirs to them.[7]

A substantial minority of male estate holders were landless or insolvent at their deaths.[8] Excluding those who transferred land to heirs during their lifetimes, this minority ranged between 11 and 27 percent of all male holders (Table 8.1, column 4). In the colonial era, upland heirs were deprived of land more often than in Wethersfield, but the differences were not large. In the 1820s about a quarter of all men in each area had no land to pass to heirs (column 4). The pattern of inter-area variation remains the same, but the proportion of estates in which all heirs were excluded from land was smaller when only fathers are considered (column 8).

These are the families in which the burden of preexisting landlessness or indebtedness deprived men of the ability to designate even one potential heir as successor to family land. Among fathers dying in the 1750s, this burden affected only those whose children were all minors. In the mid-eighteenth century, then, landlessness and indebtedness threatened family continuity only in the early phase of the family's developmental cycle. This pattern continued in the upland. Landless upland fathers were all under fifty years old when they died—considerably younger than their landed counterparts. Moreover, all of their children were minors, with the exception of one early nineteenth-cen-

---

[6] Debts receivable were simply treated as assets to be passed on to heirs. There appeared to be pressure to settle up only when these potential assets had to be realized in order to pay off creditors.

[7] In New England subsistence-plus towns, credit networks were probably symmetrical. See Michael Merrill, "Cash is Good to Eat: Self-Sufficiency and Exchange in the Rural Economy of the United States," *Radical Historian's Review* (Winter 1977): 42-46. Also see Charles S. Grant, *Democracy in the Connecticut Frontier Town of Kent* (New York: Columbia University Press, 1961), pp. 66-82; James Henretta, "Families and Farms: 'Mentalité' in Pre-Industrial America," *William and Mary Quarterly*, 3rd ser., 35 (January 1978): 14-16. Commercial agriculture towns are associated with asymmetric credit networks and a permanent money-lending class. Christopher Clark, "Household Economy, Market Exchange, and the Rise of Capitalism in the Connecticut Valley, 1800-1860," *Journal of Social History* 13 (Winter 1979): 176; Henretta, "Families and Farms," p. 16.

[8] The analysis is limited to male holders since so few females owned land at death or transferred land to potential heirs during their lifetimes. Their inclusion would exaggerate the impact of poverty on heirs. Sixty-two percent of the thirty-four female holders were landless or insolvent at death (having never passed land to heirs during their lifetimes).

TABLE 8.1

LANDLESSNESS AND INDEBTEDNESS AMONG MALE ESTATE HOLDERS

	All Male Holders				Male Holders with Children			
	Estates (N)	Usable (N)	At Least One Heir Gets Land (%)	Insolvent or Landless at Death* (%)	Estates (N)	Usable (N)	At Least One Heir Gets Land (%)	Insolvent or Landless At Death* (%)
	(1)	(2)	(3)	(4)	(5)	(6)	(7)	(8)
1750s								
Wethersfield	31	30	83	17	25	24	87	13
Upland	21	20	75	25	20	19	79	21
1770s								
Wethersfield	28	28	89	11	26	26	92	8
Upland	20	20	80	20	18	18	83	17
1820s								
Wethersfield	29	27	74	26	17	16	81	19
Upland	23	22	73	27	20	19	79	21

* Excludes those who passed land to potential heirs during their lifetimes.

tury daughter. In contrast, there was much more variability in the ages of landless Wethersfield men. Although they were also younger than their landed counterparts, the difference was not as great as in the upland, and many were over fifty when they died.[9] Moreover, after the 1750s, half the children of these landless men were adults when their fathers died.[10] Survival of the head of household past the early stages of child raising no longer continued to ensure that Wethersfield families would retain their hold on land.

Others have found that landlessness and poverty were primarily the lot of the young (or the very old) in subsistence-plus settings. For example, over half of the landless men who paid taxes in Chebacco, Massachusetts, in 1771 were under thirty years old (only 26 percent of all taxpayers were so young). Moreover, over three quarters of Cheb-

[9] In the 1750s the four upland men whose children were entirely shut out were on average sixteen years younger when they died than were fathers who had at least one child inheriting land. In the 1820s such fathers (four men) were almost nineteen years younger on average than "landed" fathers. In Wethersfield such men were only nine years younger than landed fathers in both the 1750s and the 1820s (three men at each time).

[10] The inter-area differences are not due to any overall differences in the proportions of probates who had minor children in the two areas. In the 1750s about 35 percent of probates who died in both areas had only minor children. The figures dipped to 19 percent in Wethersfield and 26 percent in the upland in the 1770s. By the 1820s the figures were 16 percent and 17 percent in Wethersfield and the upland, respectively. See Appendix B, Table B.3.

bacco men paying taxes in 1771 had, or would come to have, farms that provided a comfortable subsistence.[11] Preferential partibility made sense in such settings. When holders persisted in giving most sons at least a foothold on land, they were not irrationally putting a premium on setting up new households at the expense of continuity. Holders could reasonably expect that so long as householders survived the early, vulnerable years they would maintain or attain the status of independent producers.

Still, the data on landlessness serve to remind one that holders chose preferential partibility despite the existence of a minority who had no options. When they divided their holdings, they did so aware that such practices left new households vulnerable to indebtedness. They risked dispersion of family land to outsiders in the event that a crisis should hit, especially when new heirs were still young. It is plausible that the less egalitarian elements of preferential partibility—the short shrift to daughters, the cutting of corners on the portions of some sons, the distinctive treatment of the home lot—manifested these men's recognition of the risks and their attempts to protect against them.

According to others, in commercial agriculture towns poverty or dependence on wages was becoming the lifelong status of increasing numbers of men. Landlessness among older probates is consistent with this. So is the profile of Wethersfield probates in the 1820s: almost 30 percent of probated fathers died possessing neither shops nor even twenty acres of land (having never passed such goods to children).[12] For such men, of course, preferential partibility would have been pointless. There was no unitary productive enterprise to preserve. But the more general collapse of "favored heir plus burdens" strategies suggests that most holders no longer used family property to stave off such futures for their own children.

FAMILY SUPERVISORS

Administrators, executors, and guardians had special, legally backed authority to manage estates and household affairs, to regulate relations

---

[11] Christopher M. Jedrey, *The World of John Cleaveland: Family And Community in Eighteenth-Century New England* (New York: Norton, 1979), pp. 63-65. Also see Jackson Turner Main, "The Distribution of Property in Colonial Connecticut," in *The Human Dimensions of Nation-Making: Essays on Colonial and Revolutionary America*, ed. James Kirby Martin (Madison: State Historical Society of Wisconsin, 1976), pp. 54-104; J. Main, *Connecticut Society in the Era of the American Revolution*, Connecticut Bicentennial Series, no. 31 (Hartford: The American Revolution Bicentennial Commission of Connecticut, 1977).

[12] See Appendix B, Table B.7.

between heirs and creditors, and to coordinate the activities of appraisers, distributors, bondsmen, and others. Appointments to these supervisory positions shed light on orientations toward spouses, lineal kin,
and others. But they do so from a slightly different vantage point than
do decisions about heirship. Because they were at the center of the
flurry of the practical activities that surrounded the deaths of holders,
these appointments provide illuminating glimpses of the texture of
daily relations among immediate family members, other kin, and
neighbors.

Administrators and Executors

Administrators and executors acted as mediators among heirs (they
themselves could also be heirs), creditors, and the courts during the hiatus between the opening of probate and the distribution of estates.
They were legally responsible for ensuring that inventories and accounts of debts were rendered accurately and on time and for calling
the court's attention to a potential situation of insolvency. Basically,
administrators and executors had to account for all discrepancies between assets in the estate at death and the distributable estate.

These positions were not mere formalities. Administrators and executors stood in the shoes of the holders with regard to debts that holders had contracted before their deaths. During the sometimes considerable length of time between the opening and closing of probate,[13]
these executors and administrators also acted as auditors of daily family obligations, as well as mediators between family members and outsiders. They kept track of inventoried, perishable goods consumed by
the family, of the price of the labor of family members and the care of
children, and of all debts contracted in the daily course of maintaining
the family during the hiatus. Since the courts were generous in allowing
such expenses, the hiatus worked to the advantage of members of the
decedents' households as against preexisting creditor claims and non-
resident heirs.[14]

---

[13] In the 1750s, 30 percent of Wethersfield estates and 28 percent of upland estates
took more than five years to close, while between 37 and 44 percent of the estates took
less than three years to close. By the 1820s no more than 10 percent of the estates took
more than five years to close in either area, and 67 percent of Wethersfield and 74 percent
of the upland estates closed in less than three years. The drop in long gaps in the 1820s
may have been related to greater efficiency in closing out estates of heavily indebted decedents, a likely indication that concern for liquidity or marketability of assets had risen
among court officials. See Horwitz, *Transformation of American Law*, pp. 56-58, for
analysis of such concerns among probate court officials in other American settings.

[14] Late eighteenth-century court decisions put tighter restrictions on such generosity in

Testators could name whom they pleased as executors, but legislation guided the probate courts' appointment of administrators. In the case of intestate estates, legislation throughout the period stipulated that the widow or next-of-kin or both were to be invited first. If they refused or were incapable, the court could appoint whom it saw fit.[15] Thus the court had a great deal of discretion, as the phrase "Widow, or Next of Kin . . . or both" indicates.

As we shall see, unrelated men appeared quite frequently. Occasionally, near relations suggested substitutes when they themselves were called.[16] In other cases, non-kin entered the picture through default of kin. The order to take up letters of administration when someone other than the closest relative brought the estate to the court's attention, or when the nearest kin refused, was a blanket invitation to all kin to appear. "Neglect of Appearance" led to the appointment of non-kin. No coterie of "professional" administrators arose however. Administrators were almost always local men, not residents of the town in which the court was located, and there was no pattern of repeated appointments.[17]

By naming widows first, the legislature, in the case of administrators, displays a nonpatrilineal approach to the distribution of authority and comes down on the side of family interests over those of outsiders.[18] Court action, testators' choices, and a high rate of acceptance combined to give widows a significant presence as administrators in practice. There was an early and persistent inter-area difference in the pro-

---

the case of insolvent estates; see Zephaniah Swift, *A System of Laws of the State of Connecticut*, 2 vols. (Windham, Conn., 1795-96), 1: 438.

[15] *Acts & Laws 1750*, p. 51; *Public Statutes 1821*, p. 201. The procedure for appointing administrators when executors refused or abused their trust was similar, although not identical.

[16] As did the widow, father, and "Breathern" of Joel Loomis of Bolton. In their petition to the court they stated that they "Desist . . . Do all refuse Taking of Administration on the Estate" and asked that the judge appoint a man who was apparently a nonrelation and only a small creditor to the estate. Joel Loomis, petition, February 28, 1774, and administrative bond, March 3, 1774, folio 3432, Hartford Probate District, Estate Papers.

[17] Unrelated administrators were also always men. Although not analyzed here, local men serving as assessors, distributors, and commissioners may have formed a coterie. Unlike administrators, they received a fee for their work. My impression from handling the data was that names in these positions did repeat. The probate court represents a point of intersection between purely local and provincial administration, ordinarily handling routine, predictable traffic, not special cases irresolvable locally. It is, therefore, a potentially interesting site for examining how officials appointed by the General Assembly, virtually without a staff, attempted to maintain effective jurisdiction. They apparently not only relied on balanced and opposed interests to bring trouble spots to the court's attention, but brought into play local hierarchies to select men who could be relied upon to avoid trouble.

[18] But thoughtlessly fails to cover women's estates.

portion of widows who were administrators and executors. Widows were always a substantially stronger presence in Wethersfield. Seventy percent of them became administrators or executors in the 1750s, while only 39 percent of their upland counterparts did so. They were less likely to become administrators and executors just before the Revolution, but the inter-area differences remained large. In the 1770s, two thirds of the Wethersfield widows became executors or administrators, while only one quarter of the upland widows did. Finally, over 80 percent of the Wethersfield widows functioned in a supervisory capacity in the 1820s, while only 41 percent of the upland widows did so. The figures, in this respect, alter little, and the general pattern not at all, when only executors are examined. Both court appointed and holder-designated supervisors were always more likely to be widows in Wethersfield than in the upland. By this criterion, Wethersfield widows always had more authority than their upland counterparts.

There was, however, a split approach to the appointment of women. Although widows made strong showings, other women were virtually shut out: only eleven appeared as administrators and executors. With the striking exception of widows, the family's semipublic face—its members' several functions as "magistrates"—was male. Of course, distributors, appraisers, and commissioners were always men. All told, public authority, even petty public authority, as structured in a plethora of local offices and judicial appointments, was male. Again, widows were the exception.

Disregarding replacements for administrators and executors who resigned after they were appointed or took up their trusts, the 186 estates produced 254 first positions.[19] Table 8.2 shows the distribution of kin and others to these positions. In the presence of sons, administrators and executors were selected from within the immediate family in the great majority of upland and Wethersfield estates (Table 8.2, column 2). The widow-son pair was always the most popular in Wethersfield when both widows and sons were present (the modal category of first appointments [not shown]). In similarly structured upland families, the favored strategy was to select a son or son pair. In Wethersfield, then, widows shared authority with male heirs. In the upland, they were bypassed in favor of male heirs. When an extension beyond the nuclear family did occur, male blood relations were no more likely to appear than other kin or neighbors in either area (Table 8.2, columns 3-5).

When spouses were present, but there were no sons, Wethersfield still retained the "nucleated" pattern.[20] The spouse alone was chosen as ad-

---

[19] Illness and moving were the most frequently cited reasons for resignation.

[20] Recall that only three women had living husbands when their estates were probated. Thus "spouse" in these data is virtually synonomous with "widow."

TABLE 8.2

Administrators and Executors, by Family Structure

		Sons Present, Admin.-Exec. Include:					No Sons, Spouse Present			
	(N)	Member(s) Nuclear Fam. Only (%)	Other Male Blood (%)	Other Kin (%)	Non-Kin Only (%)	(N)	Spouse Only (%)	Other Male Blood (%)	Other Kin (%)	Non-Kin Only (%)
	(1)	(2)	(3)	(4)	(5)	(6)	(7)	(8)	(9)	(10)
1750s										
Wethersfield	20	80	5	5	10	10	70	10	10	10
Upland	10	80	10	10	0	10	10	40	20	30
1770s										
Wethersfield	21	95	5	0	0	8	63	0	0	37
Upland	15	67	7	13	13	3	33	67	0	0
1820s										
Wethersfield	15	73	13	7	7	10	100	0	0	0
Upland	16	75	0	19	6	8	25	37	13	25

ministrator or executor in no fewer than 63 percent of such Wethersfield families. By 1820 there were no extensions beyond the conjugal bond in such families; spouses alone were always chosen (Table 8.2, column 7). In sharp contrast, extensions beyond the immediate family occurred in the great majority of such upland cases in each time period. Some widows participated, but they most often shared authority with someone beyond the nuclear family. A male was brought in to supervise in these cases. Once again, when extensions did occur, paternally related men were no more likely to be selected than others (columns 8-10). Finally, when there were no spouses or sons—thirty-nine cases—no particular preference emerged. Male relatives, in-laws, and unrelated persons were all used (not shown).

Two aspects of these data stand out. First, although women, apart from widows, were bypassed, a patrilineal approach was not the dominant model for allocating the authority inherent in these positions. Even when extensions beyond the immediate family did occur, paternal uncles, brothers, and nephews did not dominate. In this respect, the appointments reinforced the cognate pattern of kin recognition found in the allocation of property, except that unrelated townsmen frequently functioned as supervisors.

Second, in Wethersfield there were fewer extensions beyond immediate families overall. This was related to a greater willingness to use widows, either in partnership with sons or alone, to see families through the period between the deaths of holders and the distributions of estates. Although Wethersfield holders were no more likely than uplanders to make wives their main heirs until at least the early nine-teenth century (and then only if there were no children), it does seem that Wethersfield widows always had greater control over the day-to-day functioning of their households. It is hard to say whether the ele-vation of the widow's position stemmed from a greater social distance from extended kin or whether a different orientation toward marriage resulted in less need to rely on kin and neighbors when male family heads died. In either case, Wethersfield households were, in this partic-ular respect, always more domestic, less permeable in their boundaries than upland households.[21]

Guardians

A core function of guardianship was, of course, to preserve and ac-count for the use of a minor's inherited property. But in the period con-sidered here, guardianship overlapped the jurisdiction of parents and masters over a child's person. In fact, in the colonial era, the statutes concerning guardianship were more preoccupied with "governing" children than with protecting their property. They mentioned only fa-therless and masterless children when directing the probate courts in mandatory procedures for selecting guardians. By 1821 the legislature firmly distinguished between jurisdiction over property and over per-sons. The probate courts could ask all masters of children who had in-herited estates and all fathers of children who had inherited estates not descending from the father's line to show cause why a guardian was un-necessary. The statute noted that when the court appointed a guardian who was neither the master nor father, the guardian's jurisdiction ex-tended to property only.[22] The implication is that a guardian of the fa-therless and masterless child had jurisdiction over the child's person. This conclusion is almost required by that portion of the statute on Masters and Servants that equates the roles of guardian and father

---

[21] But see Daniel Scott Smith, who found a declining appointment of widows as *sole* executors in eighteenth-century Hingham, Massachusetts. He argues from this that women were increasingly seen as less trustworthy managers of property. Also, Lawrence Friedman found that the combination of widow and another executor was very unpop-ular in mid- and late nineteenth-century New Jersey. See Smith, "Inheritance and the Po-sition and Orientation of Colonial Women," pp. 6, 10, 11, 13, as cited in Joan Hoff Wil-son, "The Illusion of Change: Women and the American Revolution," in *The American Revolution: Explorations in the History of American Radicalism*, ed. Alfred F. Young (DeKalb: Northern Illinois University Press, 1976), p. 417; Friedman, "Patterns of Tes-tation in the Nineteenth Century: A Study of Essex County Wills," *American Journal of Legal History* 8 (1964): 52-54.

[22] *Acts & Laws 1750*, p. 85; *Acts & Laws 1796*, p. 227; *Public Statutes 1821*, pp. 262-63.

when naming those who had authority to bind out children, "that the fathers and guardians of minors may bind them."[23]

Since the guardian did have jurisdiction over the person of the fatherless and unapprenticed child, he or she had the same general obligation to educate and employ the child as did a parent or master.[24] The way in which "government" over children by parent, guardian, and master blended can best be illustrated by a dispute case (two arose over guardianships). When Joshua Tilden of Coventry died in 1755, he had two daughters and a son, all minors. Six years later, his widow, now remarried, complained to the court that their guardian, David Lee, had abused and neglected his authority. Since the court appointed a new guardian, one can assume that it found at least some of her complaints justified. In a summons to David Lee the court noted that the charges against him were not only that the children's estates were "indangered," but that Joshua, now almost fourteen, was "wrongfully Treated": he had not been taught to read or write, or kept in suitable clothing for attending "Divine Service on the Sabbath," and was now bound-out to a person in Massachusetts Bay who was not suitable for his "Instruction."[25] The list of charges, even if these were boilerplate complaints—or, perhaps, especially if they were—indicates the broad scope of the guardian's responsibilities. Lee had the same duties of education and care as did parents. Consequently, he had the same authority to bind-out children.

Who did become guardians in this population of families? Although sixty-eight holders had minors when they died, guardians were appointed in only forty-seven families. It is likely that apprenticeship ar-

---

[23] *Public Statutes 1821*, p. 318.

[24] All masters and parents were to teach (or cause to be taught) "all such children as are under their Care and Government, . . . to Read the *English* tongue well; and to Know the Laws against Capital Offenders: And if unable to do so Much, then at least to Learn Some Short Orthodox Catechism without Book." In that large gap between universal literacy and ability to recite a catechism, one can hear the stern statement of the ideal give way to an exasperated acknowledgment of reality. See *Acts & Laws 1751*, p. 20. But no such qualifications modified the general stricture that parents and masters were to "imploy, and bring up their Children, and Apprentices in Some honest and lawful Calling, Labour, or Imployment, profitable for themselves, and the Colony." The only doubt left by this portion of the code is whether "profitable for themselves" refers to those governing or those governed. See *Acts & Laws 1750*, p. 21. In 1821 the statute was substantially the same, except that no qualification was attached to the requirement to raise literate children, and the duty of instruction in arithmetic was added—no doubt a vote of confidence in the more well-elaborated school system. See *Public Statutes 1821*, p. 107. Also see the much expanded statute on "Masters and Servants," *Public Statutes 1821*, pp. 318-21.

[25] Joshua Tilden, summons, April 28, 1761, Coventry, folio 3742, Windham Probate District, Estate Papers.

rangements had already been made in the remaining families, since all children were over ten years old by the time probate closed in most of them (sixteen out of twenty-two); it is possible, of course, that the courts failed to appoint guardians even for fatherless and masterless children.[26]

Very few guardians were appointed after the 1750s, when holders died youngest, but the data are sufficient to make some general points. Mothers were the most frequent, although by no means the universal, choice. When guardians were appointed, about one half of the mothers became guardians to their own children. Judging from the few cases available for study, Wethersfield families were somewhat more domestic than upland families in this respect also—although, again, not by any means unanimously so.[27] There was no tendency for patrilineal kin to dominate. Both widows and unrelated townsmen outnumbered children's paternal uncles, grandfathers, and other male kin in each area. All told, nineteen of the fifty-four first guardians appointed were widows, another nineteen were scattered in a variety of kin categories, and the remaining sixteen were unrelated.

Thus, when the special problems attendant upon jurisdiction over minors were not left to widows or remarried mothers and their new husbands (the most frequent single solution), they were most often handled by neighbors whose role was similar to a widely available model for governing children, that of service or apprenticeship. This adds to the evidence that patrilineal orientations were not the rule even in the colonial era. But a privatized, domestic orientation toward family life did not hold sway either, although some aspects of Wethersfield practices foreshadowed one. When a mother could claim that her own children were "orphans," and when there was no distinctive institutionalized relationship to cover the situation of the parentless child (that is, no adoption, no creation of fictive families for the purpose of nurturing and heirship), one is in the midst of an institutional and cultural world that neither regarded its children as the possession of a "line" nor had as yet resolutely singled out the conjugal family as the optimal or sacred sphere for the care of children. Between the family

[26] Stephen B. Presser writes that first apprenticeship usually fell between seven and fourteen years of age in the late eighteenth and early nineteenth centuries; see "The Historical Background of the American Law of Adoption," *Journal of Family Law* 11 (1971-72): 472. John Demos puts the range at six to eight years old for seventeenth-century Plymouth; see *A Little Commonwealth: Family Life in Plymouth Colony* (Oxford: Oxford University Press, 1971), p. 140.

[27] In the 1750s, 58 percent and 33 percent of widows (connected with estates in which guardians were appointed) in Wethersfield and the upland, respectively, became guardians; in the 1770s, 60 percent and 50 percent, respectively; in the 1820s, 50 percent and 40 percent respectively.

headed by the conjugal pair and the house of correction were interposed a series of well-codified relations involving extended kin and neighbors that could fulfill functions broadly parallel to those of parent-headed families.

FAMILY DISPUTES, FAMILY DEBTS

Conflicts among heirs rarely led to court intervention. If they arose at all, resentment or confusion about testators' wishes, or disjunctions between common-law definitions of heirship and felt equities among family members were resolved informally. Eleven scattered disputes did come before the courts, but only three cases involved core inheritance issues. The other eight cases concerned complaints and disputes about the handling of the estate during probate.

In six cases, administrators or executors were accused of stealing by other family members. For example, in one case arising from a Wethersfield estate probated in the 1770s, the widow of the holder's son charged that her brother-in-law (and then sole administrator) had inflated the indebtedness of his father's estate. She argued that if a true account were rendered, it would not require the recently authorized sale of about a third of the estate's gross landed holdings, and that, therefore, the order to sell ought to be stayed until the account was reviewed.[28] She added, "if your honors permits s^d Hosea to sell s^d Lands twill be almost the ruin of her Orphan Children."[29] This last plea, even if heartfelt, was a fillip. She was not asking the courts to vary the normal procedure for debt payments because of special hardship (in the 186 cases analyzed no such thing ever occurred), but merely to review the legitimacy of the debts.

In fact, her real complaint was that her brother-in-law had used his powers as administrator to inflate his inheritance share. Over half the administrative account in question consisted of Hosea's own notes against his father, the more typical payment to himself for chores around the farm during probate (e.g., for threshing his sister's corn), and one item, "Debt to Hosea Harris for four years and Ten months Labour & Sarvis at farming & show making after I was of Age & Before I was Married." By their father's will the two sons were to receive an equal share of the paternal land. If Hosea were able to justify these debts, his total share in his father's estate at death would have become

[28] The General Assembly granted the stay. Unfortunately, the probate documents do not record the Superior Court's determination in the matter of the account, nor did I find it in the latter court's records or files.

[29] Petitions, Estates of Deceased Persons, vol. 9, doc. nos. 207 a-b, 209 a-b, Connecticut Archives, The Connecticut State Library, Hartford.

about one and one-half times the value of that going to his deceased brother's heirs.[30] No doubt Hosea felt that he had earned the increment in virtue of special services to his father not shared by his brother or his brother's heirs. It is not surprising that Hosea's requested self-payments led to a complaint, since they constituted the largest single claim (proportionate to total debts) by an administrator or executor on his or her own behalf. But many administrators and executors were able to accumulate several pounds from shillings due for such items as "three Days work getting of wood" or "harvesting the wheat."[31]

In other cases, the administrators, executors, or their sureties initiated the complaint. They could have dual motives. If they or their children were heirs, they may have wished to retain the largest possible net estate for distribution, but they also had to explain any discrepancies between recorded outlays and net estate at the time of distribution. For example, when Josiah Welles died in 1754, leaving behind two infant sons and his wife, Anna, he and his family apparently still lived with his father and two brothers.[32] Fully ten years later, just before the Wethersfield estate was distributed, Anna, who was administrator, submitted a petition through her second husband, Ezekiel Fosdick, stating that they had a "vehement Suspicion" that Josiah's father and two brothers were withholding inventoried movables. Indeed, the father and brothers admitted as much. In response to questioning about Josiah's horse, his father testified that he had bought the horse for his son and that "my Son paid the greater part thereof in Earthen ware, and my Son used S[d] Horse During his life time and also I kept the horse after my Sons Decease and converted him to my own use untill the s[d] horse died." In answer to a series of specific questions about fourteen separate items of clothing and four empty barrels, the two brothers gave the same answer: "Converted to . . . my own use."[33]

The records do not indicate whether the brothers and father were fined for their misdeeds, and it does not appear that Fosdick sued for recovery of the items of clothing (naturally enough). But the testimony balanced the books, allowing the distributors of the estate to note that "the Reason why a Horse" was not distributed was that "Mr. John

[30] Thomas Harris, administrative accounts, one signed May 16, 1774, one exhibited May 7, 1776, Wethersfield, folio 2590, Hartford Probate District, Estate Papers.

[31] Thomas Kingsbery, account, n.d., Coventry, folio 2308 (1754), Windham Probate District, Estate Papers.

[32] He had only five acres of local land inventoried and no house. On such evidence alone, boarding or renting are also possibilities, but see the testimony cited in the text.

[33] Josiah Welles, clerk's note, November 6, 1764, Wethersfield, folio 5835, Hartford Probate District, Estate Papers.

Welles rec^d the Same & Converted him to his own Use and now not in Being."[34]

The dispute may also have arisen in part because paternal kin did not take primary responsibility for the children's care as they grew older. Indeed, shortly after the distribution of Josiah's estate, one of his sons chose his mother's new husband, Fosdick, as his guardian, and the other chose an unrelated man. We have already noted that paternal relations were not particularly favored as guardians. Yet it may have been this very fact that gave rise to tension when it came to paternal property. If paternal kin did not control children, especially when there was a remarriage, was it reasonable that they should give up control over property originally belonging to one of theirs as well? The Welles case illustrates the issue in a simple, folksy way. It must have seemed reasonable to all concerned, especially if Josiah Welles and his family had lived under his father's roof, that his grown brothers should wear his clothes and his father should use the horse he had gotten for his son. It is of at least symbolic importance that the dispute only surfaced ten years after Josiah Welles's death, once Anna had remarried, and as the boys grew up, away from their father's kin.

One is struck by what seems an extreme sensitivity concerning the "balance of payments" among family members and the unselfconscious ease with which mutual services and obligations could be given a money price. This was as true of administrative accounts in routine cases as it was in the rare disputed case. Brothers could state the price of threshing their sister's corn or sons the price of chasing after their father's cows, and mothers could calculate the price of caring for infant children.[35] Appraisers and witnesses not only could calculate the average annual revenue from a widow's dower, they could also measure the revenues against her weekly expenses, and the costs to her son for her

[34] Josiah Welles, estate distribution, exhibited November 21, 1764, folio 5835, Hartford Probate District, Estate Papers. The statute dealing with concealment of goods was less concerned with penalties for such concealment than with establishing procedures to ensure that such concealment would be discovered. See *Acts & Laws 1750*, p. 51, and *Public Statutes 1821*, p. 203. The aim almost certainly had less to do with protecting heirs' interests than it did with protecting creditors' claims. In one case involving an insolvent estate, an administrator sued his brother for recovery of $410 worth of inventoried goods. The brother was jailed. See Abel Deming, Wethersfield 1820, Hartford Probate District, Estate Papers.

[35] For example, in Union a mother was allowed 15 pounds lawful money for three years' care of her infant son; see Ebenezer Lamb, folio 2344, Windham Probate District, Estate Papers; Windham Probate Court Record Books, summary of administrator's account, June 6, 1758, vol. 3S, p. 3. In Wethersfield in 1774 nearly 8 pounds lawful money was allowed for nineteen months' care of a young child; see Timothy Hurlbutt, administrator's account, October 14, 1774, folio 3023, Hartford Probate District, Estate Papers.

care as she aged and grew ill.[36] As any reader who has been involved in probate knows, the extent of such calculations is inflated by the nature of the occasion.

But the occasion does not account for all. We should keep two points in mind. First, inheritance practices themselves involved comparable calculations: think only of retirement contracts detailing cords of wood to be delivered, of the felt need to specify that minor or unmarried children had legally enforceable use-rights in particular parts of their parents' homes, or of the zealous distributors who could map out heirs' proportional rights in haylofts, barnyards, cellars, and wells down to the necessary rights of entry and exit. Second, family relations were, for certain purposes, structured in a manner parallel to relations between neighbors. They did not constitute a firmly differentiated, hence distinctively ordered, private sphere. Thus the daily balances among family members found in these accounts have exactly the same structure as the accounts kept of transactions between neighbors. Similarly, when an administrator and son put a price on services rendered to his father, and a father specified that a favored son was to receive his inheritance only if that son did not render such an account, the calculations were like those arising from the contractual relation between master and apprentice.

It is tempting to conclude that such precision indicates a collapse in the normative consensus governing relations among family members. One of the best-known discussions of such breakdowns occurs in Michael Anderson's *Family Structure in Nineteenth Century Lancashire*. What appears to present sensibilities to be a highly developed ability to pinpoint and to calculate the price of family obligations is not, in itself, on Anderson's argument, the symptom of such breakdowns. Rather, the collapse of normative consensus is accompanied by what he calls "calculativeness": an outlook that weighs current benefits from family relationships against opportunities foregone and available elsewhere.[37] The issue is whether the balance of family claims and obligations is a fairly stable ordering of entitlements, or whether the balance shifts with conscious reference to short-run changes in conditions external to the domestic economy.

It is a mistake, then, to take "calculating" itself as an indication of such "calculativeness." For, in villages in which daily exchanges of goods and services are structured by a dense credit network, calculation is carried into the family setting. It is a concrete manifestation of

[36] James Moor, certificate, August 23, 1788, Union, folio 1499, Stafford Probate District, Estate Papers.

[37] Michael Anderson, *Family Structure in Nineteenth-Century Lancashire* (Cambridge, Eng.: Cambridge University Press, 1971), pp. 86-94, 99, 110, 135, 164.

the abstraction that the family was not yet shorn of its productive, schooling, and welfare functions. Precisely because the family was the seat of such activities, its relations were not governed by purely private or tacit norms and sentiments.

Indeed, the assumption that stability in family relations requires that actions mesh as a result of unspoken, culturally embedded accords is probably present-minded. The care with which these relations were defined, and the extent to which public authority shaped them, indicate how little an interpretation visualizing a clear line between the realm of the personal, regulated by diffuse understandings and social sanctions, and the realm of the public, governed by legal rules, suits these communities. Given the complex tasks facing household members both in regulating internal relations and relations with neighbors, it would be astonishing if this regulation took place only through tacit understanding and balancing of claims and duties. In this world, the death of a property holder was an event that called for especially detailed and explicit reaffirmations of such understandings and balances.

Finally, although this is not a facet of community life pursued here, it is likely that calculations that ordered family relations in a pattern analogous to relations between neighbors should have declined first in the more commercialized agriculture communities of the early nineteenth century. To follow the logic of Nancy Cott, Mary Ryan, and others, to the extent that households became more specialized, progressively stripped of their productive and "welfare" roles, such calculations ought to have declined—yet another aspect of the separation of the domestic from the public sphere.[38]

CONCLUSION

Possession of a freehold was a source of pride to early Americans, but the independence it conferred brought risks. The evidence on landless and indebted estates serves as a reminder that the road to a secure "competence" was strewn with obstacles even in subsistence-plus settings. The careful specification of rights in land, the selection of a few favored heirs, and the burdens characteristic of extended cognate strategies were, in part, attempts to ensure that new households were not reduced to dependence by an insufficiency of land or by the encroachment of outsiders via the mechanism of debt.

The obverse of the narrow, orderly pattern of succession to direct

[38] Nancy F. Cott, *The Bonds of Womanhood: "Woman's Sphere" in New England, 1780-1835* (New Haven: Yale University Press, 1977); Mary P. Ryan, *Womanhood in America from Colonial Times to the Present*, 2nd ed. (New York: Franklin Watts-New Viewpoints, 1979).

control over land was the otherwise fluid boundary between the internal world of the household and the public world of the town. The use of unrelated men in the supervisory positions of administrator and guardian illustrates the interpenetration of tasks carried out by family members and neighbors. So does the binding-out of children and the sensitivity to the balance of even very small debts and credits both between family members and outsiders and among family members. So long as the household was responsible for the coordination of labor and the allocation of its product, obligations among household members were calculated in a manner similar to exchanges between neighbors. Moreover, since in most households family relations involved both production and socialization, nurture and education were not sharply distinguished from the training and disciplining of labor. Though the household composed of a nuclear family normally oversaw both, the similarly structured households of neighbors could easily be substitutes. Both the orderly pattern of succession to property and the fluidity of the boundary between the household and town had the same root. Families were independent producers as well as consumers and socializing agents, and they sought to maintain that status.

CONCLUSION

This study contains two separable arguments about inheritance in early America that had previously been presented simultaneously. The first is that there was nothing unique, in the sense of distinctively modern, about family property relations in the early American North. This is, of course, the anti-exceptionalism argument; at bottom it is a "debunking" thesis. The second is that the commercialization of rural life was accompanied by basic shifts in inheritance strategies. This is a positive argument that identifies some institutional factors associated with changes in family organization in the preindustrial countryside. I will separately assess these claims and the evidence for them.

I will end with a discussion of a subject only alluded to earlier: the importance of inheritance reform in republican ideology. Taking my lead from those who stress the importance of English Country party ideology during the Revolutionary era and beyond, I argue that the constraints republican ideology imposed on legislative experiments with property were not founded on individualist premises or on a laissez-faire image of market integration. I suggest that the ideological tensions inherent in the imagery of a republic of yeomen had social parallels in the property relations found in early American family-farm communities. Moreover, just as the exceptionalist position distorts the nature of these rural relations, a "Lockean" reading of the republican ideal obscures its ideological tensions.

AMERICAN EXCEPTIONALISM AND
FAMILY PROPERTY RELATIONS

The exceptionalists assert that conditions special to the American North fostered a comparatively homogeneous culture. These conditions promoted individualist and calculative mentalities, class mobility, political recruitment based on individual achievement, and, sharpened in the Revolution, a liberal as well as egalitarian political ideology. Farmers were petty capitalists sensitive to market incentives; when local material conditions were not favorable to money-making through agriculture, rural dwellers were quick to find other sources of cash income. Material abundance and the lure of the frontier eroded parental power, encouraging the early independence of children. Inward-looking nuclear households were the center of family life; relations with extended kin and neighbors were attenuated and explicitly instrumental. In short, America was born modern.[1]

In tones variously self-congratulatory and sorrowful, analysts have used the idea of an exceptional, distinctively modern origin to account for the muted nature of class politics—for political consensus and apathy, the absence of ideology, and the hegemony of liberal values. It has encouraged us to think of the development of democratic institutions and the spread of market relations as an evolutionary process, realizing potentials present at the foundation of American society.[2]

The anti-exceptionalist position asserts that analysts of contemporary American institutions would do better to seek an alternative model of development, because there was nothing in the special conditions of early settlement and growth to promote distinctively modern social relations and values. The specific version of the anti-exceptionalism position offered here is that there was nothing in the defining regional conditions themselves—widespread family-farm ownership and land abundance among them—to reduce radically the connection between family property and life-chances. As a result, they did not produce distinctive inheritance practices. The intraregional comparison and extended time period studied here were not needed to explore this claim. Intensive analysis of colonial inheritance practices would have been sufficient.

Patterns of inheritance in colonial Wethersfield and the upland offer strong support for the anti-exceptionalist claim in the area of family property relations. The evidence is clear: extended cognate practices dominated in two types of rural towns typical of colonial Connecticut. Preferential partibility, subordination of spouses' interests, the creation of overlapping rights, and the use of family property at marriage and retirement were variants of the "favored heir plus burdens" pattern of inheritance widely adopted by family-farm holders in western Europe.

Analysis of these practices also provides a picture of family life that contradicts "born modern" imagery. They were not egalitarian, share-and-share-alike practices that dispersed property among kin. Adults inheriting homesteads shared their use with parents and unmarried

---

[1] Louis Hartz, *The Liberal Tradition in America* (New York: Harvest-Harcourt Brace, 1955); Charles S. Grant, *Democracy in the Connecticut Frontier Town of Kent* (New York: Columbia University Press, 1961); James T. Lemon, *The Best Poor Man's Country: A Geographical Study of Early Southeastern Pennsylvania* (Baltimore: Johns Hopkins University Press, 1972).

[2] Hartz, *The Liberal Tradition*; Seymour Martin Lipset, *The First New Nation: The United States in Historical and Comparative Perspective* (Garden City, N.Y.: Doubleday-Anchor, 1967).

brothers and sisters. Favored heirs routinely assumed obligations to care for parents and to provide legacies for both single and married sisters; when their married siblings died prematurely, these obligations extended to nieces and nephews and widowed sisters-in-law. Such uses and obligations might involve members of extended households. More often they reinforced links between households as sons built second houses and barns on parental homesteads and diverted revenues from inherited property to the households of their married sisters and brothers-in-law. Though probate records and deeds do not yield systematic evidence on daily management of property, there are glimpses of co-heirs cooperatively working farms, brothers and brothers-in-law jointly running mills and tanneries. In short, inheritance practices reinforced extended family relations through the creation of overlapping rights.

Extended cognate practices also provided a material foundation for patriarchal households. In virtue of inherited property, men may have had obligations to their parents and siblings, but their control over inherited property was not limited by claims created on behalf of their own wives and children. Further, most productive property went to household heads. Spouses were excluded from ownership of land; title passed to children at or before the deaths of their fathers. Though partitioning was extensive, sons were heavily favored; daughters brought far less productive property to new households than did sons. Within households, then, rights to most productive property belonged to family heads.

In sum, extensive partitioning encouraged rough equality among new households, while overlapping rights linked household to household. At the same time, preferential partibility and truncated generational depth in the creation of claims to property reinforced the internal authority of household heads. This picture more closely resembles revisionist than exceptionalist imagery of eighteenth-century family life and rural social relations. Abundance of land, the absence of sharply bifurcated rural class relations, and a weakly centralized political administration did create a rural political economy giving enormous control over local conditions to families of producers. But the result was not fluid, unstable social relations conducive to individual mobility and a competitive ethos.

Rather, these regional conditions created stable rural communities organized by complex networks of exchange among propertied households. Basic equality of standing belonged to those who could secure their livelihoods without becoming the permanent dependents of other men. Women, children, the young and single, and the minority composed of propertyless and property-poor families were denied such equality. They were the dependents who, not only as wives and children, but as wards, apprentices, and servants, were subject to the authority of heads of households. In such circumstances the family emerged as a central organizing institution: geographic and social mobility were family-sponsored; the internal organization of the household was hierarchical; and strong ties linked the households of both extended kin and neighbors.[3]

There is, however, one aspect of revisionist imagery of family life that patterns of inheritance in Wethersfield and the upland do not support. Some hold that inheritance practices displayed lineal orientations toward property.[4] Preservation of property within a narrow line of successive generations of men was not encouraged by the practices studied here. Such imagery exaggerates the inequalities among heirs and misleadingly stresses accumulative policies. Intergenerational continuity and augmentation of family property may have been a hope, but—as evidenced by extensive partitioning and, especially, unwillingness to limit sons' rights of alienation—it was subordinate to efforts to set up as many new households as possible. One need not find that the orientation to family property was lineal in order to make the case that inherited property played an important role in family life. The use of property at marriage and retirement, the subordination of spouses' claims to those of blood relations, and the distinctive treatment of land and movables, among other characteristics of extended cognate practices, all attest to the significance of inheritance for household and community organization in late colonial Connecticut.

COMMERCIALIZATION AND INHERITANCE

The comparison of inheritance patterns in Wethersfield and the upland was designed to explore the claim that marked shifts in family property relations accompanied commercialization of rural communities. Motivating the comparison was the basic, perhaps common-sense idea that urbanization and industrialization were the culmination of a long process rooted in a dynamic agrarian political economy. The more imme-

[3] Variants on this revisionist view can be found in Michael Merrill, "Cash is Good to Eat: Self-Sufficiency and Exchange in the Rural Economy of the United States," *Radical Historian's Review* (Winter 1977): 42-66; Robert Mutch, "The Cutting Edge: Colonial America and the Debate about the Transition to Capitalism," *Theory and Society* 9 (November 1980): 847-63; James Henretta, "Families and Farms: 'Mentalité' in Pre-Industrial America," *William and Mary Quarterly*, 3rd ser., 35 (January 1978): 3-31.

[4] Henretta, "Families and Farms"; John Waters, "Patrimony, Succession, and Social Stability: Guilford, Connecticut, in the Eighteenth Century," *Perspectives in American History* 10 (1976): 131-60.

diate motivation was that establishing a relationship between commercialization and inheritance would indicate the economic settings
hospitable to different forms of family life. Thus it would help to specify the opposed imageries of family organization prevailing in early
American studies.

The divergence in inheritance patterns was striking in the 1820s.
Among Wethersfield probates, extended cognate practices simply collapsed. Only a few of the poorest did not treat their heirs evenhandedly;
land and personal property were treated interchangeably; property was
no longer routinely transmitted at the marriage of children or the retirement of parents; and very few holders created overlapping rights in
property. The position of the widow improved. In short, family property was dispersed in individual, discrete bundles according to share-
and-share alike principles.

Striking as this divergence was, it provides only tentative support for
the "commercialization" thesis. The major difficulty is that though the
towns were already distinctively organized and had different relations
to regional markets in the mid-eighteenth century, no difference in inheritance patterns emerged in the colonial period. I have argued that
the simplest interpretation of this pattern of parallel, then diverging
practices is that commercialization was not associated with fundamental shifts in management of family property until a relatively advanced
stage. It is a plausible argument. But precisely because inheritance practices were similar in the colonial period, the argument relies on a small
number of cases: the practices of Wethersfield holders in the early
1820s. The argument requires further studies of late eighteenth- and
early nineteenth-century commercialized areas in order to establish sol-
idly that there was a consistent, marked departure from the pattern of
extended cognate practices.

There is a more fundamental reason for treating as exploratory the
intraregional comparison as it bears on the commercialization argument. The comparison establishes a pattern of association between inheritance strategies and differences in rural economic organization; it
is only a starting point for analyzing the dynamics producing this association. The comparison explores, but cannot resolve, two issues.

First, the distinction between subsistence-plus and commercial agriculture as used here involves several important differences in the organization of the towns and their relation to regional and export markets.
In analyzing the differences in inheritance practices that did develop,
how much weight should be given, for example, to Wethersfield's relatively complex division of labor, and how much to its more intensive,
specialized agriculture? Specialization and reliance on cash income
ought to affect inheritance practices by creating new conditions for suc-

cessful farm management, chief among them being the requirement for greater flexibility in adjusting the mix between land and capital. In short, they establish standards for viability that discourage the use of overlapping rights since these limit successors' flexibility. Occupational specialization ought to affect inheritance practices by providing alternative sources of livelihood that reduce dependence on inherited property.

The evidence permits some assessment of the relative impact of these conditions on inheritance practices. If concern for viability of the family enterprise were at work, one would expect market-dependent holders to adopt "enterprise maintenance" strategies. As before, some heirs would be favored with productive property. But the pressure to grant them greater flexibility, coupled with the alternative sources of livelihood available to other potential heirs, would confine less-favored heirs to claims in residual property. There should be, then, unburdened favored heirs and an enduring, even sharpened, distinction between productive and other property.

Yet, judging from the available evidence, this was not what happened in Wethersfield. Rather, estates were dispersed at the deaths of holders in share-and-share-alike patterns of distribution. This suggests that it was not a concern for viability under new conditions that led to diminished use of overlapping rights. Rather, local sources of employment seemed to have the greater effect on practices. They appeared to result in a very foreshortened generational perspective on the use of productive property as a direct source for maintaining social standing. Productive property supported the parental generation; but it was not used directly to set up all or some members of the next generation. Like consumption property today, it was simply converted into a "head start" or "dividend" for heirs who had largely made (or would make) their own way.

The second causal issue is common to other inheritance studies. Are inheritance practices responses to changes in local rural organization? Or do family property-management strategies contribute to changes in the economic organization of towns and their relation to nonlocal markets? The usual position is that shifts in inheritance practices are both responses to and causes of changes in rural economic and social organization.

More specifically, inheritance transfers are often thought of as a "mediating" social practice. Changes in the larger environment—in the "grid" of inheritance—alter the conditions for successful resolution of the tension between unity and provision. To continue to achieve relatively constant goals, families respond by altering their inheritance practices. These altered practices result in changes in the local distribution of property, impose new constraints on managing property, and so forth.[5] In sum, flexible inheritance practices align family goals with changing environments, but in so doing they also contribute to changes in the environment.

I do not take issue with the general position that changes in rural economic life and inheritance practices are interactive, but aspects of inheritance patterns found here suggest that the usual formulation of this position needs modification. The pattern revealed in this study does not conform to the image of highly flexible practices. Inheritance practices were not sensitive to short-run changes in local conditions. Under the increased population pressure of the 1770s, for example, there were heightened inequalities among heirs, but these were modest. Inheritance practices were basically stable in both areas in the late colonial era, and appeared to remain so in the upland in the early nineteenth century.

This stability in practices suggests that the aims underlying them not only changed little, but involved very specific understandings of the role family property played in the lives of family members. Property had to provide for the maintenance of parents and minors; nonfavored heirs were entitled to claims on revenues; and there was a reluctance to cut sons off from family land. These aims and needs did not permit great scope for varying inheritance strategies. In view of the continuity in practices, I proposed that under different local conditions, similar practices—motivated by similar, well-elaborated goals—helped to institutionalize initial differences in local economic organization. In the longer run, commercialization did result in radical shifts in inheritance practices by profoundly altering understandings concerning the role of family property in the formation of new households.

Inheritance and Revolutionary-Era Ideology

"The Best of All Agrarian Laws"

Inheritance had a central place in Revolutionary-era ideology. Of his proposals for reform of Virginia's inheritance laws, Thomas Jefferson wrote, "I considered 4 of these bills . . . as forming a system by which every fibre would be eradicated of antient . . . or future aristocracy and

[5] Lutz Berkner and Franklin Mendels, "Inheritance Systems, Family Structure, and Demographic Patterns in Western Europe, 1700-1900," in *Historical Studies of Changing Fertility,* ed. Charles Tilly (Princeton, N.J.: Princeton University Press, 1978). This is, for example, the logic implicit in much of Philip Greven's analysis; see Philip J. Greven, Jr., *Four Generations: Population, Land, and Family in Colonial Andover, Massachusetts* (Ithaca, N.Y.: Cornell University Press, 1970).

a foundation laid for a government truly republican." Certainly there is no reason to doubt the depth of his conviction in calling Virginia's new partible intestacy statute "the best of all Agrarian laws."[6] He believed that only a comparatively egalitarian distribution of land could serve as the adequate social basis for a stable republican polity. To this extent, at least, he was a good Harringtonian.

The law of inheritance became, as Stanley Katz writes, a "focal point" for efforts to guarantee the proper social foundation of a stable republic.[7] One by one, almost all the new states abolished primogeniture and entail by the end of the eighteenth century.[8] In many cases, the statutory preambles stated the double argument for inheritance reform. It was an attack on "aristocratic" accumulations: "Whereas entails of estates tend only to raise the wealth and importance of particular families and individuals, giving them an unequal and undue influence in a republic. . . ." It was also a positive program: "Whereas it will tend to promote that equality of property which is of the spirit and principle of a genuine republic. . . ."[9] Stable republics require an egalitarian foundation; properly formulated, laws of inheritance could both demolish the basis of aristocratic preeminence and actively promote wide and equal distributions of property.

The attack on "feudal" privilege surrounding these reforms is usually seen as symbolic or an excess of ideological rhetoric. The reforms attacked the instruments of "dynastic" accumulations: primogeniture and entail. But, the standard argument continues, primogeniture did not prevail even among the large landholders of the South, and the common law had already weakened the usefulness of entails as a device for maintaining dynastic accumulations. More generally, there was no true aristocracy to undermine, no Old World hierarchy to dismantle.

To be sure, an American seigneurial reaction was unlikely.[10] But, although Jefferson (and others) occasionally spoke of an "antient" or "feudal" aristocracy, he probably had other foes in mind when claim-

---

[6] *The Autobiography of Thomas Jefferson, 1743-1790* (ed. P. Ford, 1914), pp. 77-78, quoted in Stanley N. Katz, "Republicanism and the Law of Inheritance in the American Revolutionary Era," *Michigan Law Review* 76 (November 1977): 15.

[7] Katz, "Republicanism and Inheritance," p. 14.

[8] Or, as in Connecticut, they eliminated the double portion for eldest sons and greatly transformed the legal effect of entail.

[9] *The Public Acts of the General Assembly of North Carolina*, chap. 22: 1 (ed. J. Iredell, R. X. Martin Rev., 1804), quoted in Katz, "Republicanism and Inheritance," pp. 14-15.

[10] But see Rowland Berthoff and John M. Murrin, "Feudalism, Communalism, and the Yeoman Freeholder: The American Revolution Considered As a Social Accident," in *Essays on the American Revolution*, ed. Stephen G. Kurtz and James H. Hutson (New York: Norton, 1973), pp. 256-88.

ing he was fighting a Virginia "patriciate." In all likelihood, he feared the emergence of a faction whose social preeminence and undue political influence rested on manipulation of credit and political patronage. What could not be tolerated were accumulations of property that turned some into politically overweening cliques and others into dependents incapable of exercising independent political judgment.[11]

No matter who the intended target was, anti-aristocratic ideology and the inheritance reforms it engendered were ideal formulations of the inheritance strategies already pursued by New England freeholders. Their inheritance practices were not aimed at intergenerational consolidation and accumulation of family property. Judging from the families studied here, rural dwellers in family-farm areas had no use for the devices associated with dynastic strategies: primogeniture, entail, life-estates (apart from dower rights), or prototrust arrangements. Thus holders had no use for devices that constrained heirs' powers of alienation and devise by dictating the order of future succession. In short, their practices were not patrilineal.

Instead, these holders used family property to form as many new households as possible. They limited partitioning only as far as was necessary to ensure that these new households would have enough productive property to provide an independent livelihood. The inheritance strategies of New England freeholders could have served as a real model for Revolutionary-era republican legislators. Although several distinct agricultural economies existed within the countryside of the new nation, the ideology motivating the inheritance reforms overtly singled out one for special praise: family farming based on the freehold.

"The Earth Belongs in Usufruct to the Living"

Inheritance reform claimed to do more than sweep away "feudal" vestiges; it promised equality. As a practical instrument for promoting a more even distribution of wealth, the new inheritance laws were, of course, extremely limited. They did not encroach on freedom of testation, let alone restrict powers of lifetime alienation. American men, if they chose, could still practice unigeniture and could still discriminate among would-be heirs. Despite attacks on the legitimacy of "aristocratic" accumulations in republics, the reforms did not prohibit the limited dynastic practices that supported great landed estates in eight-

---

[11] J.G.A. Pocock, *The Machiavellian Moment: Florentine Political Thought and the Atlantic Republican Tradition* (Princeton, N.J.: Princeton University Press, 1975), pp. 437-39, 467-69; Pocock, "The Machiavellian Moment Revisited: A Study in History and Ideology," *Journal of Modern History* 53 (March 1981): 62-64.

eenth- and nineteenth-century England.[12] In sum, reforms did not significantly alter the permissive character of the inheritance systems that regulated the practices of most property holders.

Indeed, as Stanley Katz points out, one need only contrast these reforms with those of the French Revolution to see how little the laws actually embodied any serious attempt to promote equality through inheritance reforms. The French intestacy reform was more uniform and thorough—forbidding any inequality arising from "qualities of age or of youth, [or] from sex distinctions." And, under Robespierre, the national legislature limited both lifetime and testamentary transfers among family members. Some of these limitations on freedom of testation survived in the Napoleonic Codes.[13]

Why did republicans fail to follow the logic of their egalitarian arguments further and advocate a more thoroughgoing reform of inheritance? A few did, Jefferson and Thomas Paine among them.[14] But their proposals did not find favor. Furthermore, most did not touch on the core issue: restraints on freedom of testation in the name of promoting greater equality among the living.

Some would say simply that even the more enthusiastic advocates of a republic of yeomen were too much in the grip of Lockean natural rights principles to consider seriously any encroachment on the proprietary powers of landholders. Even if one does assume that these principles were a critical influence on the mentality of American republicans,[15] there is a problem with this view. The natural-rights tradition has at least two strands. One emphasizes the status of private property

[12] English law had long made the entail an ineffective device for supporting dynastic practices since it could be easily "barred" or broken. Large holders adopted the strict settlement instead. For a detailed discussion see, for example, Eileen Spring, "The Strict Settlement of Land in Nineteenth-Century England," *American Journal of Legal History* 8 (1964): 209-23.

[13] Katz, "Republicanism and Inheritance," pp. 21-25.

[14] Paine proposed to reduce inequality through, among other means, a sharply progressive estate tax and redistribution of the revenues. In his private correspondence, Jefferson also toyed with the idea of an estate tax, although he is better known for his advocacy of free land distribution schemes. In a draft of a Virginia bill, Jefferson proposed that seventy-five acres of land should go to every freeborn Virginia man who married. Ibid., pp. 15, 17, 19-20. Note that this is just the amount economic historians say constituted a comfortable family farm. Also note that it is not "the yeoman standing alone," but yeoman *families* that constitute the backbone of Jefferson's agrarian republic.

[15] See the current battle over Jefferson's outlook: Garry Wills, *Inventing America: Jefferson's Declaration of Independence* (New York: Random House-Vintage, 1979); Joyce Appleby, "What is Still American in the Political Philosophy of Thomas Jefferson?" *William and Mary Quarterly*, 3rd ser., 39 (April 1982): 387-90; Ronald Hamowy, "Jefferson and the Scottish Enlightenment: A Critique of Garry Wills's *Inventing America: Jefferson's Declaration of Independence*," *William and Mary Quarterly*, 3rd ser., 36 (October 1979): 503-23.

as an inherent, prepolitical right. It derives from this right maximum powers to use and dispose of property; it defines the specific powers constituting ownership as "natural" and not legitimately subject to legislation. This, of course, is the nineteenth-century reading of Locke—Locke, the individualist and uncanny anticipator of classic liberalism.

But there is another strand. Stanley Katz persuasively argues that to the extent that French and American revolutionaries applied the natural-rights tradition to inheritance, they turned it against itself. They focused on the imagery of the earth as a "common stock," deriving from it the basic right to labor on it and to appropriate the fruits of that labor. In this vein, for example, came Jefferson's famous declaration "the earth belongs in usufruct to the living." Used in this way, the natural-rights tradition helped to justify proposals for estate taxation and curbs on powers to encumber property with debt. In short, it supported the legislative redefinition of specific powers over property, and put a premium on access to property. Under these circumstances the language of natural rights no longer constituted an effective argument against further egalitarian experiments in limiting freedom of testation. If republican reformers did not pursue these experiments, it was not due to ideological constraints imposed by natural-rights theories.[16]

But two other traditions of political discourse familiar to American Revolutionary-era leaders contained ideological tensions that did pose barriers to such experiments: "country" ideology and doctrines of political economy associated with the Scottish Enlightenment. There is, of course, a very lively debate about the dominance of classical republican ideology during the revolutionary and early national periods. But it does seem that all parties to the debate at least agree that republican ideology existed in tension with other discourses, chief among them Scottish Enlightenment thought.[17] Here I wish simply to indicate how tensions characteristic of these outlooks had parallels in the organization of property relations in American family-farm communities.

"He That Can Live upon His Own"[18]

Conceptions of political liberties originating in the English Civil War and at the heart of eighteenth century Anglo-American political culture

---

[16] Katz, "Republicanism and Inheritance."

[17] Joyce Appleby, "The Social Origins of American Revolutionary Ideology," *Journal of American History* 64 (March 1978): 937, 955-57; Pocock, "Machiavellian Moment Revisited," pp. 69-71; Robert E. Shalhope, "Republicanism and Early American Historiography," *William and Mary Quarterly*, 3rd ser., 39 (April 1982): 334-35, 345-46, 350.

[18] James Harrington, as cited in J.G.A. Pocock, ed., *The Political Works of James Harrington* (Cambridge, Eng.: Cambridge University Press, 1977), p. 834.

accorded special place to the freehold.[19] However, the freehold was not thought of, or not simply thought of, as an individual right. It was considered critical to preserving an inherently fragile "balanced" or "mixed" government. The freehold was both a necessary basis for a successful defense of liberties against absolutist monarchical pretensions and a chief manifestation of the independence of aristocratic and popular (or democratic) interests from the Crown. Thus it supported not only individual autonomy, but the independence and proper balance of constituent social groups. Moreover, the inspiration for the apotheosis of the freehold came not from an abstract justification of a prepolitical right, but from a conception of liberty that equated virtue, or the fulfillment of one's nature, with active participation in the properly constructed polity. The innovation of English republican, especially Harringtonian, thought was to link the balanced constitution and the fully constituted, civic personality particularly closely to a specific form of property: the freehold.[20]

The eighteenth-century English political opposition, the "Country party," contributed a particularly fond evocation of yeoman "virtue" and the property that sustained it. The yeoman was one who could "live upon his own." His independent "competence" made him impervious to the corrupting influence of those who sought to upset the delicate political balance. And, a "competence" meant a sufficient livelihood, not a surplus. The ideal freeman, the yeoman, was not tempted by enervating luxury, a vice inimical to the vigilance required to preserve liberty.

In the English context of commercial empire and a well-entrenched Whig regime so clearly operating on patronage, evocation of the virtues of yeoman tended to be nostalgic; the country opposition tended to locate the balanced commonwealth and its virtues in past time. But in the American context, republicans who began by rejecting the very idea of a hereditary aristocracy could return to pure Harringtonian premises. They located the true commonwealth, a republic founded on scrupulous regard for the sources of yeoman independence, in the present and future. They could assert, without feeling themselves in the midst of a period of degeneration, that in a republic yeomen were the natural guardians of political liberty.[21]

Thus the American revolutionaries worked within a political culture

[19] I rely heavily on Bernard Bailyn, *The Ideological Origins of the American Revolution* (Cambridge, Mass.: Harvard University Press, 1967); Bailyn, *The Origins of American Politics* (New York: Vintage Books, 1968); Pocock, *Machiavellian Moment*.

[20] Bailyn, *Origins of American Politics*, pp. 40-52; Pocock, *Machiavellian Moment*, pp. 383-88.

[21] Pocock, *Machiavellian Moment*, pp. 514-15.

that highly valued the freehold. In the hands of radical republicans it was also a deeply agrarian and, for its time, egalitarian outlook. Its conception of liberties easily lent itself to attacks on undue accumulations of property and the dynastic inheritance strategies that supported them. Because the American family farmer seemed the real counterpart of the ideal yeoman, the tradition also lent itself to attacks on the dependency inherent in tenancy and widespread dispossession from productive property. But reverence for the freehold discouraged advocacy of restrictions on the yeoman's control over the very property that constituted both his "competence" and the republic's best defense against tyrannical usurpations.

In sum, this deeply entrenched Anglo-American political tradition imposed ideological constraints on legislative experiments with property. It did not do so because it valued liberty over equality, but, in part, because the conception of yeoman independence and the freehold that sustained it embodied egalitarian and anti-statist impulses in uneasy tension. A moment's reflection on the communities studied here suggests that family property relations displayed some of the same tensions. As a result, they posed social limits on legislative experiments with property.

It is hard to imagine that American holders would have brooked curbs on their proprietary powers. Their property-management strategies all aimed to consolidate powers over property in heads of households. Indeed, this was, in part, the corollary of the fact that their practices were not dynastic. Although extended cognate practices enforced cooperation and obligations among siblings and between adult children and their parents, male heirs were left free with respect to their own children. Patterns of partitioning and sharp distinctions between real and personal property also favored sons. Legal limitations on married women's proprietary capacities—limitations that holders did nothing to circumvent—reinforced the subordination of women's direct claims to productive property. Thus power over property was consolidated in the hands of heads of households at the expense of the predefined claims of wives as well as of children. Limitations on freedom of testation remove one set of legal supports for patriarchal household authority. If even ancestors did not impose such restrictions on new heads of households, any state-imposed restrictions would have been anathema.

Moreover, inheritance strategies reinforced a rough parity among households. They aimed not at individual equality, but at equality among families. Success was achieved when children married and became members of households founded on independently held productive property. Certainly, any limitation on powers of disposition in fa-

vor of uniform equality among individual heirs would have conflicted
with the pattern of preferential partibility that prevailed in the colonial
period and the uplands. To ensure that family property would under-
write self-sustaining households for at least some heirs and their families, holders imposed what were, from the perspective of individual
heirs, inequalities.

More generally, limitations on the proprietary powers of heads of
households were inimical to a community system in which ownership
of productive property conferred a public status. The independent
householder was one who in virtue of his property was entitled to enter
into local political life and economic exchange as an equal with others
similarly placed. He also acted in this public sphere as the "virtual"
representative of members of his household. Thus independence was,
in its reference to relations outside the household, an egalitarian social
status. It was also founded upon a conception of "competence" that depended on consolidation of proprietary powers. Community life in
family-farm areas thus posed real-enough limits on attempts to redefine
ownership.

"Beneficial Circulations"

The anti-mercantilist principles of Adam Smith and other figures of the
Scottish Enlightenment formed a second influence on the mentality of
Revolutionary-era leaders. Many valued the circulation of property
among families highly. Yet, as recent reevaluations of Scottish Enlightenment ideas and their American reception suggest, it is a mistake to
read into enthusiasm for the circulation of property a vision of social
order founded on the actions of competitive, self-interested individuals.[22]

To the contrary, the social vision sustaining the image of "beneficial
circulations" could be markedly communitarian. The stable commonwealth is built on a myriad of small social groups formed by the naturally "strong ties of friendship, acquaintance, partnership, and neighborhood" and, above all, of family—the prototype of them all.[23]
Exchange itself links not selfish, competitive individuals but those social groups that cohere in virtue of an inherent moral faculty disposing
us to "benevolent" acts. Exchange is the external expression of our social, cooperative natures and a sign of our basic condition of interde-
pendence. The idea of a naturally cohering civil society probably entails

[22] The following discussion relies particularly heavily on Garry Wills, *Inventing America*, pp. 193-217, 229-39, 284-92.

[23] Adam Smith, *Moral Sentiments*, cited in Wills, *Inventing America*, p. 288.

a conception of liberty and personality at odds with the civic, activist idea of liberty inherent in classical republican thought,[24] but it is not yet the utilitarian or laissez-faire doctrine the nineteenth century would make of it. It was not sustained by individualist premises.

Certainly, though, the enthusiasm for exchange operated as another ideological constraint on tinkering with the already well-developed individual powers defining ownership. Indeed, even those republicans who leaned heavily on neo-Harringtonian thought imagined that trade could actually sustain the wide distribution of property required in a yeomen's commonwealth. They had a horror of devices that "froze" great accumulations of property within particular families, and they imagined that unhampered ownership coupled with trade would prevent any tendency for property to accumulate unduly within families. They were well aware that a commercial society could in principle create new forms of dependency devastating to virtue. But because America was, or would soon become, a vast territory, they assumed that commerce would not unduly affect the stabilizing function of land so necessary in republics.[25]

Committed simultaneously to the idea of a yeoman's competence and to the belief that exchange could only operate to guarantee it in an agrarian empire, republicans would have been hard pressed to imagine that further market development would operate to alter radically the farm family and its relationship to land.[26] The Revolutionary generation's language of "truck, barter, and exchange" contained a dual image of markets. It focused attention on national policy with respect to regional and export trade, but it also evoked the local exchanges that reinforced well-integrated "neighborhoods." They did not foresee that a national market system would utterly transform local exchange and with it the stability of the yeoman family freehold.

This duality and failure to anticipate was reinforced by the segmented, partial character of market institutions in 1776. Subsistence and commercial agriculture areas coexisted. Family property relations in both types of rural communities quite probably seemed the real counterpart of the yeoman ideal. It was also reasonable to suppose that

[24] Pocock, "Machiavellian Moment Revisited," pp. 67-69.

[25] Pocock, *Machiavellian Moment*, pp. 534-41.

[26] I do not wish to imply that such an understanding was in its context somehow anachronistic. Neither in its fundamental premises about trade nor in its hope that in a territorial empire virtue was compatible with commerce for the predictable future was it inappropriately backward-looking, even in the early nineteenth century. But see Rowland Berthoff, "Independence and Attachment, Virtue and Interest: From Republican Citizen to Free Enterpriser, 1787-1837," in *Uprooted Americans*, ed. Richard L. Bushman et al. (Boston: Little, Brown, 1979), pp. 97-124.

the powers inherent in ownership of a freehold and the process of exchange were its foundation. As we have seen, consolidation of powers of ownership and local exchange in the context of segmented markets were compatible with strong and extended property ties among family members. They were present in retirement arrangements, in the obligations imposed on favored heirs, and in the close connection between marriage and transfers of family property characteristic of extended cognate practices. It is likely that republican leaders, when they evoked the yeoman imagery, thought that their policies strengthened just such forms of cooperation among family members and between households.

Even the economy of 1820 was not yet fully commercialized. But, as in Wethersfield, for increasing numbers "beneficial circulations" meant dependence either on distant agricultural markets or on wages and salaries. For such households it also meant dependence on distant markets for consumption goods. These developments transformed the texture of family and community life. In Wethersfield, a collapse of ties founded on family property accompanied commercialization. After the colonial period there was a radical foreshortening of generational perspective. Family property was dispersed as a "head start" or "dividend"; it was no longer used to ensure the next generation's "independent competence."

Thus the commercialization of agriculture deprived the yeoman ideal of any real social foundation, though this was still an uneven and partial development. In subsistence-plus areas, yeomen families—not individuals "doing for themselves" but families founded on an "independent competence," exchanging the "fruits of their labor"—were at the center of rural social relations.

Uneven development of market institutions corresponded to structured, persistent diversity in rural family and community organization. Any adequate understanding of the new nation and its origins, whether of change in family life, rural social relations, or political ideology, must take continuing account of this diversity. To impose on it the more uniform rhythm of social relations emerging only with a fully integrated market system, or to impose the tone of later doctrines on the ideology motivating efforts to create a system of governance compatible with this diversity, is to promote a myth of a distinctively modern past. It is to foreshorten history.

APPENDIX A

THE PROBATE POPULATION AND
GROSS WEALTH: A CHECK

In his early work covering the period 1763-88, Jackson T. Main set up a framework of expectations based on evidence from probate and tax records concerning the wealth of "subsistence-plus" and "commercial" agriculture towns in the northern colonies: the former were poorer and their wealth was more evenly distributed than the latter.[1] His recent work on Connecticut is an exploration of similar issues (using more elaborate methods for extrapolating from probated to living populations). For the colonial period, it covers dates very close to those in this study.[2] Since he has reported his unadjusted figures on wealth distribution among probates, my population of estate holders can be compared with his. The comparison establishes that the inter-area differences in the wealth of the small sample of probates in this study are in line with data derived from very large samples of probates as well as with general expectations for subsistence-plus and commercial agriculture towns.

Main's data on mean and median total wealth, value of real property, and value of personal property for his sample of estates drawn from probate districts throughout the colony for 1750-53 are presented in Table A.1. His figures for the original Hartford County alone are also included, since this is the only data he provides for 1770-74.[3] For the purpose of this comparison I have used the same population as Main's (estates of adult males) and the same currency conversion factors.[4]

---

[1] Jackson Turner Main, *The Social Structure of Revolutionary America* (Princeton, N.J.: Princeton University Press, 1965).

[2] Jackson Turner Main, "The Distribution of Property in Colonial Connecticut," in the *Human Dimensions of Nation-Making: Essays on Colonial and Revolutionary America*, ed. James Kirby Martin (Madison: State Historical Society of Wisconsin, 1976).

[3] The average value of real property was lower in Hartford County than in the colony as a whole, in part because it contained none of the fertile coastal land along Connecticut's southern border, and the original boundaries of the county included a good deal of interior upland. See ibid., pp. 71-72. Because it contained the urban state capital, this county's average and median personal wealth was much closer to the colony as a whole. Ibid., p. 76.

[4] For J. Main's discussion of colonial currency and his conversion factors, see ibid., pp. 101-102. In the 1750s, inventories were expressed in two different types of currency—

TABLE A.1

GROSS WEALTH: VALUE OF THE PROBATED ESTATES OF ADULT MALES
(Adjusted to Country Pay as of 1700)

	Total Estate			Real Estate			Personal Estate		
	Mean	Median	N	Mean	Median	N	Mean	Median	N
1750s									
Hartford Cty., 1750-54[a]	—	—	—	220	120	355	120	84	357
All Conn., 1750-53[b]	445	280	1233	319	187	1233	134	92	1233
Wethersfield, 1753-55	434	297	26	369	221	28	113	108	27
Upland, 1753-55	324	284	19	228	231	19	97	79	19
1770s									
Hartford Cty., 1770-74[a]	—	—	—	190	90	247	163	100	247
Wethersfield, 1772-74	—	—	—	282	207	22	171	97	23
Upland, 1772-74	—	—	—	171	131	15	129	97	17

[a] Figures from Jackson Turner Main, "The Distribution of Property in Colonial Connecticut," in the *Human Dimensions of Nation-Making: Essays on Colonial and Revolutionary America*, ed. James Kirby Martin (Madison: State Historical Society of Wisconsin, 1976), pp. 82-84.
[b] Ibid., p. 68.

My data for 1753-55 show that the median *total* wealth of the probated population in each of the two areas was close to the median for all Connecticut. But the spread between the mean and the median was far lower for the probated population from the upland towns, so that the average total wealth of these estates was well below the colony's. In contrast, Wethersfield's average total wealth was close to the colony's average, and the gap between the mean and median was only slightly less than the colony's. In addition, Wethersfield's probated population's slightly lower average total wealth was due to its lower average personal wealth and the relatively even distribution of the latter (as indicated by the spread between the mean and the median). Concerning real property, the average and median values of the real estate held by

"old tenor" and "lawful money." In the 1770s all inventories used lawful money. Weighing the slightly differing figures proposed in J. Main, "The Distribution of Property"; Bruce C. Daniels, "Money-Value Definitions of Economic Classes in Colonial Connecticut, 1700-1776," *Histoire Sociale-Social History*, no. 8 (November 1974): 346-51; Lawrence Henry Gipson, *Connecticut Taxation, 1750-1775*, Tercentenary Series, no. 10 (New Haven: Yale University Press, 1933); Henry Bronson, "Historical Account of Connecticut Currency, Continental Money, and the Finances of the Revolution," *Papers of the New Haven Historical Society* 1 (1865): 1-192; and the scattered evidence found in the inventories and administrative accounts themselves, I elsewhere convert all values expressed in old tenor to lawful money by dividing by eight.

Wethersfield decedents were well above that of the colony's, just as one would expect of this rich farmland community.

In contrast, the average total wealth of the upland decedents was depressed relative to the colony's by the lower average value of both personal and real estate. The value of real estate was substantially lower than that of the colony, and, therefore, dramatically lower than the average value of real property in Wethersfield estates; it was about three fifths of Wethersfield's. The real property of the upland decedents was so evenly distributed, however, that the median figure for real property in the upland was actually higher than the colony's or Wethersfield's. Indeed, in the 1750s Wethersfield's probated decedents were wealthier and the distribution of wealth among them was more concentrated than among their counterparts from the upland towns, especially with respect to real property.

In the 1770s the mean and the median values of real property for the Wethersfield estates were much higher than either the county figures[5] or those of the subsistence-plus towns: the average value of its real estate was, as it had been in the 1750s, over one and one-half times as great as the average value of real estate held by upland decedents. In the latter towns, the mean value of real property was below that of the county. In one respect there was a certain convergence. The gap between the mean and median value of real property had risen in the upland towns, although it was not as large as that of the county, while the gap in Wethersfield remained comparatively stable. Wethersfield's probated decedents were, as they had been, wealthier than their upland counterparts, but the distribution of wealth among the latter was more concentrated than it was in the 1750s. The changes in the upland may merely represent fluctuations in the probated populations. Others have found, however, that concentration of wealth increased in the first several generations of a town's settlement.

Using a subsample of towns in Hartford County, Main also supplies mean figures for the total wealth of probate populations broken down by community type: "urban," "old farming towns," "newer farm towns," and "frontier towns."[6] The probate data for 1750-55 from my

---

[5] Finding that the price of meadow land had more than doubled between the 1750s and the 1770s, J. Main deflated the stated assessed value of real property in the 1770-74 sample by one half. It is not clear that one should conclude from the resulting comparison that the colonists had grown dramatically poorer. Main himself notes that the price of land rose more rapidly than the prices of various types of personal property and that this rise was a result of more land being brought under improvement. See J. Main, "The Distribution of Property," pp. 101-102. Land's higher price tag represented a real rise in value as well as inflation.

populations are very close to the appropriate means for his 1750-54 data: compare his figure for old farming towns—415 pounds—to Wethersfield's 434 pounds, and his figure for newer farming communities—339 pounds—to that of the upland towns' 324 pounds.

⁶ Ibid., p. 92, Table 16 (based on Hartford County estates to 1719). Means presented in his text are adjusted upward by 10 percent as suggested by Main to get appropriate means for 1750-54.

PROFILE OF THE PROBATE POPULATION

DIFFERENTIAL RATES OF PROBATE

Both the colonial census of 1774 and the federal census of 1820 report town populations by age. Assuming that the mortality rates for the white adult populations in the two areas were approximately the same, Table B.1 reveals that the upland towns produced proportionately fewer probated estates than did Wethersfield. There was some difference in the age structures of the two types of towns. In Wethersfield, the oldest, densest, and most slowly growing town, 53 percent of the white population was under twenty years old in 1774 (not shown). In the upland towns, 56 percent of the white population was under twenty (close to the colonywide figure of 57 percent). If one assumes that the population over twenty years old was younger in the upland than in Wethersfield and that age-specific mortality rates were the same, this would somewhat lower the inter-area difference in the proportion of probates to total adult deaths.

One cannot definitely identify the sources of the remaining difference in representation without a great deal more independent information on the wealth and demography of towns. If it is true that small holders were less likely to go through probate than large holders, then the upland towns' lower absolute levels of wealth might account for their low

TABLE B.1

ADULT WHITE POPULATION IN WETHERSFIELD AND THE UPLAND

	1774 Pop. 20 & Over[a]		1772-74 Estates		1820 Pop. 16 & Over[b]		1820-21 Estates	
	Male	Female	Male	Female	Male	Female	Male	Female
Wether	749	823	28	4	1,015	1,207	29	7
Upland	964	1,028	20	3	1,551	1,768	23	8

[a] Figures from *The Public Records of the Colony of Connecticut*, vol. 14, Appendix, Census of 1774 (Hartford: Lockwood & Brainard Co., 1887; reprint ed., New York: AMS Press, 1968), pp. 483-91.

[b] Figures from U.S. Bureau of the Census, 4th Census, *Population for the Year 1820 in the State of Connecticut*, vol. 1 (Hartford County), vol. 2 (Tolland County).

rates of probate.[1] However, the greater homogeneity of wealth and occupational structure in subsistence-plus towns may have offset any
tendency toward low rates of participation among those who were
poor by colonywide standards. Furthermore, one suspects that the
greater economic and political self-sufficiency of the subsistence-plus
towns was associated with lower rates of probate among all types of
holders.

SEX, MARITAL STATUS, AND FAMILY STRUCTURE

Women were a small minority of probated estate holders in both
areas, particularly in the 1770s (Table B.2, column 2). At no time were
there large differences between the two areas in the percentage of female holders. Little work has been done on estimating the degree of
women's underrepresentation among probates because it is usually assumed that very few women owned significant property.[2] This perspective on the potential pool of female probates is based on two further
assumptions. First, it is assumed, probably correctly, that the legal disabilities imposed on married women account for the fact that their estates did not undergo probate. In Connecticut, unless complicated provisions were made to circumvent the common-law rule, a married
woman had no rights in most forms of personal property. In addition,
married women were not expressly granted the capacity to make wills
until 1809, though court decisions had confirmed this capacity at an
earlier date.[3] The real property owned by a woman who did not survive
her husband descended automatically to her legal heirs (subject to the
widower's right to a life estate). Indeed, in this study only three of the
thirty-four women had husbands alive at their deaths.[4] Probated
women were single or widowed.

No such disabilities applied to single and widowed women. Although there is not a great deal of work on the percentage of women
dying single or widowed, there is agreement that as a rule women outlived men as often as not and that widow remarriage was not as fre-

[1] Bruce Daniels, "Money-Value Definitions of Economic Classes in Colonial Connecticut, 1700-1776," *Histoire Sociale-Social History*, no. 8 (November 1974): 347; Alice
Hanson Jones, "Wealth Estimates for the New England Colonies about 1770," *Journal
of Economic History* 32 (March 1972): 116-18; Daniel Scott Smith, "Underregistration
and Bias in Probate Records: An Analysis of Data from Eighteenth Century Hingham,
Massachusetts," *William and Mary Quarterly*, 3rd ser., 32 (January 1975):104.

[2] By one estimate only 10 percent of free white adult women held property in their own
right; see A. Jones, "New England Colonies," p. 100.

[3] Zephaniah Swift, *A System of the Laws of the State of Connecticut*, 2 vols. (Windham, Conn., 1795-96), 1: 325-36.

[4] One from the upland in the 1770s, one each from Wethersfield and the upland in the
1820s.

TABLE B.2

PROBATED ESTATE HOLDERS: SEX, MARITAL STATUS, AND CHILDREN

	Estates (N)	Female Holders (%)	Status Known (N)	Never Married (%)	All Estate Holders Married, No Children (%)	Married, Children (%)	Female Estate Holders Never Married (N)	Married, No Children (N)	Married, Children (N)
	(1)	(2)	(3)	(4)	(5)	(6)	(7)	(8)	(9)
1750s									
Wethersfield	39	21	38[a]	13	8	79	1	1	5
Upland	25	16	25	8	0	92	1	0	3
1770s									
Wethersfield	32	13	31[b]	0	10	90	0	1	2
Upland	23	13	22[a]	0	5	95	0	0	3
1820s									
Wethersfield	36	19	36	28	19	53	5	0	2
Upland	31	26	31	16	10	74	2	3	3

[a] In the one missing case, decedent is childless, marital status unknown.
[b] In the one missing case, marital status and presence of children is unknown.

quent as had been supposed until recently.[5] A second assumption—that it was exceptional for daughters to inherit real property—supports the view that so few of these single or widowed women were property holders (and thus that so few can be counted as members of a potential population of probates).[6] The findings presented in Chapter Four suggest that this assumption needs revision. If so, the processes that account for either women's propertylessness at death or their underrepresentation as probates, apart from the legal disabilities imposed on married women, remain largely unknown.

Table B.2 (column 4) also indicates that the percentage of all estate holders who never married increased substantially in the 1820s, particularly in Wethersfield. Insofar as this change is not simply the result of improvement in the representation of (single) women among probates (column 7), it is in rough accord with, though it exaggerates, demographic shifts characterizing the region and period, shifts that included lower nuptiality and increased age at first marriage. In the 1770s, however, there were no single probates among those whose marital status is known. This is clearly a probate bias since in 1774, 22 percent of upland and 31 percent of Wethersfield men over twenty years old were unmarried.[7]

One supposes, then, that the increased presence of the unmarried among probates in the 1820s is related to several factors: underlying demographic shifts, improved representation of women, and improvement in the representation of single men. One guesses that the last may, in part, reflect the greater care taken by probate courts to oversee the estates of heavily indebted decedents. As Chapter Eight shows, these were disproportionately found among younger and childless holders. Shifts in the representation of the never-married do at least move in the same direction in both areas. The lower proportions of probated singles in the upland of the 1820s compared with Wethersfield, however,

[5] Alexander Keyssar, "Widowhood in Eighteenth-Century Massachusetts: A Problem in the History of the Family," *Perspectives in American History* 8 (1974): 83-119; Robert V. Wells, "Women's Lives Transformed: Demographic and Family Patterns in America, 1600-1970," in *Women of America: A History*, ed. Carol Ruth Berkin and Mary Beth Norton (Boston: Houghton Mifflin, 1979), pp. 16-33.

In fact, although 68 percent of Wethersfield and 79 percent of upland men seventy years old or older were married in 1774, only 37 percent of Wethersfield and 54 percent of upland women of comparable age were married. Since rates of marriage among adult men and women under seventy were much closer in both areas, this strongly suggests that widowed women remarried infrequently. See *The Public Records of the Colony of Connecticut*, vol. 14, reprint ed., ed. Charles J. Hoadly (New York: AMS Press, 1968), Appendix, Census of 1774, pp. 483-91.

[6] See, for example, A. Jones, "New England Colonies," p. 100.

[7] The colonial census of 1774 is the only one that provides data on marital status.

exaggerates the underlying slight differences in proportions married in the two areas (assuming that the 1774 census data can serve as a guide to later population structures).

Primarily as a result of these changes in the presence of the never-married, estate holders dying with children capable of inheriting were the great majority of probates in the colonial period, but dropped to under 75 percent of probates in the upland and to just over 50 percent of the probates in Wethersfield in the 1820s (Table B.2, column 6). In the colonial period, women's status paralleled that of the probated population as a whole: most had children capable of inheriting. But in the 1820s, the greater presence of the childless in the whole population was due partly to the fact that the majority of probated women were childless in both areas (Table B.2, columns 7-9).

PROBATES WITH CHILDREN CAPABLE OF INHERITING

In each time period, the percentage of Wethersfield and upland estate holders who had no minor children when they died was very similar. It was lowest in both areas in the 1750s: 25 percent of Wethersfield and 32 percent of upland families had no minor children (Table B.3). In both areas, and at all times, the majority of those with children had one or more unmarried children. Except in the 1770s, over three quarters of the holders in each area had single children to provide for (Table B.4).

One can look at the same data from the perspective of potential heirs (Table B.5). Notice that children who died before their parents, leaving their own children to represent them, amounted to about 5 percent of all children capable of inheriting. Those who were minors when their

TABLE B.3

MINOR AND ADULT CHILDREN IN THE FAMILIES OF PROBATES

	Holders with Chldrn. (N)	Family Structure Known (N)	Only Minors (%)	Some Minors (%)	All Adult (%)
1750s					
Wethersfield	30	28	36	39	25
Upland	23	22	36	32	32
1770s					
Wethersfield	28	27	19	19	63
Upland	21	19	26	5	68
1820s					
Wethersfield	19	19	16	21	63
Upland	23	23	17	22	61

TABLE B.4

MARITAL STATUS OF CHILDREN IN THE FAMILIES OF PROBATES

	Holders with Children (N)	Family Structure Known (N)	Some or All Unmarried (%)	All Married (%)
1750s				
Wethersfield	30	26	88	12
Upland	23	22	77	23
1770s				
Wethersfield	28	26	69	31
Upland	21	17	59	41
1820s				
Wethersfield	19	18	78	22
Upland	23	21	76	24

parents died were a significant minority of children capable of inheriting, and in any given time period the upland and Wethersfield percentages were similar. In addition, a high percentage of chilsen were under thirty when their parents' estates began probate. As a result, the percentage of unmarried children was considerably higher than the percentage of minors, and it was close to the percentage of children under the age of thirty in each area and at all times.

In the colonial period, the profiles of upland and Wethersfield children were similar: in both areas there was a sharp decline in the percentage of minors and unmarried young adults to be provided for. In the 1820s the profile of potential heirs diverged somewhat. The Wethersfield children had a profile similar to that of children just prior to the Revolution, while the children of upland holders were younger and more often unmarried. Despite this, the percentages of parental holders who had unmarried heirs to provide for were the same in the 1820s (78 percent in Wethersfield; 76 percent in the upland towns).

THE PROBATE POPULATION: WEALTH

The comparison with Jackson Turner Main's data establishes that the inter-area differences in the structure of wealth among the probates studied here are consistent with data drawn from much larger populations of probates (Appendix A). But that comparison considered only the wealth of male holders in the colonial period.

Table B.6 is based on all holders in this study.[8] The table displays

---

[8] These data are not directly comparable to those in Appendix A because the currency conversion factors used are different and because the data on male populations are based on slightly different age groups.

TABLE B.5
Profile of Children Capable of Inheriting

	Sex			Minors			Marital Status		Age at Death of Holder	
	Total (N)	Sons (N)	Dtrs. (N)	Predeceased[a] (%)	Status Known (N)	Minors (%)	Status Known (N)	Never Marr. (%)	Age Known[b] (N)	Under 30 (%)
1750s										
Wethersfield	151	75	76	3	141	39.0	126	64.3	112	67.9
Upland	111	58	53	5	106	46.2	97	56.7	60	67.7
1770s										
Wethersfield	158	80	78	5	144	23.6	127	40.2	134	51.5
Upland	114	53	61	5	99	19.2	83	34.9	67	44.8
1820s										
Wethersfield	109	53	56	5	106	20.8	104	41.3	91	38.5
Upland	129	63	66	6	129	27.9	118	55.9	104	61.5

[a] Predeceased their parents but were capable of inheriting through representatives.
[b] Excludes those who predeceased their parents but were capable of inheriting through representatives.

TABLE B.6

GROSS VALUE OF PROBATED ESTATES AND THE PERCENTAGE OF TOTAL
WEALTH HELD BY THE WEALTHIEST QUARTILE

	All Estates				Estates of Males Only		
	Mean	Median	Top 25%	N	Mean	Median	N
1750s							
Wethersfield	365	247	61	34	409	267	27
Upland	287	268	47	22	319	281	19
1770s							
Wethersfield	582	406	68	27	650	457	24
Upland	441	345	62	17	468	350	16
1820s							
Wethersfield	3,999	980	82	32	4,825	1,404	25
Upland	1,281	819	56	28	1,578	1,501	21

Notes: Figures for 1750s and 1770s are in pounds (Connecticut lawful money);
for 1820s in dollars. N equals number of estates for which value is known.

mean and median total wealth held at death as well as the share of total
wealth held by the top 25 percent of these holders. The most striking
fact is that at all times Wethersfield estate holders' average wealth was
substantially higher than that of the upland, and in the 1820s it was
dramatically higher. But gross wealth was also more highly concentrated in Wethersfield: the differences in median wealth were less extreme and even reversed direction. In the colonial era there was some
convergence in this respect. Wethersfield's top quartile, for example,
held over 60 percent of the wealth in both colonial time periods. In the
upland towns the share held by the top quartile rose from under 50 percent to over 60 percent, and the difference between mean and median
wealth widened. But, in the 1820s Wethersfield's top estate holders
held 82 percent of the probated wealth while the shares held by the top
quartile of upland decedents (56 percent) remained stable.[9] Note that
when the minority of female estate holders is removed, average and median wealth rises, but the inter-area differences and time trends remain
basically similar.

The poorer estate holders deserve separate attention. When land
passed to potential heirs during the decedents' lifetimes is taken into account, landless probated male holders were a small minority. Although
only 19 percent of the estate holders were women, over half the thirty-
four estate holders who died landless and had not passed land to poten-

[9] In the 1820s, even when one eliminates the two wealthiest Wethersfield estate holders, Wethersfield's average wealth ($2,228) is still almost twice that of the upland area.

tial heirs were women. Only 10 percent of the men were landless (of men with children, only 7 percent).

In farm communities such as these, however, landlessness is a crude measure of the welfare of those who held the least wealth. If one owned no other significant form of productive property, one would have slipped into a condition of dependency well before the threshold of landlessness. Conversely, though he may also have owned only a house and a few acres, a skilled artisan owning his shop could maintain his status as an independent producer.

Table B.7 indicates those among the probated adult males who would have had to hire themselves out or rent land in order to live. It excludes those men who were known to have been unmarried, under thirty years old, and living with their parents. The inventories of the remaining men who died holding less than forty acres[10] (and had never

TABLE B.7

OWNERSHIP OF LAND AND OTHER PRODUCTIVE PROPERTY BY MALE PROBATES

	All Men				Men with Children		
		Own 40 Acres or More	Dependent			Own 40 Acres or More	Dependent	
	(N)	(%)	−40A (%)	−20A (%)	(N)	(%)	−40A (%)	−20A (%)
1750s								
Wethersfield	31	74	26	(19)	25	80	20	(12)
Upland	21	67	33	(14)	20	65	35	(15)
1770s								
Wethersfield	28	78	22	(14)	26	81	19	(12)
Upland	19	95	5	(5)	17	94	6	(6)
1820s								
Wethersfield	27	52	48	(44)	17	65	35	(29)
Upland	23	70	30	(17)	20	75	25	(10)

Note: Dependent men are those who are land-poor or landless and own no other significant productive property. Figures exclude young adults still dependent on their parents.

[10] New England historians use sixty to eighty acres as the range for a "comfortable" or "complete" working farm. See Clarence Danhof, *Change in Agriculture in the Northern United States, 1820-1870* (Cambridge, Mass.: Harvard University Press, 1969), pp. 136-38; Kenneth Lockridge, *A New England Town: The First Hundred Years. Dedham, Massachusetts, 1636-1736* (New York: Norton, 1970), p. 149n (relying on estimates by Charles Grant and James Lemon); Darret B. Rutman, "People in Process: The New Hampshire Towns of the Eighteenth Century," in *Family and Kin in American Urban Communities, 1780-1920*, ed. Tamara Hareven (New York: Franklin Watts-New Viewpoints, 1977), pp. 27-28. J. Main also writes that fifty acres was the minimal-subsistence

passed land to potential heirs in amounts that pushed their total holdings over forty acres) were examined for evidence of ownership of significant productive property apart from land, farming implements, and
livestock, such as shops and mills. If they did not own such productive
property, these smaller holders and landless men were classified as "dependent." Since information on age was incomplete, a few young men
still dependent on their parents may be present. Therefore, comparable
information for married men only is presented.

One might assume that a table constructed with these criteria might
illegitimately classify professionals as "dependent" men. Interestingly
enough, among professionals only one held under forty acres of land.
He was a judge from Willington who died in 1821 owning enough personal property to place him among the wealthiest, although he owned
no land or other productive property. He is not included in Table B.7.
The other professionals (the one doctor, the several ministers and merchants, etc.) all held over forty acres. All were also practicing farmers
even if, for some, farming could not be defined as a "primary occupation." This is consistent with the findings of others.[11] Although a
profession conferred authority and standing in its own right, in these
communities substantial land holdings normally accompanied such authority.

The artisan (either self-identified or judged to be an artisan from the
inventory's listing of tools and raw materials) who was land-poor and
who owned no shop is included in this table of men dependent on other
men. There is only a thin line between such a man and the artisan or
artisan-farmer who, though he was land-poor, is excluded from this
table because he owned a "shop" (often in back of the house and worth
very little). In the colonial period, there were only three of the former
type. All other colonial artisans and artisan-farmers (thirteen more)
owned their own shops or also owned substantial land.[12] In the 1820s

---

family farm in the colonial period, see *Connecticut Society in the Era of the American
Revolution*, Connecticut Bicentennial Series, no. 21 (Hartford: The American Revolu-
tion Bicentennial Commission of Connecticut, 1977), p. 58. James Lemon, *The Best Poor
Man's Country: A Geographical Study of Early Southeastern Pennsylvania* (Baltimore:
Johns Hopkins University Press, 1972), p. 91, gives a higher estimate.

[11] J. Main, *Connecticut Society*, pp. 39-42, 44-52. Throughout this study farmers are
identified independently of their landholdings at death so that the landless or land poor
who may have rented or had use-rights in land are not tautologically and mistakenly defined as nonfarmers. The presence of livestock and farming implements (for example,
plows but not hoes or rakes) was used to identify farmers.

[12] This corresponds with Main's data. He found that although artisans were on the
whole not as wealthy as farmers, they were almost as well off, and were often part-time
farmers. See J. Main, *Connecticut Society*, pp. 31-32, 35-38.

the upland produced two such probated men and Wethersfield four (of thirteen artisans from both areas).

Two things stand out in Table B.7. First, the probated population in the 1770s contained very few who could be called dependents. In the upland only one adult estate holder held under forty acres and no other productive property. Recall that in this period the probated population in both areas contained the fewest women and the fewest childless persons. This is a special population, restricted largely to independent farm families. It is certainly unlikely that the decline in the proportion of probated smaller holders in both areas reflected any such change in the communities in which they died. (The debate concerning concentration of land in the colonial period is always whether it rose or remained stable; no one proposes that it dropped.)

Second, although in the 1750s Wethersfield decedents were doing better than their upland counterparts (particularly those who had children), positions had reversed by the 1820s. Almost half of Wethersfield men in the 1820s (44 percent) held under twenty acres and owned no other productive property. This is a substantially higher percentage even than that for men holding under forty acres in the 1750s. Taking into account that Wethersfield's more intensive farming practices created different thresholds of viability by the 1820s, the percentage of upland decedents holding under forty acres (30 percent) was still substantially lower than that of Wethersfield decedents holding under twenty acres. The gap was smaller but still present for men who had children. In this area, the figures more nearly resembled those of the populations of the 1750s.

Complete and Incomplete Estates.   The depth of documentary coverage obtained from the probate records varied. Once administrators and executors were appointed, their first duty was usually to take an inventory of all the decedent's assets. Although there was a slight lapse in the Revolutionary period, in other periods almost all complied with the requirements (Table B.8, column 2).

The last step in the probate process varied. When estates were intestate and solvent, the men whom the courts assigned to distribute the estates were required to make reports precisely describing the property distributed to each heir. However, when the interested parties came to an agreement among themselves, the courts simply recorded it. If the intestate estate was insolvent, commissioners, also assigned by the courts, submitted returns detailing the apportionment of property among creditors.[13] The filing of one of these three documents usually

[13] *Acts & Laws 1750*, pp. 52, 101; *Public Statutes 1821*, pp. 206, 209-10.

TABLE B.8
INVENTORIED AND COMPLETE ESTATES

	(N)	Estates Inventoried (%)	All Estates Incomplete (%)	Testate Incomplete (%)	Intestate Incomplete (%)
	(1)	(2)	(3)	(4)	(5)
1750s					
Wethersfield	39	95	31	60	13
Upland	25	88	36	58	15
1770s					
Wethersfield	32	85	41	63	19
Upland	23	74	43	67	18
1820s					
Wethersfield	36	89	25	41	11
Upland	31	94	19	36	6

signaled the end of probate. Normally, the probate of an intestate estate was not legally complete unless this occurred.

The procedure for testate but insolvent estates was the same as that for insolvent, intestate estates. In the colonial period, the routine end of probate for solvent and testate estates is unclear. An estate distribution apparently was not required so long as the named executor was able and willing to carry out his or her responsibilities.[14] The later statutes clearly state that the administrator's duty to submit an account of expenses and estate liabilities applied to the executor as well, but the 1750 code was ambiguous.[15]

Assuming that the account of expenses and liabilities was the normal end of probate for testate estates, Table B.8 (column 3) indicates that the rates of completion of probate were very similar in Wethersfield and the upland. The highest rates of completion occurred in the 1820s, the lowest in the 1770s, but in all periods it was largely the testate estates that were incomplete (columns 4-5). In the colonial period about 60 to 67 percent of the testate estates lacked administrative accounts or estate distributions, while between 81 and 87 percent of the intestate estates were complete.[16] In the 1820s the percentage of incomplete testate

[14] *Acts & Laws 1750*, p. 50; *Public Statutes 1821*, p. 208.
[15] *Acts & Laws 1750*, pp. 51-52; *Acts and Laws 1796*, p. 168; *Public Statutes 1821*, pp. 201-202.
[16] Thus the dip in the 1770s had nothing to do with potential interruptions caused by the Revolution. If this had been the case, rates of completion for intestate estates would have fallen also.

estates in each area dropped to well below half, but they were still completed far less often than intestate estates.

Regardless of the state of the law, the lack of recorded accounts of liabilities or estate distributions (mainly for testate cases) creates certain difficulties when the absolute value of shares taken by heirs is of concern. Fortunately, most of the analysis here rests on proportional shares taken (for example "to my two sons, two thirds of my real estate; to my four daughters, one third of my real estate"). When the value of the share taken is of interest and information on net estate is absent, the study made the following assumptions. Since real estate sales to pay off debts were carefully supervised in all periods, it was assumed that indebtedness did not reach to real property unless such a sale took place. The inventoried value of the real estate was assumed to be the net value. The exception concerned the five testators who designated a specific piece of land to be sold for debts. In these cases it was assumed that debts did not exceed the value of such property and that nothing remained of such property once debts were covered. Since creditor claims were to be satisfied out of personal property first, the value of shares of personal estates was coded missing whenever explicit information on net value was unavailable.[17]

[17] When creditor claims threatened to deprive widows of household necessities, the courts were required to exempt certain personal property from creditor claims. *Acts & Laws 1750*, p. 102; *Public Statutes 1821*, p. 211. In such cases, we know the exact amount and kind of personal property the widow received and that no potential heir got personal property. When such distributions of widow's necessaries were not ordered and when real estate sales did not occur, one can be fairly confident that creditor claims did not reach to the entire personal estate, and one can in good conscience retain information on proportional shares in net.

SOURCES AND A NOTE ON
SIGNIFICANCE TESTING

PROBATE RECORDS

The folios containing the Estate Papers are grouped by probate district. The estate papers for the towns and dates included in this study are filed under the following districts: Wethersfield, in the Hartford Probate District; Bolton, in the Hartford District in the colonial period, then in the Andover District (Vernon in the 1820s, the Stafford District); Coventry, in Windham in the colonial period, then also in Andover; Willington in 1753-55 in Hartford, thereafter in Stafford; Union in 1753-55 in Windham and Pomfret, thereafter in Stafford. ("Parent" and subsequently formed districts relevant to the given towns were checked and an occasional misfiled estate was found. However, others may have gone undetected.)

A search of the relevant indexes generated the probate population. The indexes (Inventory Control Books) for each district are organized alphabetically by decedent, but they contain columns listing the town in which the decedent died and the date the estate began probate. Thus it was a relatively straightforward matter to locate those upland and Wethersfield estates that began probate in the targeted years. (The exception concerns the Hartford probate district. The Inventory Control Book does not cover estates after 1820. A more tedious search of a card index to this district's Estate Papers produced the Wethersfield estates for the year 1821.) The standard for inclusion was the date the first probate document was exhibited or recorded. For testate cases this document was the will or the executor's bond; for intestate cases, the bond accompanying the letters of administration. If the last was absent, the date the inventory was exhibited was used. In several cases the indexes led to estates that had begun probate a year or two earlier than listed. These were excluded. To compensate, I checked the estates listed for two years following the targeted dates. Consult the "Descriptive Report," rev. 1976, Connecticut Archives, Record Group Four, Probate Courts, for a detailed description of these and other parts of The Connecticut State Library's (Hartford) holdings on probate courts.

Along with the land records, the Estate Papers provided a main source of data on inheritance practices and on the decedents' wealth.

The Estate Papers also yielded a good deal of genealogical information about the decedents and closely related kin. The 186 estates involved about 1,100 documents from the Estate Papers series. Forms that mirrored fairly closely the "natural" ordering of the original documents insured consistency in data collection.

Wills, codicils, and estate distributions were the basic sources on property transferred at death. Supplementary documents on the distribution of property included court orders of "widow's necessaries" (when debts exceeded movable property) and heir agreements. Inventories and administrator's or executor's accounts of liabilities were the key documents for information on wealth. In Connecticut, inventories covered all real and personal property, including debts receivable. Accounts included not only the decedent's lifetime debts, but probate expenses and household expenses accumulating during the period of probate. Supplementary documents concerning assets and liabilities included commissioner's returns (reports of debts and debt payments for insolvent estates) and court returns on land sales (when debt exceeded personal estate). Any given file might also contain papers relating to guardianship and to disputes (summons, petitions, and even summaries of testimony).

The individual files of the Estate Papers vary greatly in depth. A search of the relevant probate district *Court Record Books* supplemented the data drawn from the Estate Papers. These clerks' summaries of proceedings contain information that parallels that of the Estate Papers, so that one can get information on original papers that have been lost. In addition, the indexes for The Connecticut State Library's collection of manuscript materials on the state legislature provided parallel evidence on estate sales of real property.[1]

THE GENEALOGICAL SOURCES

Published genealogies and vital records (the latter available for Bolton and Coventry) and the Connecticut State Library's Barbour Collection of Connecticut Vital Records supplemented the biographical information provided by the probate records themselves. I searched for (1) the dates of birth, marriage, and death of the decedent, the decedent's spouse(s), and the decedent's children; (2) the maiden names of

---

[1] Estates of Deceased Persons, Index, "Connecticut Archives," RG 1, The Connecticut State Library, Hartford. In the colonial period the law required the approval of the General Assembly for all estate sales of real property. The General Assembly routinely granted such petitions (which were accompanied by the probate court's certificate stating the exact amount by which debts exceeded the value of personal property). By 1820 powers to authorize sale of real property had been settled entirely on the probate courts. See *Acts & Laws 1750*, p. 54; *Public Statutes 1821*, p. 205.

the decedent (or decedent's spouse) and the decedent's mother; (3) the names of the marriage partners of the decedent's children; and (4) the names of the decedent's siblings. If there were no children capable of inheriting, I also looked for the marital status and names of marriage partners of siblings, and whether they had children. There was considerable variation among decedents in the depth of genealogical information available, and generally, more information was missing for holders from the subsistence-plus towns.

THE LAND RECORDS

The land records—deeds organized by town and chronologically within towns (with grantor and grantee indexes)—were the central source for evidence of lifetime transfers of real estate.[2] A scan of these records covered all deeds carrying the names of the decedents as grantors or grantees, signed within the decedents' lifetimes, and involving transfers of land in the town of the decedents' last residence (approximately 2,900 in number). The last restriction may introduce a bias against finding lifetime transfers of "newcomers." However, the majority of "inheritance-like" transfers among longtime residents occurred within ten years of their deaths. This was in part because the retirement contract arrangement was prevalent and in part because demographic factors made even the marriage portion an event that occurred relatively late in the decedents' lifetimes.

In order to cope with the sheer numbers of transactions and the bias in the biographical data, the study limits the empirical question to be addressed by systematic quantitative analysis. Coding included only transfers between the decedent and (1) those who inherited at the decedents' deaths and their representatives and spouses; (2) relations of the same degree of kinship as actual heirs and their representatives and spouses; and (3) all children, whether or not any children were heirs. Coding included purchases of property by these potential heirs. Thus the question that can be answered systematically is the extent to which lifetime transfers affected or altered the distribution of property and the creation of rights among heirs. What cannot be addressed systematically are the property arrangements the holder may have made with all kin.

Ancillary sources on lifetime transactions include references to prior transactions mentioned in the wills and estate distributions themselves. These are particularly useful as sources for information on movable es-

---

[2] Available on microfilm at The Connecticut State Library. The original deeds remain, for the most part, with the offices of Town Clerk. They were filmed by the Genealogical Society, Church of Jesus Christ of Latter-day Saints, Salt Lake City, Utah.

tates given to daughters as marriage portions and on arrangements made between estate holders and their spouses. These lifetime transfers of personal property are otherwise poorly documented. There is, then, an underestimate of the total wealth transferred to married daughters.

Significance Tests. The text builds the case for an overall pattern of parallel inheritance practices in the colonial period and diverging practices thereafter. It relies mainly on an analysis of the magnitude of inter-area differences in the percentage of holders engaged in given inheritance practices. For the most important data and tables, however, I have also presented the results of chi-square tests of independence, a popular measure of the statistical significance of relationships found in contingency tables. Assuming for the moment that these tests are appropriate, they reinforce the general finding of similarity, then divergence. In the colonial era, when the inter-area differences in practices were small, the tests uniformly indicate that these differences were not statistically significant. In the 1820s, despite the small number of cases, the large inter-area differences were significant (or approached significance) at generally accepted levels.

But the use of the tests raises the question, what population is represented by these estate holders and in what sense are they a sample of that population. There is certainly no sample of subsistence-plus and commercial agriculture towns. Thus one should not infer from these tests that the data are a sample of, for instance, an imagined population of probates from all subsistence-plus and commercial agriculture towns in New England.[3] Neither are these data a random sample of probated holders from Wethersfield and the upland towns; the study analyzes the entire population of probates from these towns for the selected years. In a looser sense, though, the data are representative of a larger population of probates from these particular communities. If one views the time periods selected as a sample of years, one can visualize the data as a sample (though not a *random* sample) of probates from the given towns.

There is debate concerning the applicability of significance tests to data not based on a random sample. The conservative position is that my "population" for statistical purposes is the probated holders from

---

[3] One must decide on substantive grounds what "universe" Wethersfield and the upland towns represent. This decision involves a series of analytical commitments about the nature of the early American countryside and what distinctions within it are likely to "count." Given the lack of consensus concerning northern rural social organization, the conceptual "universe" to which these towns belong will be subject to debate. The criteria I have used to distinguish Wethersfield from the upland are, I believe, of sufficient power to warrant generalization. But only future research will tell how far.

the selected years and towns. Since there is data on the entire population, statistical tests of significance are at best irrelevant. But statistical tests of significance are widely used on less rigorous samples. Given this conventional practice, I have presented the tests because they are particularly important when "sample" sizes are small. For those who accept the broader use, they provide straightforward additional support for the case that the inter-area pattern of similarity and divergence is not the result of quirky data; it should hold up for larger populations of probated estate holders.

BIBLIOGRAPHY

Adams, Sherman W., and Stiles, Henry R. *The History of Ancient Wethersfield*, 2 vols. Reprint ed. Somersworth: New Hampshire Publishing Co., 1974.

Anderson, Michael. *Family Structure in Nineteenth-Century Lancashire*. Cambridge, Eng.: Cambridge University Press, 1971.

——. "Sociological History and the Working Class Family: Smelser Revisited." *Social History*, no. 3 (October 1976): 317-34.

——. *Approaches to the History of the Western Family, 1500-1914*. London: Macmillan, 1980.

Anderson, Terry L. "Economic Growth in Colonial New England: 'Statistical Renaissance'." *Journal of Economic History* 39 (March 1979): 243-58.

Andrews, Charles M. *The Connecticut Intestacy Law*. Tercentenary Series, no. 2. New Haven: Yale University Press, 1933.

Appleby, Joyce. "The Social Origins of American Revolutionary Ideology." *Journal of American History* 64 (March 1978): 935-58.

——. "What is Still American in the Political Philosophy of Thomas Jefferson?" *William and Mary Quarterly*, 3rd ser., 39 (April 1982): 387-410.

Arensberg, Conrad M., and Kimball, Solon T. *Family and Community in Ireland*. Cambridge, Mass.: Harvard University Press, 1940.

Auwers, Linda. "Fathers, Sons, and Wealth in Colonial Windsor, Connecticut." *Journal of Family History* 3 (Summer 1978): 136-49.

Bailyn, Bernard. *The Ideological Origins of the American Revolution*. Cambridge, Mass.: Harvard University Press, 1967.

——. *The Origins of American Politics*. New York: Vintage Books, 1970.

——. "Politics and Social Structure in Colonial Virginia." In *Colonial America: Essays in Politics and Social Development*, pp. 119-43. 2nd ed. Ed. Stanley N. Katz. Boston: Little, Brown, 1976.

Ball, Duane E., and Walton, Gary M. "Agricultural Productivity Change in Eighteenth-Century Pennsylvania." *Journal of Economic History* 36 (March 1976): 102-17.

Bell, Daniel. *The End of Ideology*. Rev. ed. New York: Free Press, 1965.

Berkner, Lutz. "The Stem Family and the Developmental Cycle of the Peasant Household: An Eighteenth Century Austrian Example." *American Historical Review* 77 (April 1972): 398-418.

——. "The Use and Misuse of Census Data for the Historical Analysis of Family Structure." *Journal of Interdisciplinary History* 5 (Spring 1975): 721-38.

——. "Inheritance, Land Tenure, and Peasant Family Structure: A German Regional Comparison." In *Family and Inheritance: Rural Society in Western Europe, 1200-1800*, pp. 71-95. Ed. Jack Goody, Joan Thirsk, and E. P. Thompson. Cambridge, Eng.: Cambridge University Press, 1976.

Berkner, Lutz, and Mendels, Franklin. "Inheritance Systems, Family Structure, and Demographic Patterns in Western Europe, 1700-1900." In *Historical Studies of Changing Fertility*, pp. 209-25. Ed. Charles Tilly. Princeton, N.J.: Princeton University Press, 1978.

Berthoff, Rowland. "Independence and Attachment, Virtue and Interest: From Republican to Free Enterpriser, 1787-1837." In *Uprooted Americans: Essays to Honor Oscar Handlin*, pp. 97-124. Ed. Richard L. Bushman et al. Boston: Little, Brown, 1979.

Berthoff, Rowland, and Murrin, John M. "Feudalism, Communalism, and the Yeoman Freeholder: The American Revolution Considered As a Social Accident." In *Essays on the American Revolution*, pp. 256-88. Ed. Stephen G. Kurtz and James H. Hutson. New York: Norton, 1973.

Bidwell, Percy Wells, and Falconer, John I. *History of Agriculture in the Northern United States, 1620-1860*. Reprint ed. New York: Peter Smith, 1941.

Bronson, Henry. "Historical Account of Connecticut Currency, Continental Money, and the Finances of the Revolution." *Papers of the New Haven Colony Historical Society* 1 (1865): 1-192.

Brookes, George S. *Cascades and Courage: The History of the Town of Vernon and the City of Rockville, Connecticut*. Rockville, Conn.: T. F. Rady, 1955.

Brown, Richard D. "Modernization and the Modern Personality in Early America, 1600-1865: A Sketch of a Synthesis." *Journal of Interdisciplinary History* 2 (Winter 1972): 21-28.

Bruchey, Stuart. *The Roots of American Economic Growth, 1607-1860: An Essay in Social Causation*. New York: Harper Torchbooks, 1968.

Bushman, Richard L. *From Puritan to Yankee: Character and the Social Order in Connecticut, 1690-1765*. New York: Norton, 1970.

————. "The Great Awakening in Connecticut." In *Colonial America: Essays in Political and Social Development*, pp. 334-44. 2nd ed. Ed. Stanley N. Katz. Boston: Little, Brown, 1976.

————. "Family Security in the Transition from Farm to City, 1750-1850." *Journal of Family History* 6 (Fall 1981): 238-56.

Clark, Christopher. "Household Economy, Market Exchange, and the Rise of Capitalism in the Connecticut Valley, 1800-1860." *Journal of Social History* 13 (Winter 1979): 169-89.

Cole, J. R. *History of Tolland County, Connecticut*. New York, 1888.

Cole, John W., and Wolf, Eric R. *The Hidden Frontier: Ecology and Ethnicity in an Alpine Valley*. New York: Academic Press, 1974.

Connecticut General Assembly. *Acts and Laws of His Majesty's English Colony of Connecticut in New England in America*. New London, 1750.

————. *Acts and Laws of the State of Connecticut in America*. Hartford, 1796.

————. *The Public Records of the Colony of Connecticut from October 1772 to April 1775 Inclusive*, vol. 14. Reprint ed. Ed. Charles J. Hoadly. New York: AMS Press, 1968.

————. *The Public Statute Laws of the State of Connecticut. Revised 1821*. Hartford, 1821.

————. *Register and Manual, 1919*. Hartford, 1919.

————. *Register and Manual of the State of Connecticut, 1889*. Hartford, 1889.

————. *Roll of State Officers and Members of the General Assembly of Connecticut from 1776-1881*. Hartford, 1881.

Connecticut, Office of the Secretary of State. *Statistics of the Condition and Products of Certain Branches of Industry in Connecticut for the Year Ending October 1, 1845*. Hartford, 1846.

Cook, Edward M., Jr. *The Fathers of the Towns: Leadership and Community Structure in Eighteenth Century New England*. Baltimore: Johns Hopkins University Press, 1976.

Cooper, J. P. "Patterns of Inheritance and Settlement by Great Landowners from the Fifteenth to the Eighteenth Centuries." In *Family and Inheritance: Rural Society in Western Europe, 1200-1800*, pp. 192-327. Ed. Jack Goody, Joan Thirsk, and E. P. Thompson. Cambridge, Eng.: Cambridge University Press, 1976.

Cott, Nancy F. *The Bonds of Womanhood: "Woman's Sphere" in New England, 1780-1835*. New Haven: Yale University Press, 1977.

Creighton, Colin. "Family, Property, and Relations of Production in Western Europe." *Economy and Society* 9 (May 1980): 129-67.

Curtiss, George. *History of the Congregational Church of Union, Connecticut*. N.p., 1914.

Danhof, Clarence. *Change in Agriculture in the Northern United States, 1820-1870*. Cambridge, Mass.: Harvard University Press, 1969.

Daniels, Bruce C. "Money-Value Definitions of Economic Classes in Colonial Connecticut, 1700-1776." *Histoire Sociale-Social History*, no. 8 (November 1974): 346-51.

————. *The Connecticut Town: Growth and Development, 1635-1790*. Middletown, Conn.: Wesleyan University Press, 1979.

————. "Economic Development in Colonial and Revolutionary Connecticut: An Overview." *William and Mary Quarterly*, 3rd ser., 37 (July 1980): 429-50.

Day, Clive. *The Rise of Manufacturing in Connecticut, 1820-1850*. Tercentenary Series, no. 44. New Haven: Yale University Press, 1935.

Deen, James, Jr. "Patterns of Testation: Four Tidewater Counties in Colonial Virginia." *American Journal of Legal History* 16 (1972): 154-77.

Degler, Carl N. *At Odds: Women and the Family in America from the Revolution to the Present*. Oxford: Oxford University Press, 1981.

Deming, Dorothy. *The Settlement of the Connecticut Towns*. Tercentenary Series, no. 6. New Haven: Yale University Press, 1933.

Demos, John. *A Little Commonwealth: Family Life in Plymouth Colony*. Oxford: Oxford University Press, 1971.

Demos, John, and Boocock, Surane Spence, eds. *Turning Points: Historical and Sociological Essays on the Family*. Supplement, *American Journal of Sociology* 84. Chicago: University of Chicago Press, 1978.

Elder, Glen. "Approaches to Social Change and the Family." In *Turning Points: Historical and Sociological Essays on the Family*, pp. S1-S38. Ed.

John Demos and Surane Spence Boocock. Supplement, *American Journal of Sociology* 84. Chicago: University of Chicago Press, 1978.

Friedman, Lawrence M. "Patterns of Testation in the Nineteenth Century: A Study of Essex County Wills." *American Journal of Legal History* 8 (1964): 34-53.

————. *A History of American Law.* New York: Simon and Schuster, Touchstone, 1973.

Fuller, Grace P. "An Introduction to the History of Connecticut As a Manufacturing State." *Smith College Studies in History* 1 (1915): 10.

Gagan, David P. "The Indivisibility of Land: A Microanalysis of the System of Inheritance in Nineteenth-Century Ontario." *Journal of Economic History* 36 (March 1976): 126-41.

Geisey, Ralph. "Rules of Inheritance and Strategies of Mobility in Prerevolutionary France." *American Historical Review* 82 (April 1977): 271-89.

Gipson, Lawrence Henry. *Connecticut Taxation, 1750-1775.* Tercentenary Series, no. 10. New Haven: Yale University Press, 1933.

Goode, William J. "Family and Mobility." In *Class, Status, and Power*, pp. 582-601. 2nd ed. Ed. Reinhard Bendix and Seymour Martin Lipset. New York: Free Press, 1966.

Goody, Jack. "Strategies of Heirship." *Comparative Studies in Society and History* 15 (January 1973): 3-20.

————. "Introduction." In *Family and Inheritance: Rural Society in Western Europe, 1200-1800*, pp. 1-10. Ed. Jack Goody, Joan Thirsk, and E. P. Thompson. Cambridge, Eng.: Cambridge University Press, 1976.

Gordon, Michael. "Introduction." In *The American Family in Social-Historical Perspective*, pp. 1-16. 2nd ed. Ed. Michael Gordon. New York: St. Martin's, 1978.

Grant, Charles S. *Democracy in the Connecticut Frontier Town of Kent.* New York: Columbia University Press, 1961.

Greene, Evarts B., and Harrington, Virginia D. *American Population before the Federal Census of 1790.* New York: Columbia University Press, 1932.

Greven, Philip J., Jr. *Four Generations: Population, Land, and Family in Colonial Andover, Massachusetts.* Ithaca, N.Y.: Cornell University Press, 1972.

————. *The Protestant Temperament: Patterns of Child-Rearing, Religious Experience, and the Self in Early America.* New York: Knopf, 1977.

Habbakuk, H. J. "Marriage Settlements in the Eighteenth Century." *Transactions of the Royal Historical Society*, 4th ser., 32 (1950): 15-30.

————. "Family Structure and Economic Change in Nineteenth-Century Europe." *Journal of Economic History* 15 (1955): 1-12.

Hajnal, J. "European Marriage Patterns in Perspective." In *Population in History*, pp. 101-43. Ed. D. V. Glass and D.E.C. Eversley. London: Edward Arnold, 1974.

Hammond, Charles. *The History of Union, Connecticut.* Comp. Harvey M. Lawson. New Haven, 1893.

Hamowy, Ronald. "Jefferson and the Scottish Enlightenment: A Critique of

Garry Wills's *Inventing America: Jefferson's Declaration of Independence.*"
William and Mary Quarterly, 3rd ser., 36 (October 1979): 503-23.

Hareven, Tamara. "Family Time and Industrial Time: Family and Work in a
Planned Corporation Town, 1900-1924." In *Family and Kin in American
Urban Communities, 1780-1920*, pp. 187-207. Ed. Tamara Hareven. New
York: Franklin Watts, New Viewpoints, 1977.

Harrington, James. *The Political Works of James Harrington.* Ed. J.G.A. Pocock. Cambridge, Eng.: Cambridge University Press, 1977.

Harris, Marshall. *Origins of the Land Tenure System in the United States.*
Ames: Iowa State College Press, 1953.

Hartz, Louis. *The Liberal Tradition in America.* New York: Harvest-Harcourt
Brace, 1955.

Haskins, George L. "The Beginnings of Partible Inheritance in the American
Colonies." *Yale Law Review* 51 (May 1942): 1280-1315.

————. "The Legal Heritage of Plymouth Colony." In *American Law and the
Constitutional Order: Historical Perspectives*, pp. 38-45. Ed. Lawrence M.
Friedman and Harry N. Scheiber. Cambridge, Mass.: Harvard University
Press, 1978.

Henretta, James. "Families and Farms: 'Mentalité' in Pre-Industrial America."
William and Mary Quarterly, 3rd ser., 35 (January 1978): 3-31.

————. "Wealth and Social Structure." In *Colonial British America*, pp. 262-
89. Ed. Jack P. Greene and J. R. Pole. Baltimore: Johns Hopkins University
Press, 1984.

Hofstadter, Richard. "The Myth of the Happy Yeoman." *American Heritage*
(April 1956), pp. 43-53.

Homans, George C. *English Villagers of the Thirteenth Century.* New York:
Norton, 1975.

Horwitz, Morton J. *The Transformation of American Law, 1790-1860.* Cambridge, Mass.: Harvard University Press, 1977.

Howell, Cicely. "Peasant Inheritance Customs in the Midlands, 1280-1700."
In *Family and Inheritance: Rural Society in Western Europe, 1200-1800*, pp.
112-55. Ed. Jack Goody, Joan Thirsk, and E. P. Thompson. Cambridge,
Eng.: Cambridge University Press, 1976.

Jedrey, Christopher M. *The World of John Cleaveland: Family and Community in Eighteenth-Century New England.* New York: Norton, 1979.

Jones, Alice Hanson. "Wealth Estimates for the American Middle Colonies."
Economic Development and Cultural Change 18 (1970): 9-172.

————. "Wealth Estimates for the New England Colonies about 1770." *Journal of Economic History* 32 (March 1972): 98-127.

Jones, Eric L. "Agricultural Origins of Industry." *Past and Present*, no. 40 (July
1968): 58-71.

————. "Afterword." In *European Peasants and Their Markets*, pp. 327-60.
Ed. William Parker and Eric L. Jones. Princeton, N.J.: Princeton University
Press, 1975.

Katz, Stanley N. "Republicanism and the Law of Inheritance in the American
Revolutionary Era." *Michigan Law Review* 76 (November 1977): 1-29.

Keim, C. Roy. "Primogeniture and Entail in Colonial Virginia." *William and Mary Quarterly*, 3rd ser., 25 (October 1968): 545-86.

Kerber, Linda. *Women of the Republic: Intellect and Ideology in Revolutionary America*. Chapel Hill: University of North Carolina Press, 1980.

Keyssar, Alexander. "Widowhood in Eighteenth-Century Massachusetts: A Problem in the History of the Family." *Perspectives in American History* 8 (1974): 83-119.

Kirby, Ephraim. *Report of Cases Adjudged in the Superior Court of the State of Connecticut from the Year 1785 to January 1789*. Reprint ed. Hartford, Conn.: N.p., 1962.

Ladurie, Emmanuel Le Roy. "Family Structures and Inheritance Customs in Sixteenth Century France." In *Family and Inheritance: Rural Society in Western Europe, 1200-1800*, pp. 37-70. Ed. Jack Goody, Joan Thirsk, and E. P. Thompson. Cambridge, Eng.: Cambridge University Press, 1976.

Laslett, Peter. *The World We Have Lost*. 2nd ed. New York: Scribner's, 1973.

Laslett, Peter, ed., assisted by Richard Wall. *Household and Family in Past Time*. Cambridge, Eng.: Cambridge University Press, 1972.

Lemon, James T. *The Best Poor Man's Country: A Geographical Study of Early Southeastern Pennsylvania*. Baltimore: Johns Hopkins University Press, 1972.

———. "Spatial Order: Households in Local Communities and Regions." In *British Colonial America*, pp. 86-122. Ed. Jack P. Greene and J. R. Pole. Baltimore: Johns Hopkins University Press, 1984.

Levine, David. *Family Formation in an Age of Nascent Capitalism*. New York: Academic Press, 1977.

Levine, David, and Wrightson, Keith. *Poverty and Piety in an English Village: Terling, 1525-1700*. New York: Academic Press, 1979.

Levy, Barry. " 'Tender Plants': Quaker Farmers and Children in the Delaware Valley, 1681-1735." *Journal of Family History* 3 (Summer 1978): 116-55.

Levy, Michael Bruce. "Liberalism and Inherited Wealth." Ph.D. dissertation. Rutgers, The State University of New Jersey, 1979.

Lipset, Seymour Martin. *The First New Nation: The United States in Historical and Comparative Perspective*. Garden City, N.Y.: Doubleday-Anchor, 1967.

Locke, John. *Two Treatises of Government*. Rev. ed. Ed. Peter Laslett. Cambridge, Eng.: Cambridge University Press, 1960.

Lockridge, Kenneth A. "Land, Population, and the Evolution of New England Society, 1630-1790." *Past and Present*, no. 39 (April 1968): 62-80.

———. *A New England Town: The First Hundred Years. Dedham, Massachusetts, 1636-1736*. New York: Norton, 1970.

———. "Social Change and the Meaning of the American Revolution." In *Colonial America: Essays in Politics and Social Development*, pp. 403-39. 2nd ed. Ed. Stanley N. Katz. Boston: Little, Brown, 1976.

Lockwood, James. *Religion the highest Interest of a civil Community, and the surest Means of its Prosperity: An Election Sermon*. New London, 1754.

————. *Man mortal: God everlasting, and the sure, unfailing Refuge and Felicity of his faithful People, in all Generations.* New Haven, 1756.

Main, Gloria L. "Probate Records As a Source for Early American History." *William and Mary Quarterly*, 3rd ser., 32 (January 1975): 89-99.

————. "Inequality in Early America: The Evidence from Probate Records of Massachusetts and Maryland." *Journal of Interdisciplinary History* 7 (Spring 1977): 559-81.

Main, Jackson Turner. *The Social Structure of Revolutionary America.* Princeton, N.J.: Princeton University Press, 1965.

————. "The Distribution of Property in Colonial Connecticut." In *The Human Dimensions of Nation-Making: Essays on Colonial and Revolutionary America*, pp. 54-104. Ed. James Kirby Martin. Madison: State Historical Society of Wisconsin, 1976.

————. *Connecticut Society in the Era of the American Revolution.* Connecticut Bicentennial Series, no. 21. Hartford: The American Revolution Bicentennial Commission of Connecticut, 1977.

Medick, Hans. "The Proto-Industrial Family Economy: The Structural Function of Household and Family during the Transition from Peasant Society to Industrial Capitalism." *Social History*, no. 3 (October 1976): 291-315.

Mendels, Franklin F. "Proto-Industrialization: The First Phase of the Industrialization Process." *Journal of Economic History* 32 (March 1972): 241-61.

————. "Agriculture and Peasant Industry in Eighteenth Century Flanders." In *European Peasants and Their Markets*, pp. 179-204. Ed. William Parker and Eric L. Jones. Princeton, N.J.: Princeton University Press, 1975.

Merrick, John. *Recollections of John Merrick, a Native of Willington, 1833-1865.* Ed. Isabel Weigold. Storrs, Conn.: Parousia Press, 1978.

Merrill, Michael. "Cash is Good to Eat: Self-Sufficiency and Exchange in the Rural Economy of the United States." *Radical Historian's Review* (Winter 1977): 42-66.

Milsom, S.F.C. *Historical Foundations of the Common Law.* London: Buttersworth, 1969.

Minor, William (Mrs.). *Coventry in Retrospect, 1712-1963.* N.p., n.d.

Morgan, Edmund. *The Puritan Family: Religion and Domestic Relations in Seventeenth Century New England.* Rev. ed. New York: Harper Torchbooks, 1966.

Morris, Richard. *Studies in the History of American Law.* 2nd ed. New York: Octagon Books, 1964.

Mutch, Robert E. "Yeoman and Merchant in Pre-Industrial America: Eighteenth Century Massachusetts As a Case Study." *Societas* 7 (Autumn 1977): 279-302.

————. "The Cutting Edge: Colonial America and the Debate about the Transition to Capitalism." *Theory and Society* 9 (November 1980): 847-63.

Nash, Gary B. "Social Development." In *Colonial British America*, pp. 233-61. Ed. Jack P. Greene and J. R. Pole. Baltimore: Johns Hopkins University Press, 1984.

Nelson, William E. *Americanization of the Common Law: The Impact of Legal Change on Massachusetts Society, 1760-1830*. Cambridge, Mass.: Harvard University Press, 1975.

Nettels, Curtis P. *The Emergence of a National Economy, 1775-1815. The Economic History of the United States*, vol. 2. White Plains, N.Y.: M. E. Sharpe, 1962.

Newell, William H. "The Wealth of Testators and Its Distribution: Butler County, Ohio." In *Modeling the Distribution and Intergenerational Transmission of Wealth*, pp. 95-138. Ed. James D. Smith. Chicago: University of Chicago Press, 1980.

Norton, Mary Beth. "The Myth of the Golden Age." In *Women of America: A History*, pp. 37-47. Ed. Carol Ruth Berkin and Mary Beth Norton. Boston: Houghton Mifflin, 1979.

————. *Liberty's Daughters: The Revolutionary Experience of American Women*. Boston: Little, Brown, 1980.

Olsen, Albert Lavern. *Agricultural Economy and the Population in Eighteenth Century Connecticut*. Tercentenary Series, no. 40. New Haven: Yale University Press, 1935.

Parsons, Francis. "Elisha Williams: Minister, Soldier, President of Yale." *Papers of the New Haven Colony Historical Society* 7 (1908): 188-217.

Parsons, Talcott. "The Kinship System of the Contemporary United States." In *Essays in Sociological Theory*. Rev. ed. New York: Free Press, 1964.

Pease, John C., and Niles, John M. *Gazetteer of the States of Connecticut and Rhode Island*. Hartford, 1819.

Peterson, Maude G. "Historic Sketch of Coventry, Connecticut." Program, Bicentennial Celebration. Coventry, 1912.

Pocock, J.G.A. "Virtue and Commerce in the Eighteenth Century." *Journal of Interdisciplinary History* 3 (Summer 1972): 119-34.

————. *The Machiavellian Moment: Florentine Political Thought and the Atlantic Republican Tradition*. Princeton, N.J.: Princeton University Press, 1975.

————. "The Machiavellian Moment Revisited: A Study in History and Ideology." *Journal of Modern History* 53 (March 1981): 49-72.

Powell, Richard R., and Rohan, Patrick J. *Powell on Real Property*. One-vol. ed. New York: Mathew Bender, 1968.

Presser, Stephen B. "The Historical Background of the American Law of Adoption." *Journal of Family Law* 11 (1971-72): 443-516.

Pruitt, Bettye Hobbes. "Self-Sufficiency and the Agricultural Economy of Eighteenth Century Massachusetts." *William and Mary Quarterly*, 3rd ser., 41 (July 1984): 333-64.

Rabkin, Peggy A. "The Origins of Law Reform: The Social Significance of the Nineteenth-Century Codification Movement and Its Contribution to the Passage of the Early Married Women's Property Acts." *Buffalo Law Review* 24 (Spring 1975): 683-760.

Rassmussen, Wayne D., ed. *Agriculture in the United States: A Documentary History*, vol. 1. New York: Random House, 1975.

Root, Marvin. "History of Coventry through the Revolutionary Period." Typescript. Hartford: The Connecticut State Library, 1958.

Rosenfeld, Jeffry P. *The Legacy of Aging: Inheritance and Disinheritance in Social Perspective.* Norwood, N.J.: Ablex, 1979.

Rothman, David. *The Discovery of the Asylum.* Boston: Little, Brown, 1971.

Russell, Howard S. *A Long, Deep Furrow: Three Centuries of Farming in New England.* Hanover, N.H.: University Press of New England, 1976.

Rutman, Darret B. "People in Process: The New Hampshire Towns of the Eighteenth Century." In *Family and Kin in American Urban Communities, 1780-1920,* pp. 16-37. Ed. Tamara Hareven. New York: Franklin Watts-New Viewpoints, 1977.

Ryan, Mary P. *Womanhood in America from Colonial Times to the Present.* 2nd ed. New York: Franklin Watts-New Viewpoints, 1979.

————. *Cradle of the Middle Class: The Family in Oneida County, New York, 1790-1865.* Cambridge, Eng.: Cambridge University Press, 1981.

Salmon, Marylynn. "Equality or Submersion?: Feme Covert Status in Early Pennsylvania." In *Women of America: A History,* pp. 92-113. Ed. Carol Ruth Berkin and Mary Beth Norton. Boston: Houghton Mifflin, 1979.

————. " 'Life, Liberty and Dower': The Legal Status of Women after the American Revolution." In *Women, War and Revolution,* pp. 85-106. Ed. Carol R. Berkin and Clara M. Lovett. New York: Holmes & Meier, 1980.

————. "The Property Rights of Women in Early America: A Comparative Study." Ph.D. dissertation, Bryn Mawr, 1980.

————. *Women and the Law of Property in Early America.* Chapel Hill: University of North Carolina Press, 1986.

Sartori, Giovanni. "Concept Misinformation in Comparative Politics." *American Political Science Review* 64 (December 1970): 1033-53.

Schumacher, George. *The Northern Farmer and His Markets during the Late Colonial Period.* New York: Arno, 1975.

Shalhope, Robert E. "Republicanism and Early American Historiography." *William and Mary Quarterly,* 3rd ser., 39 (April 1982): 334-56.

Shammas, Carole. "How Self-Sufficient Was Early America?" *Journal of Interdisciplinary History* 8 (Autumn 1982): 247-73.

Smith, Daniel Blake. *Inside the Great House: Planter Family Life in Eighteenth Century Chesapeake Society.* Ithaca, N.Y.: Cornell University Press, 1980.

Smith, Daniel Scott. "Parental Power and Marriage Patterns: An Analysis of Historical Trends in Hingham, Massachusetts." *Journal of Marriage and the Family* 35 (August 1973): 419-28.

————. "Underregistration and Bias in Probate Records: Analysis of Data from Eighteenth Century Hingham, Massachusetts." *William and Mary Quarterly,* 3rd ser., 32 (January 1975): 100-10.

————. "A Malthusian-Frontier Interpretation of United States Demographic History before 1815." In *Urbanization in the Americas.* Ed. Woodrow Borah, Jorge Hardoy, and Gilbert Stelter. Ottawa: University of Ottawa Press, 1980.

Smith, Henry, C., comp. *Centennial of Vernon-Rockville*. Rockville, Conn.:
T. F. Rady, 1908.

Snydacker, Daniel. "Kinship and Community in Rural Pennsylvania, 1749-
1820." *Journal of Interdisciplinary History* 8 (Summer 1982): 41-61.

Spring, Eileen. "The Strict Settlement of Land in Nineteenth Century England." *American Journal of Legal History* 8 (1964): 209-23.

Spufford, Margaret. *Contrasting Communities: English Villagers in the Sixteenth and Seventeenth Centuries*. Cambridge, Eng.: Cambridge University
Press, 1974.

————. "Peasant Inheritance Customs and Land Distribution in Cambridgeshire from the Sixteenth to the Eighteenth Centuries." In *Family and Inheritance: Rural Society in Western Europe, 1200-1800*, pp. 156-76. Ed. Jack
Goody, Joan Thirsk, and E. P. Thompson. Cambridge, Eng.: Cambridge
University Press, 1976.

Stiles, Ezra. *Extracts from the Itineraries and Other Miscellanies of Ezra Stiles,
D.D., LL.D., 1755-1794, with a Selection from His Correspondence*. Ed.
Franklin Bowditch Dexter. New Haven: Yale University Press, 1916.

Stinchcombe, Arthur. "Agricultural Enterprise and Rural Class Relations." In
Class, Status, and Power, pp. 182-90. 2nd ed. Ed. Reinhard Bendix and Seymour Martin Lipset. New York: Free Press, 1966.

Stone, Lawrence. *The Family, Sex, and Marriage in England, 1500-1800*. New
York: Harper Colophon, 1979.

————. "Family History in the 1980's: Past Achievements and Future Trends."
Journal of Interdisciplinary History 7 (Summer 1981): 51-87.

Sussman, Marvin B.; Gates, Judith N.; and Smith, David T. *The Family and
Inheritance*. New York: Russell Sage, 1970.

Swift, Zephaniah. *A System of the Laws of the State of Connecticut*, 2 vols.
Windham, Conn., 1795-96.

Thirsk, Joan. "The Debate about Inheritance." In *Family and Inheritance: Ru-
ral Society in Western Europe, 1200-1800*, pp. 177-91. Ed. Jack Goody,
Joan Thirsk, and E. P. Thompson. Cambridge, Eng.: Cambridge University
Press, 1976.

Thompson, E. P. "The Grid of Inheritance: A Comment." In *Family and Inheritance in Western Europe, 1200-1800*, pp. 328-60. Ed. Jack Goody, Joan
Thirsk, and E. P. Thompson. Cambridge, Eng.: Cambridge University Press,
1976.

Tilly, Louise, and Scott, Joan. *Women, Work, and the Family*. New York:
Holt, Rinehart, and Winston, 1978.

Tocqueville, Alexis de. *Democracy in America*. Ed. J. P. Mayer. Trans. George
Lawrence. New York: Doubleday-Anchor, 1969.

Trumbach, Randolph. *The Rise of the Egalitarian Family: Aristocratic Kinship
and Domestic Relations in Eighteenth Century England*. New York: Academic Press, 1978.

U.S. Bureau of the Census. *Population for the Year 1820 in the State of Connecticut*, vol. 1: *Hartford County*; vol. 8: *Tolland County*. Photostats of the
Original Returns of the Assistant Marshalls.

————. *Aggregate Value and Produce and Number of Persons Employed in Mines, Agriculture, Commerce, Manufactures, & etc. 1840.* Reprinted as *American Industry and Manufactures in the Nineteenth Century,* vol. 4. Elmsford, N.Y.: Maxwell Reprint, 1970.

Vann, Richard T. "Wills and the Family in an English Town: Banbury, 1550-1800." *Journal of Family History* 4 (Winter 1979): 346-67.

Verdon, Michel. "The Stem Family: Toward a General Theory." *Journal of Interdisciplinary History* 10 (Summer 1979): 87-105.

————. "Shaking Off the Domestic Yoke, or the Sociological Significance of Residence." *Comparative Studies in Society and History* 22 (January 1980): 109-32.

Waters, John. "The Traditional World of the New England Peasant: A View from Seventeenth Century Barnstable." *New England Historical and Genealogical Register* 30 (January 1976): 3-21.

————. "Patrimony, Succession, and Social Stability: Guilford, Connecticut, in the Eighteenth Century." *Perspectives in American History* 10 (1976): 131-60.

Wells, Robert V. *The Population of the British Colonies in America before 1776: A Survey of the Census Data.* Princeton, N.J.: Princeton University Press, 1975.

————. "Family History and Demographic Transition." In *The American Family in Social-Historical Perspective,* pp. 516-32. Ed. Michael Gordon. New York: St. Martin's, 1978.

————. "Women's Lives Transformed: Demographic and Family Patterns in America, 1600-1970." In *Women of America: A History,* pp. 16-33. Ed. Carol Ruth Berkin and Mary Beth Norton. Boston: Houghton Mifflin, 1979.

Williams, Elisha [Philalethes]. *The Essential Rights and Liberties of Protestants. A Seasonable Plea for the Liberty of Conscience, and the Right of private Judgment, In Matters of Religion, Without any Controul from human Authority. . . .* Boston, 1744.

Willington Historical Society, comp. *Chronology of Willington, Connecticut, 1727-1927.* Storrs, Conn.: Parousia Press, 1977.

Wills, Garry. *Inventing America: Jefferson's Declaration of Independence.* New York: Vintage Books, 1979.

Wilson, Joan Hoff. "The Illusion of Change: Women and the American Revolution." In *The American Revolution: Explorations in the History of American Radicalism,* pp. 383-445. Ed. Alfred F. Young. DeKalb: Northern Illinois University Press, 1976.

Wolf, Stephanie Grauman. *Urban Village: Population, Community and Family Structure in Germantown, Pennsylvania, 1683-1800.* Princeton, N.J.: Princeton University Press, 1976.

Yasuba, Yasukichi. *Birth Rates of the White Population in the United States, 1800-1860: An Economic Study.* Baltimore: Johns Hopkins University Press, 1962.

Zuckerman, Michael. *Peaceable Kingdoms: New England Towns in the Eighteenth Century.* New York: Knopf, 1970.

INDEX

accumulation, intergenerational: not the aim in Wethersfield and the upland, 47, 65, 72, 74; patrilineal practices and, 30-32, 33-34, 82

Adams, James Camp, 51

Adams, John 15

administrators and executors: appointments to the positions of, 145-48; duties of, 40n33, 143-44, 152-53, 187-88; supervision of household finances by, 144, 151-52, 153-54

agricultural enterprise type, 3

agriculture: in Connecticut, 14-15, 18-19; diversified, 4, 8, 20; economic development and, 3-4; surpluses in, 4, 7-8

agriculture, commercial: effect of on inheritance practices in Europe, 35-37, 101; effect of on inheritance practices in Wethersfield, 38, 62, 77-79, 80-81, 83, 91, 100-101, 132, 136-37, 157, 161-62; and subsistence-plus agriculture, defined and discussed, 11-13; and subsistence-plus agriculture towns, wealth of compared, 173, 175-76; in Wethersfield, 13, 17, 19-20, 22, 74-75. *See also* commercialization

alienation, powers of: in colonial, Connecticut, and English law, 25-26, 92, 126, 128, 139-40, 165-66; and inheritance practices, in Wethersfield and the upland, 84, 99, 108-109, 116-17; limited for married women, 122-23, 124; restraints on, in patrilineal inheritance practices, 26, 32, 82-83

American exceptionalism thesis: and inheritance, xv, 28-30, 38, 62, 79-81, 102, 158-60; and modernization theory, xiii-xiv; and rural economic life and values, 5-10, 157-58

American North. *See* family-farm communities; middle colonies; New England

Andover, Mass., 29, 34, 60, 104

Andover Probate District (Conn.), 191

Andrus, Nancy and Sybil, 124

annuities, as substitutes for dower, 130

anti-exceptionalism. *See* American exceptionalism thesis

apprentices. *See* servants and apprentices

artisans, 47, 74; number of, 186-87

Barnstable, Mass., 30

Berlin, Conn., 16n

Blackstone, Sir William, 123

Boardman family, 18

Bolton: agriculture and textiles in, 21; soil and topography of, 17

Boston, Mass., 13, 40-41n

Buck, Abigail, 93

Bulkley family, 18

Bulkley, Joseph, 78, 79, 97

Bunce, Eunice, 129-30

calculativeness, 153-55

charitable bequests, 53, 57

Chebacco, Mass., 100n34, 142

children: capable of inheriting, defined, 42n; under Connecticut law of intestacy, 49, 63; unborn, 65; dying before parents, 42n, 181; heir selection and, 53, 54; percentage of probates having, 43, 181-82. *See also* daughters; sons

children, minors: governance of, under Connecticut law, 148-49; guardians of, 148-51, 153; joint ownership for, 92, 93-94; parental indebtedness and, 141-42; percentage of, 181-82; price for care of, 153n35; use-rights for, 84

children, unmarried: percentage of, 182; use-rights for, 84

commercialization, 171-72; and comparative analysis, xiv-xv, 160-61; and inheritance, causal relations between, 161-63; and inheritance by women, 36-37, 132, 136-37; in New England and middle colonies compared, 10-11; and patriarchal households, 134-37. *See*

Library of Congress Cataloging-in-Publication Data

Ditz, Toby L., 1951-
Property and kinship.

Bibliography: p.
Includes index.
1. Inheritance and succession—Connecticut—History.
2. Property—Connecticut—History. 3. Family—
Connecticut—History. 4. Kinship—Connecticut—
History. I. Title.
HB715.D58 1986   333.33   86-5051
ISBN 0-691-04735-9 (alk. paper)